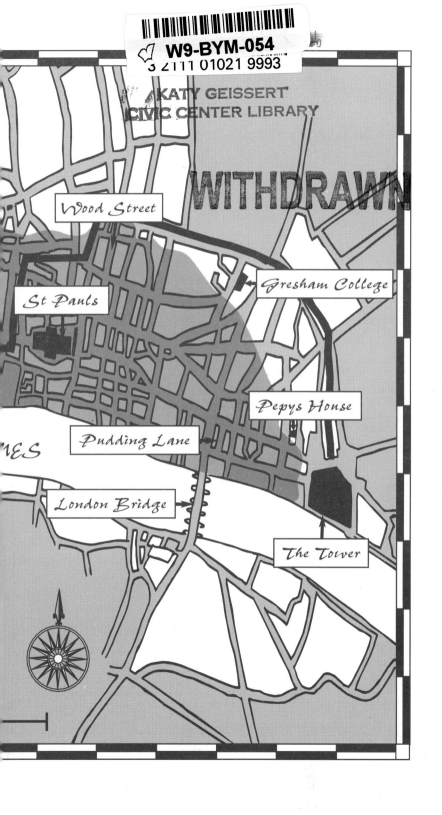

Wood Street

Gresham College

St Pauls

Pepys House

Pudding Lane

London Bridge

The Tower

THAMES

Blood and Justice

Blood and Justice

The seventeenth-century Parisian doctor who made
blood transfusion history

Pete Moore

JOHN WILEY & SONS, LTD

Published in 2003 by John Wiley & Sons Ltd, The Atrium, Southern Gate, Chichester, West Sussex PO19 8SQ, England

Telephone (+44) 1243 779777

Email (for orders and customer service enquiries): cs-books@wiley.co.uk
Visit our Home Page on www.wileyeurope.com or www.wiley.com

Other Wiley Editorial Offices

John Wiley & Sons Inc., 111 River Street, Hoboken, NJ 07030, USA

Jossey-Bass, 989 Market Street, San Francisco, CA 94103-1741, USA

Wiley-VCH Verlag GmbH, Boschstr. 12, D-69469 Weinheim, Germany

John Wiley & Sons Australia Ltd, 33 Park Road, Milton, Queensland 4064, Australia

John Wiley & Sons (Asia) Pte Ltd, 2 Clementi Loop #02-01, Jin Xing Distripark, Singapore 129809

John Wiley & Sons Canada Ltd, 22 Worcester Road, Etobicoke, Ontario, Canada M9W 1L1

British Library Cataloguing in Publication Data

A catalogue record for this book is available from the British Library

ISBN 0-470-84842-1

Typeset in 9.5/13pt Photina by Mathematical Composition Setters Ltd, Salisbury, Wiltshire
Printed and bound in Great Britain by Biddles Ltd., Guildford and King's Lynn
This book is printed on acid-free paper responsibly manufactured from sustainable forestry in which at least two trees are planted for each one used for paper production.

Contents

Plates   vii
Note on sources   viii
Acknowledgements   ix
'Cast', and people mentioned, in order of appearance   x

1   A Vital Fluid   1

2   Building on Harvey   17

3   English Infusion   36

4   Scientific Society   53

5   English Transfusions   67

6   Denis' Route to the Top   91

7   Precedence and Prison   108

8   Playing Catch-Up   132

9   Mauroy Mystery   149

10   The Great Debate   161

11   Mistake, Malice or Murder?   194

Notes   211
Timeline   214
Bibliography   219
Further reading   224
Index   225

Plates

Plate 1 Jean-Baptiste Denis.   6

Plate 2 Frontispiece of *De Humani Corporis Fabrica*
      (Andreas Vesalius).   21

Plate 3 William Harvey's diagram of arm and valves.   28/29

Plate 4 Letter from Francis Potter to John Aubrey, 5 December
      1652, Bodleian Library, Oxford, Aubrey MS 6, F.61R,
      showing a diagram of a bladder.   38

Plate 5 Richard Lower (1631 – 1691), anatomist. Oil painting
      by Jacob Huysmans.   48

Plate 6 Illustrations of cannulae in *Tractatus de Corde*
      (Richard Lower).   75

Plate 7 Gresham College.   82

Plate 8 Arundel House.   83

Plate 9 'Sheep to Man' (Purmann, 1705).   99

Plate 10 'Dog to Man' (Scultetus, 1693).   100

Plate 11 *Philosophical Transactions*, Issue Number 27
      (Oldenburg, 1st edn).   109

Plate 12 *Philosophical Transactions*, Issue Number 27
      (Oldenburg, 2nd edn).   111

Plate 13 Henry Oldenburg.   116

Plate 14 Oldenburg's translation of a letter from Denis.   127

Plate 15 Illustration in the 1672 publication of reports from
      Denis' Parisian conferences.   143

Plate 16 First illustration of a syringe injection.   145

Plate 17 Front page of a French pamphlet giving court
      sentencing at Chastelet.   201

Note on sources

*A*ll of the people who have walked through the pages of this book are authors of, or are mentioned in, research papers and letters written in the 1660s. This book does not set out to be a traditional scholarly work linking all text to the relevant references, but all of the factual material relating to the experiments with blood and the circulation were drawn from the primary sources listed in the Bibliography at the back of the book.

Throughout this book, quotes from these sources have been 'translated' into a more modern version of English. The intention has been to retain the overall style of the entries, while making them easier to read.

Acknowledgements

As far as I can see, no book written by a single person without the help of others would be worth reading. I'm therefore pleased to acknowledge that I did not write this book alone, and that I am extremely grateful to those who helped me out along the way. The historical scholars A. Rupert Hall and Marie Boas Hall gave me a much needed injection of enthusiasm halfway through the writing, as well as lending me the wealth of their historic know-how, and Professor Michael Hunter pointed me towards some great leads at the beginning of the project as well as commenting on some of the script. In addition, consultant haematologist Dr John Amess helped tidy-up my understanding of the science of blood transfusion reactions.

Researching the material for this book involved working in a number of archive libraries, and I would particularly like to thank the staff in the Royal Society library for their friendly assistance in finding ancient documents. Finally, my prime reader Adèle, agent Mandy Little, commissioning editor Sally Smith, copy-editor Caroline Ellerby, production editor Amie Jackowski Tibble and picture-researcher Benjamin Earl all worked hard to give you, the reader, a book that is worth picking up and not putting down until it is finished. Thank you.

'Cast', and people mentioned, in order of appearance

Chapter 1

Jean-Baptiste Denis (c1640–1704)
Mathematician, astronomer, philosopher and part-time medic. History records him as the first person to transfuse blood into a human being.

Louis XIV (1638–1715)
The 'Sun King' of France who came to the throne at the age of five and oversaw an exciting phase of French artistic and academic life.

M. Lamoignon
Son of the First President of the Parliament of Paris, Guillaume de Lamoignon (1617–1677) and Denis' lawyer.

Henri Louis Habert de Montmor (c1600–1679)
Wealthy French patron of early scientific research.

Ducs d'Enghien
French dignitary.

Louis Charles d'Albert Duke de Luynes (1620–1690)
Distinguished writer with interests in natural philosophy as well as being a French dignatory.

Charles de Chaulnes (1625–1698)
French dignitary.

René Descartes (1596–1650)
French philosopher and mathematician, usually seen as the father of modern philosophy.

Girard Desargues (1591–1661)
French mathematician.

Pierre Gassendi (1592–1655)
French mathematician, physicist and religious philosopher who was a strong advocate of the experimental approach to science. He was an early critic of Descartes.

Blaise Pascal (1616–1662)
French mathematician, physicist and philosopher who pioneered the theory of probability.

Jean Chapelain (1595–1674)
French poet and critic, and original member of the Académie Française. By all accounts his poetry was poor.

Paul Emmerey (died 1690)
Surgeon who worked as Denis' technician in developing ways of performing blood transfusions.

Antoine Mauroy (c1633–1668)
French house servant who in all probability was mad from having syphilis, and died after receiving transfused blood.

Perrine Mauroy
Antoine's wife.

Homer (eighth century BC)
Greek epic poet who is believed to have written the *Iliad*, which tells the story of the fall of Troy, and the *Odyssey*, which tells of the subsequent wanderings of Odysseus.

Cain and Abel
Sons of Adam and Eve described in the Biblical book of Genesis. Cain kills Abel when he becomes jealous that God accepts Abel's meat sacrifice and dismisses his sacrifice of grain.

Asclepius (thirteenth century BC)
Ancient Greek physician who became revered as a god. His daughter, Hygeia, gave her name to the word 'hygienic'.

Pythagoras (c560–480 BC)
Mathematician, astronomer and mystic who was born on the Greek island of Samos and founded a secret society at Croton in southeast Italy.

Empedocles (fifth century BC)
Greek philosopher and poet from Sicily, who also worked as a doctor and statesman.

Plato (c428–348 BC)
A pupil of Socrates, and now seen as one of the most important philosophers of all time.

Hippocrates (*c*460–377 BC)
Greek doctor working on the island of Kos who is regarded as the father of medicine. He formed a code of practice under which medical practitioners could work ethically – the Hippocratic oath.

Aristotle (384–322 BC)
Greek philosopher who came to be one of the most important and influential figures in Western thinking.

Polybus (*c*205–123 BC)
Probably Hippocrates' son-in-law and author of *De Natura Hominis*, an ancient medical textbook.

Anton van Leeuwenhoek (1632–1723)
Dutch fabric merchant who had a passion for creating and using early microscopes. He created some 550 lenses, many of which were of very high quality. He was elected as a Fellow of the Royal Society in 1680.

Claudius Galen (*c*130–201)
Greek philosopher and anatomist who, when working in Rome, developed a model demonstrating what blood was and how it worked.

Marcus Aurelius (121–180)
Roman Emperor.

Chapter 2

William Harvey (1578–1657)
Son of a farmer who married the daughter of the King's physician and discovered that blood circulates around the body.

Andreas Vesalius (1514–1564)
Flemish anatomist, the son of a pharmacist, who after studying at Louvain, Paris and Padua became the founder of modern anatomy.

Johann Stephan von Calcar (1499–1546)
Artist and illustrator who worked with Andreas Vesalius.

Michael Servetus [alias Michael Villeneuve] (1511–1553)
Spanish theologian and physician who was born in Tudela but worked largely in France and Switzerland. He got into trouble because he denied the Trinity and the deity of Jesus Christ and was burnt at the stake by Calvin.

John Calvin (1509–1564)
Born in France, he became the chief Reformer of Geneva who is best known for his teachings on the absolute authority of God.

Matteo Realdo Colombo (1516–1559)
Italian physician who described the anatomy of the heart and the large blood vessels that are attached to it. He was the first person to point out that the heart's valves were one-way devices.

King James I of England (1566–1625)
Son of Mary Queen of Scots. He became King James VI of Scotland in 1567, but was also King James I of England from 1603.

King Charles I (1600–1649)
Second son of James I of England, and beheaded after the English Civil War.

Thomas Howard, Earl of Arundel (1586–1646)
English statesman who is best remembered for his art collections, including the Arundel Marbles that his grandson gave to the University of Oxford.

Ferdinand II (1578–1637)
Born in Graz, Austria, the Holy Roman Emperor from 1619.

John Aubrey (1626–1697)
Anecdotalist and gossip who recorded highly personal views about notable people in his book *Brief Lives*. He became a Fellow of the Royal Society in 1663.

Hieronymus Fabricus (c1533–1619)
Italian anatomist born in Aquapendente who became professor of anatomy at Padua. His work was heavily based on Galenic and Aristotelian understandings of how the body works.

Robert Boyle (1627–1691)
Predominantly interested in what is now known as chemistry, this Irishman was one of the founding fathers of modern science. He was elected as a Fellow of the Royal Society in 1663.

Galileo Galilei (1564–1642)
Italian astronomer and physicist whose meticulous work studying planets and stars with his telescope set new standards for investigation and observation of the universe, but also led him into conflict with church authorities.

Johannes Walaeus
Dutch anatomist and founder of experimental physiology in mainland Europe. He followed Harvey's experiments and descriptions of the circulation and added a few of his own. Walaeus was more concerned about the chemical aspects of blood than was Harvey.

Caspar Hoffmann (1572–1648)
German physician living in Nuremberg. He believed that Aristotle had given a better account of the way that the body worked than had Galen, and held views very similar to Harvey's in terms of the way he thought the heart worked.

Marcello Malpighi (1628–1694)
Born near Bologna, he studied medicine and became professor of theoretical medicine at Pisa. He was an extraordinary lecturer in theoretical medicine at Bologna and the first professor of medicine at Messina. In 1691 he became chief physician to Pope Innocent XII. He pioneered the use of microscopes and became a Fellow of the Royal Society in 1669.

Henry Oldenburg (1619–1677)
German émigré to England who became the first secretary to the Royal Society.

Chapter 3

Francis Potter (1594–1674)
Reclusive Church of England clergyman and inventor who became a Fellow of the Royal Society in 1663.

Publius Ovidius Naso (Ovid) (43 BC – AD 17)
Having been trained in law in Rome, he gave his whole energy to poetry and wrote more poetry than any other Latin poet.

Ralph Bathurst (1620–1704)
President of Trinity College, Oxford, from 1664, he was a physician to the Navy and Chaplain to the King. He was elected a Fellow of the Royal Society in 1663.

Christopher Wren (1632–1723)
Famous architect who started out working in astronomy and anatomy, and was a founder member of the Royal Society. He was buried in his largest building, St Paul's Cathedral in London.

John Wilkins (1614–1672)
One of the original members of the Royal Society, this clergyman was fascinated by mathematics.

Oliver Cromwell (1599–1658)
Lord Protector of England from 1653 until his death in 1658.

Richard Cromwell (1626–1712)
Briefly succeeded his father as Lord Protector of England but was forced to abdicate in 1659.

John Crosse (c1620–fl.1693)
Boyle's Oxford landlord.

William Petty (1623–1687)
English philosopher, physician and founder member of the Royal Society who is best known for his contribution to statistics.

Robert Wood (c1621–1685)
Physician who researched areas of mathematics and was elected as a Fellow of the Royal Society in 1681.

Henry Pierrepoint (1606–1680)
First Marquis of Dorchester.

Timothy Clarke (c1620–1672)
Educated at Balliol College, Oxford, he worked as a physician in London, living at St Martin-in-the-Fields. He was an original Fellow of the Royal Society.

Richard Lower (1631–1691)
Elected to the Royal Society in 1667 after assisting Thomas Willis in his work and pioneering methods for transfusing blood between animals.

Thomas Willis (1621–1675)
Physician elected a Fellow of the Royal Society in 1663.

Peter Sthael (–1675)
German chemist and friend of Robert Boyle.

Samuel Pepys (1633–1703)
Famous diarist who worked as a civil servant and became a member of the Royal Society in 1665.

Charles II (1630–1685)
After returning from exile in France, he became King of Scotland and England in 1660.

Anthony Wood (1632–1695)
English antiquary who studied at Merton College, Oxford, from 1647 to 1652.

Johann Sigismund Elsholtz (1623–1688)
German physician who wrote a text book showing how to inject solutions into the bloodstream.

Chapter 4

Francis Bacon (1561–1626)
London-born philosopher and statesman who was educated at Trinity College, Cambridge, before studying law at Gray's Inn, London. He insisted on the need to substantiate an argument with discernible facts, rather than resting on the authority of ancient thinkers.

Ismael Boulliau (1605–1694)
French mathematician and astronomer.

Peiresc and **Pierre Dupuys**
French seventeenth-century academic historians.

Samuel Sorbière (1615–1670)
French clergyman and physician who was educated by his uncle, Samuel Petit, in Paris, the subject of jealousy when he was elected to the English Royal Society in 1663.

François Bernier (1620–1688)
French physician whose letters are translated into English and published as 'Travels in the Mogul Empire AD1658–1668'. This book gives an insight into life in India during the Mogul era.

Aurangzeb (1658–1707)
Indian Moghul emperor who alienated the Hindu members of his empire and ended up living in exile.

Robert Hooke (1635–1703)
Born on the Isle of Wight, he worked as an architect and performed experiments in physics. An original member of the Royal Society.

Thomas Aquinas (1225–1274)
Italian scholar, philosopher and theologian, who reconciled Aristotle's science with Christian doctrine.

John Wallis (1616–1703)
Clergyman and mathematician who was an original Fellow of the Royal Society.

Jonathan Goddard (c1617–1675)
Physician who became closely associated with Cromwell, and was a founder Fellow of the Royal Society.

Robert Moray (1608–1673)
He fought as a soldier and worked as a courtier and diplomat. At the same time he performed research in chemistry and studied metals, minerals and natural history. A founder Fellow of the Royal Society.

Gilles Personne de Roberval (1602–1675)
French mathematician who began studying at the age of 14. A founding member of the Académie Royale des Sciences.

Voltaire (1694–1778)
Satirical writer who became a member of the Royal Society in 1743.

Chapter 5

Johann Daniel Major (1634–1693)
German physician whose medical textbook included instructions on how to inject solutions into patients.

Daniel Coxe (1640–1730)
By profession an adventurer, but also performed experiments in chemistry and medicine. He was elected a Fellow of the Royal Society in 1665 and made an Honorary Fellow of the Royal College of Physicians in 1680.

Thomas Coxe (1615–1685)
Having been the physician to the parliamentary army, he switched allegiance and in 1665 became a physician to the King. An original Fellow of the Royal Society.

William Croune (1633–1684)
Born in London, he worked as a physician in the city and was an original Fellow of the Royal Society.

Thomas Millington (1628–1704)
Oxford mathematician and a friend of Robert Boyle.

John Beale (1608–1683)
Clergyman who was Rector of Yeovil, Somerset, from 1660 to 1682, and was elected to the Royal Society in 1663.

Walter Charlton (1620–1707)
Born in Shepton Mallet, Somerset, a physician who researched areas of medicine and natural philosophy. An original member of the Royal Society.

Richard Zouche (1590–1662)
Oxford academic.

Lady Ranelagh (1614–1691)
Robert Boyle's sister.

Gilbert Sheldon (1598–1677)
Elected a Fellow of the Royal Society in 1665, at which point he was the Archbishop of Canterbury, a post he held from 1663 to 1677.

Elizabeth Billings (1640–1669)
Samuel Pepys' wife.

Thomas Shadwell (1642–1692)
Satirical playwright who wrote 13 comedies and three tragedies. Succeeded John Dryden as Poet Laureate in 1689.

Edmund King (1629–1709)
London surgeon who studied chemistry and had a passing fascination with blood transfusion.

Chapter 6

Claude Perrault (1613–1688)
Influential Parisian physician and one of the founding members of the Académie Royale des Sciences. In June 1667 he led a team of researchers invited to dissect a shark and a lion at the royal menagerie.

Louis Gayant (died 1673)
Parisian surgeon.

Isaac Newton (1642–1727)

Mathematician and natural philosopher who on two occasions was Member of Parliament for Cambridge University, was Master of the Mint from 1699 until his death, and elected a Fellow of the Royal Society in 1672.

Denis de Sallo (1626–1669)

Founding editor of the Parisian magazine, *Journal des Sçavans*.

Matthaeus Gottfried Purmann (1648–1711)

Surgeon who performed the first transfusion of blood into a human in Germany, taking the blood from a lamb.

Johann Scultetus (fl. 1682)

Dutch surgeon and anatomist.

Leonard Landois (1837–1902)

German physiologist who started looking for a scientific understanding of the reactions that occur when blood from different animals is mixed.

Karl Landsteiner (1868–1943)

Nobel Prize-winning scientist who discovered the concept of blood groups. He was elected a Fellow of the Royal Society in 1941.

Chapter 7

Dom Robert de Gabets (fl. 1667)

Benedictine friar who Denis claimed gave him the idea of transfusing blood.

Henry Bennet (1618–1685)

First Earl of Arlington, educated at Westminster School and Christ Church, Oxford. Retired to Suffolk after holding the post of Lord Chamberlain.

Oswald Mosley (1896–1980)

English politician who resigned from the Labour government to become leader of the British Union of Fascists. He had a vision of a politically and financially united Europe.

John Milton (1608–1674)

English poet who studied at Cambridge.

Richard Jones (1641–1712)

Robert Boyle's nephew who became the first Earl of Ranelagh.

Dorothy West (died 1665)
Oldenburg's first wife.

Dora Katherina (c1652–)
Oldenburg's second wife.

Joseph Williamson (1633–1701)
Barrister, statesman, assistant to Lord Arlington, and an original Fellow of the Royal Society.

Henri Justel (1620–1693)
Frenchman who switched nationality and became English in 1687. A frequent correspondent of Oldenburg and Boyle. Elected a Fellow of the Royal Society in 1681.

Seth Ward (1617–1689)
Bishop of Salisbury who researched areas of astronomy and was an original Fellow of the Royal Society.

John Martin (fl. 1680)
Oldenburg's publisher.

Baron Bond (–1667)
A Swedish nobleman who became ill while visiting Paris.

Christina Wasa (1626–1689)
Queen of Sweden from 1640 until her abdication in 1654.

Pierre Michon Bourdelot (1610–1685)
French doctor who worked for a time as physician to Queen Christina of Sweden.

Chapter 8

Arthur Coga (c1645–unknown)
First person in England to receive transfused blood.

Daniel Whistler (1619–1684)
Physician educated at Trinity College, Oxford, and who worked in Oxford, London and Sweden. An original Fellow of the Royal Society, and died of pneumonia.

Philip Skippon (1641–1691)
Elected a Fellow of the Royal Society in 1667, a virtuoso who travelled extensively with John Ray.

John Ray (1627–1705)
English clergyman, botanist, zoologist and entomologist who was elected a Fellow of the Royal Society in 1667.

Pope Innocent VIII (1432–1492)
Born Giovanni Battista Cibò, he had a chequered history as a youth, but was generally liked when he became Pope.

Abraham Myere of Balmes
Shadowy physician who appears to have offered medical advice to Pope Innocent VIII.

Marsilio Ficino (1422–1499)
Italian philosopher – head of the Platonic Academy in Florence.

Count Ferencz Nadasdy
Elizabeth of Bathroy's husband.

Elizabeth of Bathroy (1575–1613)
Evil woman who decided that bathing in virgins' blood would maintain her beauty.

Dorottya Szentes and Darvula
Two of Elizabeth of Bathroy's servents.

Iilona Joo
Elizabeth of Bathroy's nurse.

Matthias II
King of Hungary from 1609–1619, excommunicated from Rome in 1609.

Andreas Libavius (1546–1616)
German chemist.

Pauli (Paolo) Manfredi (fl. 1668)
Italian researcher.

Johannes Colle (1558–1631)
Professor of medicine at Padua, Italy.

Francesco Folli (1624–1685)
Italian physician.

Georg Abraham Mercklino
German seventeenth-century physician who advocated blood transfusion.

Balthasar Kaufmann
Colleague of Gottfried Purmann.

Lorenz Heister (1683–1758)
German surgeon who worked in the battlefields before becoming professor of anatomy and surgery at the University of Altdorf in 1709, and later moved on to be the professor of medicine and botany. His book on surgery was translated into many languages, including Japanese.

Regner de Graaf (1641–1673)
Dutch anatomist who gave his name to Graafian folicles, the fluid-filled cavities left in the ovaries after they release eggs.

Johannes van Horne (1621–1670)
Dutch physician who worked with Graaf. His father was one of the first directors of the Dutch East India Company, and as such would have been highly influenced by the wars with England.

Fabritius
Physician working in Dantzig, Spain.

Carlo Fracassati
Italian anatomist working at Pisa.

Jean Dominique Cassini (1625–1712)
Italian investigator who had a go at transfusing blood and was elected a Fellow of the Royal Society in 1672.

Chapter 9

Denis Dodart (1634–1707)
Parisian physician from a wealthy background. His main work was entitled *Mémoires pour Servir a l'Histoire des Plantes*, and presented ideas on how speech was created in the mouth.

Pierre de Bourger (1698–1758)
Parisian physicist.

Guillaume-Hugues Vaillant (1619–1678)
Parisian churchman.

Monsieur de Veau
Parisian priest.

Steen Willadsen (1944–)
Dustch scientist who was the first person to produce a mammalian clone.

Monsieur Bonnet
Parisian priest called on to assess Mauroy's state of mind.

Chapter 10

Henry Sampson (1629–1700)
Nonconformist minister who had to leave his parish at St Michael's Framlingham because of his refusal to be ordained after the Restoration. Sent a letter to Edmund King in January 1668 replying to King's questions about blood transfusion.

Louis de Basril (16th–17th century)
Parisian physician.

Claude Tardy (fl. 1667)
Parisian physician.

Louis Gadroy (1642–1678)
Parisian physician.

Pierre-Martin de la Martinière (1634–1676)
Outspoken opponent of blood transfusion who masterminded the attack on Denis' technique and wrote numerous pamphlets attacking Denis and his work.

George (Guillame) Lamy (1644–1683)
Parisian physician and opponent of Denis.

Jan Baptiste van Helmont (1579–1644)
Highly controversial physician who started to question ancient modes of thought regarding medical practice.

Paracelsus (1493–1541)
Maverick German alchemist and physician who challenged established beliefs, and who supposedly only lectured when he was half-drunk. His real name was Theophrastus Bombastus von Hohenheim, but he changed this to one implying that his work was beyond that of the Roman physician Celsus.

George Ent (1604–1689)

Anatomist and physician who was an original Fellow of the Royal Society and became the president of the Royal College of Physicians in 1663.

Chapter 11

André D'Ormesson

Parisian magistrate.

CHAPTER ONE

A vital fluid

A stave struck the floor three times, demanding attention from the assembled crowd. The effect was a brief lull in the hubbub, followed by a resumption of the cacophony. Three more times the stave hit the marble tile, each assault more strident than the one before. 'S'il vous plaît,' called the official in the clipped accent that marked him as a resident of Paris. 'S'il vous plaît,' he repeated, spacing each word and ensuring that his call was noticed. The case before them was serious – after all, accusations of murder should never be taken lightly, particularly in such unusual circumstances. The date was Saturday, 17 April 1668. The place, Le Grand Chastelet, the central court in Paris, a fantastic building in the heart of the city on the banks of the River Seine.

In the centre of one small group stood Jean-Baptiste Denis, one of a number of science-minded medics who had the acquaintance of King Louis XIV. Denis had been born into a family that moved on the edge of royal circles, but was never in a position to gain full acceptance. His father was Louis XIV's chief engineer, who had made a name for himself designing and building water pumps. Now aged about twenty-seven, Denis had a superb mind and had obtained a bachelor's degree in theology before going on to study medicine at Montpellier. He had recently been awarded a doctorate in mathematics, and had returned to his native city of Paris, assuming the position of professor of mathematics and natural philosophy, and dividing his time between his major interests of mathematics and astronomy. As a hobby he dabbled in medical research. Like so many hobbyists he had hoped that one day this pastime would strike gold. Instead it had brought him to court – on trial for murder.

The legal professionals surrounding him wore black gowns and square hats with one corner pointing forward, casting a triangular shadow across their faces like a raptor's beak. They included Denis' lawyer, M. Lamoignon, the son of the First President of the Parliament of Paris. Denis wore his carefully contoured wig that ended in a tightly rolled curl just above the collar of his long dark-brown jacket and gently frilled shirt – a dresscode that marked him as a man of learning. He grimaced in annoyance at the sight of splashes of mud or unmentionable excrement that had spattered the pristine white stockings which rose from highly polished black high-heeled shoes sporting large, square, silver buckles. This was a critical day, and Denis wanted the Sergeant charged with reviewing the case to be in no doubt as to his status.

Alongside him stood a powerful collection of friends, including Henri Louis Habert de Montmor, first Master of Requests to Louis XIV. Their dress-sense was as far from drab as was possible. They wore huge wigs that sent curls cascading down elaborately frilled shirts, and massively sleeved coats covered in the most ornate needlework.

In the gallery sat a man and a woman, both of whom were present as witnesses. Both were patients who had received the treatment Denis had developed, and both were adamant that it had cured them. The woman claimed that prior to the treatment she had been partially paralysed, but was now cured. Evidence – living proof. That was important. Equally important was the presence of other dignitaries such as the ducs d'Enghien, de Luynes, and de Chaulnes, their circle of friends and courtiers. Even if a case started to look thin, such an impressive line-up of supporters packing the gallery provided a greater hope of winning.

The official struck again, this time lashing out at the surface of the table, creating a sharp 'crack'. The chatter of the crowd dropped to whispers, though some laughed at the man's attempts to create order. Denis' mind, however, was jolted by the memory of an urgent knocking at his door one evening a few months earlier, which represented the start of this unfortunate episode.

Meeting Mauroy

It had been late, and Sunday had just rolled into the early hours of Monday, 19 December 1667. Denis, as was often the case, was sitting in his library considering some of his latest observations and calculations on the movement of various planets, when he heard a carriage pull up at the door. He was a sombre-looking gentleman, for whom generous meals were beginning to make their mark on his waistline and, despite his youth, middle-age was beginning to show itself in the appearance of ample flesh around his lower jaw and deep-set crescent-shaped creases framing his mouth. He continued working, scratching the side of his roman nose, so deep in concentration that he had forgotten about the visitor. A few minutes later his servant appeared, announcing that Monsieur de Montmor had sent for him. Denis narrowed his eyes and, filled with a combination of alarm and excitement, tried to determine why he was being summoned at this time of night. After all, Paris in 1667 wasn't the safest place to wander around the streets after dark. But then again, de Montmor wasn't the sort of person to make idle requests.

With an annual income of 100,000 livres, the 67-year-old French aristocrat Henri de Montmor had personal financial independence, with sufficient surplus for expensive hobbies, the main one of which was new science. Using this wealth he had founded the Académie Montmor in 1657, which had become a meeting place for intellectual talent including the likes of the innovative mathematician and friend René Descartes, Girard Desargues, the Professor of mathematics at the Collège Royale in Paris, Pierre Gassendi, mathematician, physicist and religious philosopher and Blaise Pascal, as well as people like French poet and critic Jean Chapelain. These notables met weekly at the spectacular Hôtel de Montmor, standing at what is now number 79 rue du Temple, half-a-mile north of the river level with Notre Dame, in what is now Paris' third arrondissement.

At the beginning of 1667 the group was in the process of disbanding, some of the members having been invited to join the newly formed Académie des Sciences, but in scientific circles Montmor still held considerable influence. Denis abandoned his work, spent a few minutes carefully rearranging his clothes, and with the assistance of his servant tugged his wig on over his closely cut hair. Checking himself in the mirror, he pulled at his collars, readjusted his wig and, deciding all was well, he left. To his relief he discovered that Montmor's servant had come with a closed carriage. But he was taken by surprise when he climbed inside to find it already occupied by Paul Emmerey, a talented surgeon and anatomist who had also tagged onto the group. At the peak of his career, Emmerey was recognised as one of the most capable teachers of surgery and anatomy, and having been born in Saint Quentin, Paris, rose to become the Provost of the Parisian Society of Surgeons. Finding that neither knew the nature of the summons, both men said nothing as the carriage rattled noisily along cobbled streets, passing the Hotel de Ville before heading east along rue du Temple.

Veering sharply left through the gates, the carriage stopped in an open courtyard and its two passengers headed straight for the door. On arrival they were shown into the high-ceilinged library where they were met with a few shouts of welcome. The ornate room was already full of fashionable gentlemen, strutting around and standing about in order that their flamboyant costumes could be seen to greatest effect. At the far end of the library, tied to a chair, was a man, his hair matted and wet, his face grazed, and in marked contrast to the other occupants of the room, he was without clothes. A cloak had been draped around his shoulders, but it slipped to the floor every now and then as he fought to free himself.

The captive was 34-year-old Antoine Mauroy, a man-servant who lived in a village about 10 miles from the centre of Paris. For seven or eight years he had suffered from bouts of insanity, each lasting 10 or more months. During these episodes he became violent, and had a tendency to run around the streets naked, whenever possible setting fire to buildings. Unsurprisingly, he soon became notorious in the district.

About a year earlier, during one of his sane periods, he had married Perrine, a young woman who was persuaded to believe that his insanity had been a passing illness and that he was now cured. The marriage appeared to have started well, but sadly after a few months his behaviour deteriorated. Initially his wife had managed to contain him, and despite being attacked on a number of occasions, she and friends had tied him down for his own safety as well as that of those around him.

There were plenty of people willing to give advice about treatments and remedies for Antoine's condition. Quite clearly something was causing this outrageous behaviour, and according to the principles followed by most practitioners at the time, the strongest possibility was that Antoine's blood was to blame. Maybe he simply had too much of it, or he had an appropriate amount, but it had become contaminated. Either way, the best thing to do would be to remove some.

Local physicians and barbers had 'bled' him on eighteen separate occasions, a technique that was assumed to let out bad blood, restore a healthy balance and enable recovery. They had also given him forty or more 'baths', each filled with different combinations of herbs, chemicals and other active ingredients. Nothing had changed. Taking a similar tack they had strapped innumerable potions to his forehead. But all to no avail. In response he repeatedly broke free, and ran off.

On this particular dark midwinter evening, Mme Mauroy had been scouring the streets and alleys, fields and ditches, searching for him, or even hoping to find telltale signs of his destructive passing. She was, however, unaware that this time he had made it as far as central Paris and been detained by nightwatchmen. For some reason this sad man had been brought to the attention of Montmor. Whether out of a sense of pity or curiosity we will never know, but, unable to find a place in a suitable hospital, Montmor had taken him home, and then called in his friends.

His idea was as simple as it was radical. Over the last few months he knew that two of the members of his academy, Denis and Emmerey, had been experimenting with the idea of swapping blood between different animals. In the mid-seventeenth century, any thinking about the body centred around the idea that a person's blood contained vital elements of their spirit. This gave rise to a new possibility. Might draining his own, sinfully damaged blood, and replacing it with pure, innocent blood from a docile animal, cure the behaviour of a wild and dangerous man? Could the blood of a lamb, for example, literally wash away a man's sins?

As Denis and Emmerey walked into the room, all heads turned towards them and conversation dropped to a murmur. The men stepped forward and bowed in respect to Montmor and his assembled friends, acknowledging their nods with warm smiles and waves of their hats. Montmor beckoned them over towards Mauroy, and the three stood together while Montmor filled them in with the case history as he saw it. Their task, he informed them, was to see if they felt this man was a suitable candidate for a transfusion.

The stakes were high. Among the gathered crowd there were certainly many who hoped this would be the case, in order that they would be able to witness the experiment and another amazing stride forward in the rapidly expanding field of scientific medicine. Others were either

Plate 1 Jean-Baptiste Denis. Reproduced by permission of the Musée d'Histoire de la Médecine.

deeply sceptical or totally outraged. If anything terrible happened to the patient, the whole of Paris would know about it, and Denis' livelihood, maybe even his life, would be in danger. If the experiment was successful, Denis was sure that he could sign his name in history.

Playing with fire

But what if it went wrong? Today, the whole concept of moving blood from an animal to a person seems bizarre. Many would also view it as unethical in terms of both the risk to the patient and the use of the donor animal, which would probably bleed to death during the process. But to appreciate the reason for the taste of fear in Denis' mouth at the time, we need to understand his reverence for blood.

Like most of the people gathered in Montmor's apartment, Denis was not one of the ignorant conmen or dangerous quacks who set up business in dingy back streets of towns and cities in seventeenth-century Europe. His knowledge of theology and the magical wisdom of the Graeco-Roman world taught him that blood played a fundamental role as a mediator between humankind and the gods. It was a symbol around which spirituality and superstition, sacred teachings and folklore all mingled. No one toyed with blood.

However, blood was more than just a symbol. Blood was life. Any physician handling blood was manipulating the very life of the person. This conclusion came from one simple observation. Slit an animal's throat, or a human's for that matter, and watch what happens. As the blood gushes out, the person starts to become faint, running low on their vital spirit. Once drained of all his or her blood, the person has no life left in his or her body. Quite obviously, life leaves with the blood. Therefore blood contained life.

This rationale underpins many of the earliest recorded events that involve or make statements about blood. One such incident occurs in writings attributed to the Greek epic poet Homer, whose eighth-century BC story, the *Odyssey*, recounts the aftermath of the Trojan War. At one point in the book, Homer's hero Odysseus finds himself in a spot of trouble and, taking the advice of a witch, summons the dead oracle Tiresias. Odysseus hopes that this soothsayer will be able to solve his problems. In a daring move, Odysseus enters Hades and pours an offering of milk, honey, wine and the blood of a sacrificial ram. This blood wins the day, and as the spirits of the dead drink this 'black, steaming' blood, so they regain their memories of life on earth, regain their vital breath of life for a brief moment, and give Odysseus the help he needs. Blood had, at least temporarily, restored Tiresias' life.

While the sixteenth and seventeenth centuries were marked by a new phase in human thought that wanted to question mythical understanding, most of its philosophers still took biblical teaching seriously. Throughout the biblical texts were clear warnings not to take blood lightly. The book of Leviticus has an emphatic prohibition against consuming blood, 'because the life of every creature is in its blood', and in Genesis' account of Abel's murder, God confronts his guilty brother Cain, saying: 'Your brother's blood cries out to me from the ground'. Denis' theological scholarship would have reinforced his awareness of the need for caution.

Was Denis seriously contemplating pouring blood from an animal into a person? Yes he was, convinced that this sacrificial gift had a chance of restoring health. Denis looked at Mauroy. He studied the appearance of his skin and looked for signs of any physical disease that would make the procedure particularly dangerous. His colleague, Emmerey, bent down to join in the examination. Neither of them were part of the old school of physicians who made diagnoses from a distance. Both wanted to base their decisions on hard evidence. The crowd also pressed forward, looking for signs that would enable them to make diagnoses of Mauroy's condition and formulate a strategy for treating him. Many announced their conclusions with loud bravado. The cynic might suggest that it is very easy to be certain that your treatment will work when you know that there is no way you are going to have it put to the test!

The initial examination was pleasing. Mauroy looked to be physically fit. There were no obvious signs of disease or illness. It seemed that only his soul was in turmoil. Surely the best treatment would be to tackle the seat of the soul, to tackle his blood. After all, blood was the place where a person's individuality resided. Blood contained the reason you were the person you were. If your personality was disordered, then what better than to remove some of it and replace it with a spirit of calm and order.

The possibilities seemed very real; but so too did the dangers. Again the stakes were high. Would it be ethical to employ a treatment that altered a person's nature? If someone's personality and characteristics have been given by his or her creator, does any physician have the moral authority to wade in and alter them? This is a question that has shown up frequently since science began to vent its learning and theories on living systems, especially when those systems are human beings. Put crudely, was the proposed experiment 'playing God'?

The debate would probably have been very similar to the one played out recently with regard to the genetic manipulation of plants and animals, and the more heated exchanges that have accompanied discussion of the possibility of human cloning. In all these situations there is a fear that humankind might be using science to take control of areas outside our jurisdiction. Among the God-fearing population of the seventeenth century there would have been a more uniform anxiety that some ordained rules were about to be bent or broken. Who has the authority to decide the personality of an individual, except God?

This would not have been a minor consideration, but a serious dilemma. Hadn't everyone been made the way they were by God? If this theory of transfusing blood worked, wouldn't it alter the person's nature? Wouldn't it alter the person that God had made? Wasn't this outside the scope of action that any moral physician was allowed to work within? Denis would have been well aware of critics who were already sharpening their knifes. He was potentially in a no-win situation. If the treatment failed, he could be accused of reckless disregard for life. If it worked, he would be indicted for usurping God's authority. In Eden, Eve had bitten the apple of knowledge of good and evil – now, for many in the room, there was every indication that evil was about to take the upper hand.

Medicine, it would have been argued, can cure sickness, but here a person's unruly behaviour was about to be tackled by altering his temperament. This was an attempt to change his very nature. And what was potentially more shocking was that the experimenter-physicians were considering doing it by introducing a few pints of calf blood into his system. In so doing, they wanted to introduce the docile, calm and altogether loveable spirit of an innocent calf into this disreputable vagabond. But if they succeeded, would he still be a human being, or would he now be a hybrid – a human-calf?

The equivalent twenty-first-century discussion revolves around the transport of genes from one species to another, and asks how many genes it is necessary to move from a pig to a human before the human becomes part-pig? Or, conversely, how many genes must be moved from a human to a pig before the pig should be afforded human rights? Indeed, there is a distinct similarity between the two scenarios – genes and blood. In the seventeenth century, Denis and co-workers would have believed that your blood is an essential component of who you are. Modern science sees reproduction as a mingling of genes. By this reckoning, genes are the new blood.

In good humour

Clearing the ethical ground to ensure a relatively high degree of safety from the risk of censure from members of the religious community and the public, was one issue. But Denis also needed to consider the medical fraternity's current treatment strategies. Letting blood out was their business, not putting it in. This was an era ruled by the art and craft of phlebotomy. Many of the medical community stood to lose their source of income if his ideas worked, however no one seemed certain as to whether the theory of transfusion went with, or against, the current theory of health, disease and blood.

To understand the radical nature of Denis' proposal, we need to pause for a moment and take a look at the prevailing understanding of blood. In the mid-seventeenth century, people were still highly influenced by the philosophical mindset that had originated in ancient Greece. In the thirteenth century BC, the physician Asclepius had taught that all diseases were purely spiritual issues and should be treated by prayer and the offering of sacrifices to the gods. But by the sixth century BC new ideas were emerging.

Thinkers like Pythagoras, and statesman and doctor Empedocles, became fascinated with the number four. They were convinced that this number was so powerful because the entire cosmos had been built using four component parts. This notion of four-part divisions permeated Plato's work. He believed that all creatures came in one of four types. Firstly there were the original gods and children of gods that the craftsman had created. Secondly, certain men and women who were simpleminded but otherwise inoffensive, were turned into birds. Thirdly, those that were dull-witted and incapable of complex thought became animals. Fourthly, the most ignorant men and women became lizards and snakes, and the really stupid were turned into fish and oysters. Indeed, this mindset has continued; we talk of the four ages of man and divide the year into four seasons, and we even partition hours into quarters.

These Greek philosophers suggested that since humans were part of the cosmos, their bodies (their microcosms) must function like everything else (the macrocosm). Consequently, they felt that any explanation of how a healthy body operated should rest on a four-part physical system, and any discussion of disease needed to make sense of four elementary substances – earth, air, fire and water.

Philosophers like Pythagoras and Empedocles maintained that these elements represented qualities of heat, cold, wet and dry. For example, earth was generated by mixing coldness and dryness, and fire was a combination of heat and dryness. Furthermore, they maintained that a person's temperament, his or her intelligence and perception of reality were highly influenced by the relative proportions of earth, air, water and fire in their bodies. Consequently, an understanding of health and medical practice evolved around notions of treating perceived imbalances in a person's make-up.

In the fifth and fourth centuries BC, Hippocrates and his fellow Hippocratic doctors integrated the idea of the four basic elements with another prevalent notion – that of humours. Whenever food was consumed, there were elements in the diet that could not be digested and used by the body. If these 'humours' were not eliminated, they would build up and cause disease. Initially, they believed that there were two humours – bile and phlegm. Bile was then divided into two types – yellow bile and black bile. This gave three humours. However, if humours existed, there must be four of them. After much head-scratching, the doctors of the day decided to add blood to the list. Blood was different from the original three humours in that, unlike black and yellow bile and phlegm, it had a positive influence on the body. As to their sources within the body, phlegm came from the brain, while blood originated in the heart. The liver produced black bile, and the yellow bile came from the spleen.

So it was that blood began to assume a fundamental role, for not only was it one of the humours, but it was also charged with the task of maintaining the body's vital balance – of keeping the right proportions of air, water, earth and fire. Blood acted by communicating with the pores that were thought to be on the outer surface of the body. These pores allowed the four elements to diffuse into and out of the blood, which could then travel into the tissues and organs in the centre of the body and restore any region that was currently unbalanced. Most importantly, blood would make sure that the balance was maintained in the vicinity of the heart – the seat of people's thinking.

Blood was the perfect tissue in the body. It was warm, indicating that it was full of life, and played a role in all aspects of life, from respiration to nutrition, digestion to thought. The idea became known as the haemocentric (blood-centred) view of life. This fitted well with Aristotle's notion that emotions were wrapped up in blood, for example timidity was a consequence of a person having thin blood, and the blood becoming too cold was also to be feared.

The concept was refined even further by Hippocrates' son-in-law Polybus, who, in his book *De Natura Hominis*, formed a four-part system that underpinned medical practice right through to the seventeenth century and beyond. Polybus summarised his ideas in a simple table:

Humour	Season	Qualities
Blood	Spring	Heat and humidity
Yellow bile	Summer	Heat and dryness
Black bile	Autumn	Cold and dryness
Phlegm	Winter	Cold and humidity

As Denis' colleagues would have been taught during their medical education, this gave a structured approach to treating illness. If a person was too cold or lacked humidity, then he or she should drink wine as this was known to help a person get warm, a benefit that must have come from an increase in the amount of blood. Blood 'letting' also became codified within this scheme of medicine. While on occasions it could be used for reducing heat in a person with fever, letting was normally seen as beneficial because it had a chance of removing the nasty humours that mingled with the blood. Hippocrates and his followers were convinced that menstrual bleeding and nose bleeds were the body's natural way of restoring balance and maintaining health. Therefore blood letting, not blood infusion, became a key way of restoring balance for an extremely wide range of conditions.

Linked to life

Most seventeenth-century physicians would also have believed that blood was the source of new life. Aristotle had coined the idea that new life started when refined blood from the man and the woman, semen and menstrual blood, came together. Denis and his colleagues would have had no evidence causing them to question this. They were around just a few decades before the Dutch fabric merchant Anton van Leeuwenhoek peered through his collection of pioneering microscopes and discovered sperm in samples of semen. For Denis' friends, playing with blood was playing with the very stuff of life.

The link between blood and life was further strengthened by the last serious alteration to the scheme of beliefs that developed prior to the seventeenth century. This was introduced by the Greek philosopher and anatomist Claudius Galen in the second century AD, who had studied medicine in the city of Pergamum, in what is now western Turkey. Galen had become chief physician to the gladiators stationed in Pergamum, and was a prolific writer. During his career he produced some 500 books and treatises on all aspects of medical science and philosophy. His views fitted well with those of the early Christian believers and became incorporated into the thought patterns of Christian-dominated cultures for the next 1,500 years. So much so that if anyone questioned them, he or she would be in for a rough time – this would be effectively questioning the church.

Galen moved to Rome as physician and friend to the Emperor Marcus Aurelius. Working with gladiators gave him ample access to wounded bodies, and tending to half-butchered men at the Colosseum allowed him to observe blood at first-hand. This was an unusual situation, in that he was looking at healthy people who had only just been harmed, rather than those in different stages of disease, or battle victims who may have reached a physician hours or days after receiving an injury. From his observations he drew a critical conclusion. There were, he said, two types of blood: one was bluish in colour and tended to flow gently from the cut end of the vessels that contained it, the other was bright red and prone to spurt from its vessels.

This theory of two different types of blood caused Galen to develop a more complex idea than had held sway up to this point. He concluded that blood was formed in the liver. After all, a chunk of liver looks very much like congealed blood, and if it is mashed up it creates a liquid mush that has similarities to blood. This blood was formed directly from the digested elements of food, and as such blood was the means by which nutrients became distributed throughout the body and carried in veins.

Arteries, on the other hand, carried a form of blood that had been refined in the furnace-like facility of the heart. This purified blood now contained a new substance, one that was weightless but absolutely essential. This was 'vital spirits'. However, there was one further complication to this theory – that some blood containing vital spirits was sent up to the head. Here it was further refined and became 'animal spirits', which enabled thought and was distributed through the body in nerves. For Denis' contemporaries, this high value of blood would have only increased their anxiety about any medical procedures that used blood in a new way. By playing with blood, he was playing with life itself.

Towards a decision

From Denis' point of view, transfusion was just a different approach to the task of restoring a correctly balanced set of humours. As far as he could see, it also held the advantage of doing this at the same time as maintaining a normal volume of blood. His plan was to remove some of the unbalanced blood from the diseased person and replace it with balanced blood from a healthy animal. This meant that the patient would not be stripped of the nutritious properties of the blood, and there would be a good volume of blood on which the heart could imprint the person's vital and animal spirits.

It was obvious that Mauroy was not in 'good humour'. The small knots of physicians around the library pushed forward to examine the patient, but were generally disappointed by the lack of data. There was no indication that the man was physiologically cold, which could have indicated an excess of phlegm, but they didn't expect to see that, not in a mad man. What would have been useful would have been a good stool sample. Runny diarrhoea would have been taken as a firm indicator of excess yellow bile, and too much yellow bile, as everyone knew, could boil the brain, causing all sorts of mental imbalance. On the other hand, dark masses in a solid stool could indicate excess black bile. Those associated with the College of Physicians were certain of what they would do – they would bleed him. Granted, he had been bled before, but probably not severely enough, or the blood had been taken from the wrong place. After all, was there any indication that the man had been bled until he was unconscious? It's a fair bet that, at this point, several of the physicians were playing their fingers over the catches on the beautifully crafted boxes that contained exquisite sets of razor-sharp, bloodletting tools!

This then would have been the predominant view of the medical community in Paris, and would have coloured most of the discussion as the early hours of the morning ticked by. Denis was fully aware that his concept of giving a patient blood, of taking blood from one animal and giving it to another, was sending shockwaves through the established order. He argued, though, that while it was a novel method, it could still be seen as a way of restoring a person's balance – it just did so in a more active manner than phlebotomy alone. Furthermore, if it worked, the technique could be a universal panacea; learn to perform it and you could potentially cure almost any disease. With such a reward in prospect, who could possibly want to stand in the way of anyone trying to push the method forward?

As Denis and Emmerey looked at their potential patient, they would have been weighing up whether his bloodline needed altering. They would have been questioning in their minds whether Mauroy's madness and violence could be tempered by an injection of an altogether gentler spirit. They would have been wondering whether this was their opportunity to startle the sceptics and make a name for themselves, to boot.

There is no way of knowing whether his decision would have been different had he foreseen the chain of events that were about to result in the death of his patient. But it does seem likely that he would have had an inkling that the action would cause jealous consternation over the seas in England. No true pioneer flinches in the face of a challenge, and Denis could already see the headlines. Prestige before the age of 30 – it was just the sort of meteoric rise to fame that should be expected of a genius.

CHAPTER TWO

Building on Harvey

The seventeenth century was both exciting and frustrating. Denis was caught up in the excitement of questioning the previously unquestionable – intellectual revolution was in the air. However, he was hampered by the fact that the recognised ways of conducting this sort of quest were only just beginning to emerge.

The key issue was progress, and the question was how to break the shackles that bound enquiring minds to Aristotelian patterns of thought, in which ideas and argument were more important than physical observations. The Renaissance had been a first step, but if anything it had reinforced the respect for this ancient mode of thought; people had rejuvenated Greek philosophy, given it a new lease of life and let it inspire a new generation of understanding. But this new understanding was still based on rhetoric rather than measurement. Consequently, there was little room for experiment-based pursuit of knowledge.

Worse than this, there was a growing body of opinion that, in many instances, the old conclusions were wrong. When people did perform experiments, take measurements and then try to make sense of their findings, they all too often found that ancient theories did not hold water. The Aristotelians dismissed this on the basis that any deviation from ancient teaching was bound to provide false understandings. Those who were bold enough to venture beyond these ancient confines saw it as proof of the need to take a new look at life.

The seventeenth century was therefore witness to a tentative dawn of a new freedom, and the 'curious' – as this generation of thinkers often referred to themselves – cautiously started to shake themselves free. This wasn't a matter of instantly casting all ancient knowledge aside, but rather of insisting that every idea should be tested by experiment. The curious made great claims that they accepted ideas, new or old, only when they had experimental evidence for each theory.

So it was this new spirit of discovery that set the scene for Denis' work. If Greek theory and biblical theology had been the only sources of information, it is doubtful that he would have ever given a second thought to the idea of transfusing blood. Except for a few fanciful mythical or historic events, he would have had no reason for believing that it would be anything other than a dangerous and possibly even immoral thing to try. But Denis was also aware of the work of William Harvey. In 1624 this English physician and surgeon had published a shockingly novel idea. Written in Latin, *De Motu Cordis (The Motion of the Heart)* cast aside the centuries-old Galenic concept of blood flow. Harvey had no particular problem with the idea that food was turned into chyle in the stomach, and that this chyle became blood when it was taken into the liver. However, he differed in what happened next. Galen had maintained that the blood then moved to the heart, where some was passed from the right ventricle to the lungs, while the rest moved through pores in the central dividing septum, into the left ventricle, and from there was drawn to the needy parts of the body and used up. Instead, Harvey demonstrated that blood constantly circulated around the body.

Harvey still had little idea of why blood actually chased round and round, and many of the arguments he used to reach his conclusion could now be seen as wildly inaccurate and verging on the amusing. But as Denis read Harvey's book, he, like many others, realised that this work raised new possibilities for the way physicians might handle blood, one of which was transfusion.

Demonstrating that blood circulates was only one of the reasons why this work was so important. The second was that in pursuing his theory, Harvey showed how he was deeply set in Greek tradition, but at the same time breaking new ground in what was on the way to becoming modern science. Debates continue in the twenty-first century about whether he was an ancient or a modern.

Born on 1 April 1578, in Folkestone, Kent, Harvey was the eldest of seven children. He was short, had olive-coloured skin, a round face and, by all accounts, a short temper. His eyes were small and black, almost certainly making him distinctly short-sighted, and the long raven-black hair of his youth turned progressively more white so that by the time he was 60, there were no black strands left. Being born the son of a yeoman farmer meant he was comfortably off, but not rich. Being bright, his family sent him to study medicine at Caius College, Cambridge. Following a typical career path, he then spent the better part of three years working at Padua University in Italy, the foremost centre of medical excellence in the world. The combined experience would have given him an exceptional grounding in Galen's understanding of the body, but would have also exposed him to many of those who were beginning to question the ancient conclusions.

While at Padua, Harvey would have learnt of Renaissance physician Andreas Vesalius, one of the first to question the unquestionable. Originally from Belgium, Vesalius studied medicine in Paris, where he began making careful dissections of bodies. Arguably, his most important move was to climb off the lecturer's chair. When he started his studies, lecturers tended to sit at a distance, reading directions from a textbook and waving a long stick in the general direction of interesting features inside the body, while some lesser mortal did the nasty business of cutting and pulling. In an age when appearance was everything, few people with learning and dignity wanted to get their hands dirty, or come too close to a smelly, rotting corpse. Moreover, there was still the ancient Greek legacy of thought that intellectual people should not get involved in manual work, which should be left to the lower class of labouring technicians.

Getting stuck in, literally, had allowed Vesalius to take a fresh look at old ideas. Try as he might, he could find no pores in the chambers of the heart. He recognised the indentations in the septum that Galen had recorded, but could not force blood, or any other liquid, from one side to the other. In his own words:

> Not long ago I would not have dared diverge a hair's breadth from Galen's opinion. But the septum is as thick, dense, and compact as the rest of the heart. I do not see therefore, how even the smallest particle can be transferred from the right to the left ventricle through it.[1]

There was now a problem. If these pores didn't exist, the whole of Galen's system failed. To get around this, most physicians started to assume that the blood could dissolve through the solid wall, though experiments showed that this did not happen if one side of a heart was filled with blood and pressure applied to it. Versalius therefore believed there must be some other solution, but died 60 years before the problem was resolved. Working with his assistant Johann Stephan von Calcar, Vesalius did, however, publish *De Humani Corporis Fabrica*, a book of intricate diagrams detailing the blood vessels in the body – a text that would have been an essential part of Harvey's education.

Although this started to chip away at the foundations of Galenic belief, there remained many unanswered questions. For example, all the evidence pointed towards there being two different types of blood. Dark-blue blood moved in thin-walled vessels – veins – and bright-red blood travelled in thick-walled arteries. We now know that the thick walls of arteries enable them to transmit the pressure pulse around the body, but this has come from the realisation that the heart acts as a pump. Galen thought that the active phase of the heart's behaviour was when it expanded. This expansion, he believed, caused it to attract blood to it. All of the rest of the body then attracted blood to it in order to satisfy the needs of individual organs. This concept is similar to watching ink seep into a dry tissue paper, where blank paper attracts the fluid.

It would be easy to suggest that cutting a vessel and watching blood pour, or spurt, out is proof enough that blood moves around the body. But, while the observation that blood poured out was undisputed by Renaissance philosophers and all thinkers who came before them, the Renaissance school saw it simply as evidence that the system was full, and consequently under pressure. In itself it provided no evidence that blood circulated around the body; after all, a similar result can be obtained by making a hole in the side of a pipe that is transporting water from one place to another.

Lectures and conversation over dinner may have also brought a second person to Harvey's attention, namely Michael Servetus, though the few people who did know of him would have probably spoken his name only after dropping their voices a little. This Spanish physician had described the anatomy of the heart and pointed to the four large vessels that came from it. He had also correctly suggested that the muscles of the heart relax as the organ fills with blood, and that they contract when it empties. This alone was revolutionary.

Servetus also made crude attempts at measuring blood flow, and came to the additional conclusion that the amount of blood travelling

Plate 2 Frontispiece of *De Humani Corporis Fabrica* (Andreas Vasalius). Reproduced by permission of Lane Medical Library Special Collections, Stanford University.

to the lungs was far more than they needed to satisfy their own demand for nutrition. More radically, he believed that blood flowed back from the lungs to the heart, but while he noted this down as an illustration in a theological text, there is no evidence that he recognised the significance of his findings.

Sadly for Servetus, he fell into an argument with the dogmatic French theologian John Calvin over the nature of God. Challenging Christian teaching was dangerous, and he was marked as a heretic in France, Spain and Geneva. When Servetus tried to convert Calvin to the view that Jesus was not the Son of God, he effectively signed his own death warrant. Even going into hiding and assuming the pseudonym Michael Villeneuve didn't save him. He decided to call in on Calvin in person while on the way from Paris to Rome. At this point Calvin was living in Geneva, and far from being willing to discuss issues, he had Servetus arrested on his arrival. His trial was brief and Servetus soon lit up the sky as he burnt at the stake. It was a reminder, if one was needed, that ideas could get one into trouble.

Harvey would have also encountered the work of Italian surgeon Matteo Realdo Colombo, a contemporary of Versalius, having succeeded him as professor of surgery at Padua in 1554. Colombo's chief claim to fame was the discovery that blood passed through the lungs, and he recorded this in an anatomical text book. The book also stated that the heart acted like a pump, actively expelling blood into the great arteries. The idea was basically correct, but it was so extreme and revolutionary that few took it seriously. In any case, Colombo was a professor of surgery, and 'proper' doctors had little time for these rough-and-ready technicians. His book was well known, but Colombo had little direct evidence to support his conclusion, and was unable to make use of the newly emerging scientific approaches to plead his case. This raises the question of how often a person fails to gain recognition because their ideas come ahead of their time?

Arriving back in England in the summer of 1602, Harvey settled in London, and soon became part of the establishment. The Queen's physician was looking for a husband for his daughter, Elizabeth Browne. Harvey made a perfect match. The suit was good for Harvey as his wife came with money and with access to the King. Consequently he didn't have to push his medical work too hard for a living, and had plenty of time for research. The increasingly close liaison that he formed with

King James I of England, and then King Charles I, meant that he spent quite a bit of his life on the move, acting as a diplomat. Observation and discovery were, however, always high on his agenda. On one trip accompanying Thomas Howard, the Earl of Arundel, to meet the Austrian-born Holy Roman Emperor Ferdinand II, he complained at the lack of wildlife to study:

> By the way we could scarce see a dog, crow, kite, raven or any bird, or anything to anatomise: only some few miserable people, the relics of the war and the plague, whom famine had made anatomies before I came.

He travelled with King Charles on military campaigns against the Scots in 1639, 1640 and 1641, and when the Civil War broke out, he seldom left the King's side. History records that Harvey was present at the battle of Edgehill in October 1642, the event that marked the start of hostilities. Even with the sounds of war echoing in his ears, Harvey was not easily separated from his books, and soon after the first shots were fired he led the 12-year-old Prince of Wales and 10-year-old Duke of York under a nearby hedge, took out a pocketbook and read. 'But,' explains seventeenth-century gossip John Aubrey, 'he had not read very long before a bullet of a great gun grazed on the ground near him, which made him remove his station'.[2]

After the indecisive battle, Harvey moved with the king to his base in Oxford, even though his wife and home were in Coombe in Surrey. Still, as Aubrey records, he wasn't about to be deprived of companionship:

> I remember he kept a pretty young wench to wayte on him, which I guesse he made use of for warmth-sake as King David did, and tooke care of her in his Will, as also of his man servant.[3]

Thus it was this strange mixture of circumstance and local politics that caused Oxford to be the base for much of Harvey's scientific work. It was also his close friendship with the King that brought royalty into the centre of scientific research in England, as Charles frequently came to the demonstrations that Harvey laid on. This friendship also gave Harvey access to the King's herd of deer, which enabled his work to progress in later years.

After years of formal education, Harvey was convinced that the body worked on similar principles to the rest of the cosmos – it was a microcosm. Just as the sun was central to the solar system and gave life to the world, so he believed that the heart was at the centre of the body and was the source of its life. In the opening remarks in *Exercitatio Anatomica de Motu Cordis et Sanguinis in Animalibus* (more commonly called *De Motu Cordis*), the book that Harvey eventually wrote, detailing his work, he expands on this theme, likening the heart not only to the sun, but to his benefactor King Charles I. The opening of Harvey's most famous book reads:

> Most illustrious King! The animal's heart is the basis of its life, its chief member, the sun of its microcosm; on the heart all its activity depends, from the heart all its liveliness and strength arise. Equally is the king the basis of his kingdoms, the sun of his microcosm, the heart of the state; from him all power arises and all grace stems.

The question was how did the heart perform this function? One difficulty Harvey and his contemporaries faced was how to study the heart. One approach was to work at dissecting dead animals, but then they could only stare at an immobile heart and it was consequently difficult to establish what it did. Alternatively they could try to open the chests of living animals, but here these pioneering anatomists found that the hearts were beating so fast that they couldn't make out its individual movements. Harvey likened the situation to trying to work out how a musket works. The sequence of movements starts with pulling the trigger and ends with the bullet firing out of the barrel. But the chain of events that links the two occurs so rapidly that tracing it is almost impossible. The only hope is to slow the system down.

To achieve this he based many of his observations on the hearts of animals that were dying, where the heart was consequently beating very slowly, or snakes, which always have slow heart-rates. Now he could see that the pulses in arteries came immediately after the heart contracted. He was now certain that the pulse was due to blood moving into the vessels.

By careful observation, Harvey found that blood entered the right side of the heart from the *vena cava*, the vein that collects blood from the organs of the body, including the liver. When it contracted it forced this blood into the lungs. The blood then returned to the left side of the heart, and from there it was pumped via the aorta into the arteries around the body.

Again Harvey's training in ancient Greek philosophy came into action. Aristotle had concluded that there was too much water running in the earth's rivers. Without performing any calculations of flow rates or volumes, this ancient philosopher decided that the world did not contain enough water for it to simply flow from the top of mountains into the sea without it returning from the sea to the top of the mountain:

> It is clear that, if anyone should wish to make the calculation of the amount of water flowing in a day and picture the reservoir, he will see that it would have to be as great as the size of the earth or not far short of it to receive all the water flowing in a year.

Aristotle realised that the sun's energy caused sea water to evaporate. It rose in the air, cooled and then fell as rain on the mountains. This water collected in the form of streams, trickled into rivers and rushed into the seas. It was a cycle of activity.

From his observations, Harvey became convinced that there was too much blood flowing through the heart to be explained by Galen's one-way flow from the liver to the extremities. Maybe, he thought, there was a similar cycle of activity:

> But not finding it possible that this could be supplied by the juices of the ingested aliment without the veins on the one hand becoming drained, and the arteries on the other getting ruptured through the excessive charge of blood, unless the blood should somehow find its way from the arteries into the veins, and so return to the right side of the heart, I began to think whether there might not be a Motion, As It Were, In A Circle.[4]

Harvey drew inspiration from the macrocosm. In the same way that the sun heats the seas and causes evaporation, the heart could heat the blood. As it rushed through the arteries it gave out this heat and the nutrition that it contained. Thus it cooled and needed to return to the heart in order to be reinvigorated. If this sort of process occurred in the macrocosm, the weather, then it was safe to assume that it could be happening in the microcosm, the body. For Harvey, the *vena cava* was the 'headspring, the cellar and cistern of the blood'.

Evidence from guesstimates

To prove the point, Harvey did a series of incredibly rough but ingenious calculations. Based on a few observations he suggested that the heart's ventricles could hold anything between one-and-a-half and three ounces of blood. He then estimated that when the heart contracted it expelled anything between one-eighth and a third of this volume. Finally he said that the heart beats between 1,000 and 4,000 times per hour. Once he had the numbers, the calculation was easy.

$$\frac{\text{volume of left}}{\text{ventricle}} \times \frac{\text{proportion of}}{\text{blood expelled}} = \frac{\text{volume of blood}}{\text{passed per beat}}$$

$$\frac{\text{volume of blood}}{\text{passed per beat}} \times \frac{\text{number of beats}}{\text{per half-hour}} = \frac{\text{volume passing through}}{\text{the heart in half an hour}}$$

Harvey's conclusion was that at least 500 ounces of blood moved through the heart in half an hour (about 16 kilograms). It turns out that this number is extremely inaccurate, as the true volume passing through an adult human's heart when he or she is resting is more like 4 kilograms per minute (120 kilograms per half-hour). But even Harvey's value was enough to convince him that there was not enough blood in the body for this to be moving in one direction. It must be circulating.

This was the early 1600s, there were no microscopes and it was therefore impossible for Harvey to see the capillaries that linked the arteries to the veins. All the same, Harvey became increasingly convinced that blood must circulate, and the results of a series of experiments helped to confirm his convictions. To start with he took a snake, opened its skin and squeezed its *vena cava*. The heart turned white and became smaller, its beat slowing. Clearly, blocking this vein prevented blood flowing into the heart. Its activity and colour were restored, however, as soon as he took his finger off the vein. Conversely, if he compressed the artery leading from the heart, Harvey saw the heart swell and turn deep red. Occluding the artery was preventing blood leaving the heart. This was more evidence of the direction in which the blood flowed through the heart.

Harvey then showed that blood flowed through arteries in the arm. To do this he tied a bandage tightly around his arm. The pulse in the wrist disappeared. He had cut off the flow. Instead, there was a regular throbbing at the site of the bandage, which Harvey attributed to the blood 'trying to burst through an impediment to its passage and reopen the channel'.

He then relaxed the bandage just a little. Blood flowed into the arm but couldn't escape. The veins in the arm filled up and stood out. One of Harvey's tutors in Italy, Hieronymus Fabricus of Aquapendente, had previously proposed that the lumps seen in veins were valves, but had not been able to suggest why these were present. Harvey noted:

> The finder out of these portals did not understand the use of them, nor others who have said the blood by its weight should fall downward: for there are in the jugular vein those that look downward and do hinder the flow of blood upwards.

Harvey was gathering evidence that the valves ensured that blood could travel only in one direction – flowing to the heart. Blood from the head travelled down the jugular vein through the downward-pointing valves, while blood from the legs and lower body rose through the upward-pointing valves in the rest of the veins. This was completely contrary to expectation. Blood, after all, was supposed to move from the liver to the rest of the body through veins, thus moving in the opposite direction. Harvey was convinced that the only explanation of his findings was that blood circulated around the body.

Just before his death, Harvey met the super-rich Irish pioneer of discovery, Robert Boyle, who recorded their conversation:

> I remember that when I asked our famous Harvey, in the only discourse I had with him (which was but a while before he died), what were the things which induced him to think of the circulation of the Blood? He answered me, that when he took notice that the valves in the veins of so many several parts of the body, were so placed that they gave free passage of the blood towards the heart, but opposed the passage of the venal blood the other way: he was invited to imagine, that so provident a cause as nature had not plac'd so many valves without design: and no design seemed more probable, than that, since the blood could not well, because of the interposing valves, be sent by the [veins] to the limbs, it should be

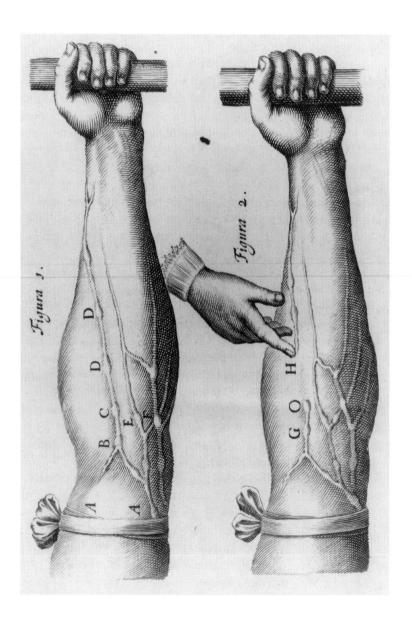

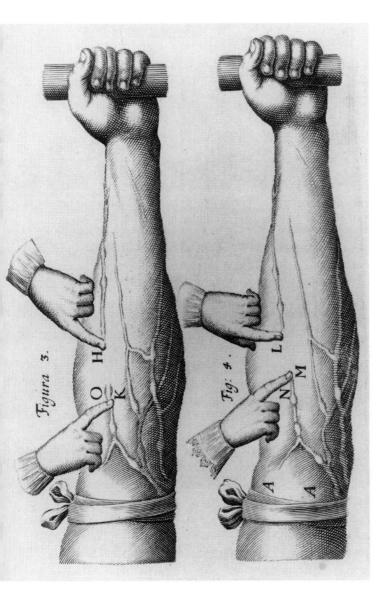

Plate 3 William Harvey's diagram of arm and valves. Reproduced by permission of Lane Medical Library Special Collections. Stanford University.

sent through the arteries, and returned through the veins, whose valves did not oppose its course that way.

When this revolutionary concept was published, opinion was divided. If Harvey was right, this meant that the whole of the underlying theories of health and medicine might need to be revised. Unsurprisingly, this met considerable resistance, and in places, downright opposition. There is plenty of evidence that Harvey delayed publishing his ideas for a few years while he grew in confidence. It wasn't long before the idea was widely accepted.

Harvey was distinctly aware of the enormity of his work. In the first chapters of *De Motu Cordis* he confidently discusses the critical findings that convinced him that blood did indeed move from veins into arteries through the heart. In chapter eight, he is more cautious. As he moves on to air his concept of a circulating system, he expresses his fears:

> But what remains to be said upon the quantity and source of the blood which thus passes is of a character so novel and unheard-of that I not only fear injury to myself from the envy of a few, but I tremble lest I have mankind at large for my enemies, so much doth wont and custom become a second nature. Doctrine once sown strikes deep its root, and respect for antiquity influences all men. Still the die is cast, and I place my trust in my love of truth and the candour of cultivated minds.

His anxiety was well founded; after publishing *De Motu Cordis*, Harvey complained that there was a distinct drop in the number of patients who were prepared to come to him for medical advice. He once told Aubrey that the gossip among common folk around town was that he was 'crack-brained', but that he was personally convinced the real problem was that physicians were spreading malicious gossip because they were jealous of his findings. If truth be told, few people had a kind word for his medical skills in any case, so his lack of medical practice was probably not a great loss to the community.

Though many scientists die before their radical ideas are accepted, Harvey had the distinct fortune to come up with his idea when he was young, and then live to see his 80th birthday. This was sufficient time for the concept to be tested by others and gain credence from most of those involved in science and medicine.

Ancient or modern?

So was Harvey an ancient thinker who based his work on philosophical argument, or a modern scientist working with experiments and careful measurements? To start with, his main guiding principles were drawn from two key ancient expectations. The first, as we have seen, was his belief that the body would operate as a microcosm of the rest of the world. The second was that the body had been carefully designed – everything in the body could only be present because God had made it and put it there. Like many of his time he saw anatomy as a branch of theological study:

> The examination of bodies has always been my delight, and I have thought that we might thence not only obtain an insight into the lighter mysteries of nature, but there perceive a kind of image or reflection of the omnipotent Creator himself.

In *De Motu Cordis* he comments on the relative size of the heart's ventricles and the vessels that are attached to the heart 'for nature doing nothing in vain, would never have given them so large a relative size without a purpose ...'.

Looking at the way Harvey reached his conclusions shows that he had scant regard for measuring anything carefully. As was the case for the rest of his contemporaries, he didn't see any benefit in making careful measurements. His estimates of blood flow through a heart were wildly inaccurate, even though it may have been easy for him to measure volumes more carefully and monitor how frequently a heart beats in a minute to a high degree of accuracy. Harvey was more interested in the intellectual argument than detailed measurements, and as such he came to the right conclusions on faulty data.

Maybe he was just a few years ahead of his time. While Harvey was working on the heart, Galileo Galilei was developing ways of using careful measurements and accurate calculations to study the universe, the macrocosm. However, Galileo had yet to publish his work, and Harvey was therefore not in a position to borrow this rigorous approach and adapt it to physiology.

Harvey was living and working at a crossroads in philosophy. He was using rational debate to form theories, and then performing rudimentary experiments to see if they matched reality. Harvey refuted strongly any notion that he was one of the newly emerging medical fraternity, saying that in comparison with Aristotle these pretenders were mere 'shit breeches'. From the viewpoint of the twenty-first century, he could be seen as a late ancient, or an early modern, or better still, a bridge between the two.

When looking at Denis' work we will find that while he claimed to be part of the new world of questioning and discovery, he too made little or no serious attempt to take measurements, and seemed to be lax at making detailed observations. In Denis' case, however, this is more likely to be an indication of his cavalier attitude to detail than a particular reflection on the philosophy underlying his work.

Driven by ebullition

If blood was circulating around the body, something must be driving it. The generally accepted view was that any pressure in the system came from 'ebullition'. Ebullition is the term used to describe the expansion that happens to milk or honey when it is put into a saucepan and heated on a cooker. Just as it reaches boiling point, the liquid froths up, and if one is not careful, rapidly rises to the top of the pan and overflows. The same would happen to a pan full of blood, were you to attempt to boil it. Galen, and those who came after him, believed that the heart's key function was to heat the blood. The resulting ebullition caused the blood's volume to increase, forcing it out into the arteries. The increased pressure inside the heart caused by this ebullition was the reason why the heart rhythmically increased in volume. According to Galen, the heart was a chamber that attracted blood and then had the job of acting as a heater.

Over the waters in France, Descartes quickly adopted Harvey's notion of a blood flowing around a system of tubes into his mechanical view of life. Even so, Descartes held onto some of the ancient theories, in that he still believed that the heart's expansion was due to the ebullition of blood within it. As Denis was a close follower of Cartesian thought, there is every reason to believe that he would have shared this understanding of the system.

Harvey thought hard about this, and then performed an experiment. He took equal volumes of blood from an artery and from a vein, placed them in two identical jars and watched what happened. In both cases blood clots formed. Over a few minutes the surface of both became the same colour. But more importantly for Harvey, both the arterial and the venous blood remained at the same volume. The arterial blood did not shrink as it cooled. If the arterial vessels were under pressure, or arterial blood was driven around the vessels because heat in the heart had caused ebullition, then as it cooled its volume should have reduced. After all, taking boiling milk off the cooker allows the froth to subside. As this change did not occur, Harvey concluded that ebullition was a figment of people's imaginations. No one knows what Denis thought of this experiment, or whether he cared much. When he looked at the blood system he was much more keen to see what he could do with it than to find out how it worked.

Others, such as Dutch anatomist Johannes Waleus, tried other ways of tying circulation into the prevailing understanding that the heart heated the blood. Waleus came to the conclusion that blood circulated in order to be kept in perfect condition – dark venous blood went into the right side of the heart and bright-red pulsing arterial blood came chasing out of the left side. For Waleus, the explanation was simple; blood was heated in the heart, and then 'condensed' as it became more concentrated in the rest of the body. For, he said, nothing in it is warmer than the heart and nothing is cooler than the surface. This, he thought, allowed for the possibility that blood was refined in the same way that chemists purify liquids by repeatedly boiling them and condensing the vapour.

Closing the loop

Those sceptical of Harvey's ideas pointed to two critical flaws in his theory. Firstly, there was the lack of any evidence of connections between arteries and veins, and secondly there was nothing to demonstrate what would push blood back to the heart from the extremities. As the physician Caspar Hoffmann of Nuremberg, Germany, put it, how did Harvey explain the way that blood passed from the arteries to the veins?

Even if invisible passages existed, how did Harvey explain the movement – what was the driving force?

Only four years after Harvey's death, in 1661 Italian physiologist Marcello Malpighi found the missing link, though it would take decades for people to work out that it was the pressure of muscles squeezing veins that forced blood back to the heart. Having been born the year Harvey published *De Motu Cordis*, Malpighi went on to study Aristotelian philosophy at the University of Bologna. Life was not straightforward for Malpighi: his father, mother and paternal grandmother all died while he was studying, and he consequently had to leave the university for a couple of years while he looked after his three younger sisters and sorted out the family's finances. Two years later he was back and working hard, eventually combining a medical career with an interest in science.

Malpighi's pursuit of science was controversial. He began to question Galen, and therefore lost a number of opportunities for promotion, though he was eventually fêted for his work and became a personal friend of the Pope. Much of Malpighi's work was devoted to peering down some of the world's earliest microscopes, and drawing what he saw. In 1661 he published his first book, which, among other things, announced his observation that there was a network of tiny vessels in the lungs of frogs. Calling these capillaries, he went on to speculate, correctly, that they might be the missing link in Harvey's circulation, the tubes that connected arteries to veins. In scientific circles this discovery finally put an end to the idea that blood turned into flesh at the end of veins. However, it took many decades before knowledge and acceptance of the demise of this Galenic idea spread throughout the medical community, and even longer before it came to interest the public at large.

His discovery soon won Malpighi a pseudo English citizenship. Scientists in England were distinctly possessive of their work and their claims to fame, and central to this fame was Harvey's groundbreaking evidence for the theory of circulation. They were therefore keen that any new work that added more detail to this would find a home on English soil. It is not surprising, then, that by 1667 Henry Oldenburg, secretary to England's most prestigious research organisation, the Royal Society, had started communicating by letter with Malpighi on behalf of the Society. Quite clearly Malpighi was a scholar, and his observation of capillaries was unlikely to be his only contribution to science and medicine. The best way, therefore, that England had of keeping his research within its scientific family was to invite Malpighi to become a fellow of the Royal Society. He accepted and added his signature to the growing list of scientific worthies in 1669.

The last piece of the circulation puzzle was now in place, yet still no one knew what blood was actually doing. This information was enough for many people around Europe to scratch their heads and see what they could do with a circulating blood system. When Denis approached the issue he was less concerned with the underlying physiology than with seeing if this new knowledge could modify medical practice.

CHAPTER THREE

English infusion

Claiming that blood circulated fundamentally questioned all understanding of what blood was, and what it did. Scientists in Oxford began to assess two possible routes of investigation – infusion and transfusion. In about 1639, the year before Denis was born, Oxford scholar Francis Potter began to consider the ideas of transfusing blood from one animal to another. He claimed that this occurred while he was thinking about an event that occurs in Publius Ovidius Naso's story of Jason and the Argonauts. In Ovid's tale, Medea restored the youth of Jason's aged father by giving him a brew incorporating moonlight and hoar frost, bits of owls, tortoises, wolves, stags and crows. Medea poured her brew into his mouth while letting his blood flow from a cut in his neck. According to legend, the old man's youth was instantly restored; his white hair resumed its former black colour, his veins filled with blood and his paleness was replaced with a healthy complexion.

Potter wondered if there could be any way of replacing old and worn blood. Trying to solve recurrent illness was a personal issue, as he regularly suffered from epileptic fits. His 27 years at Trinity College, Oxford, encompassed the siege of the city, and it was through this period of history that Potter scribbled remarks on the sides of his note books commenting on the number of times that Harvey came to look at the hens' eggs that were incubating in the college. This was because Harvey was looking at the way that chick embryos develop in the egg, and was making almost daily visits to the chambers of his colleague Ralph Bathurst. By 1651, Potter and Harvey had become good friends, and the two enjoyed stretching the thinking of one another. This proved particularly useful for, in contrast to Harvey, Potter never had much interest in reading.

Once the siege was over, Potter moved to the Rectory in Kilmington in Somerset, where he dressed like a monk or old-time pastor and lived alone, pleased to get away from the bustle of a courtier-laden city. He was a passionate gardener, and his long, pale face could often be seen above the tall, immaculately kept, square-cut box hedges. He also set up a private laboratory and carried out a series of experiments. He loved inventing machines, working both as carpenter and blacksmith to turn his dreams into reality. One of his machines was a complex pulley mechanism specially designed to make light work of heaving barrel-sized buckets from his exceptionally deep well. Aubrey was one of his few close friends, and was particularly impressed by the contraption. Potter was also obsessed with theological work aimed at revealing that the Pope was the antichrist, and in his only book, *Interpretation of the Number 666*, like many others he sought to make mathematical sense of the number of the Beast in Revelation.

In his parsonage, Potter began pursuing his aim to collect blood from one hen and then inject it into another. But he hit two problems. Firstly he had difficulty drawing blood, and secondly it tended to clot before he could pass it into another animal. Trying to perform the experiment on hens was not the best idea because the animals are so small, and getting pipes inside any vessels was extremely difficult.

On 7 December 1652, Potter wrote to Aubrey describing the situation:

Worthy Sir,

I am sorry that I cannot at the moment give you a better account of the experiment that you want to know about. I am as yet frustrated in ipso limine (The problem being my lack of experience – as I have never attempted such thing upon any creature before) for although I have tried many times, I cannot strike the vein so as to make it bleed in any considerable quantity.

I have made a little clear transparent vessel from the claw of a pullet. It looks a bit like a bladder, and I have fastened an ivory pipe to one of its necks. I have inserted this pipe into a vein in the lowest joint of a leg. It is a large vein and stands out well. However, I can only get 2 or 3 drops of blood to come through the pipe into the bladder.

I would have sent this bladder and pipe to you in my letter, but I was afraid that the letter might get lost. Instead I have done a rough drawing of it so that you can understand what I am trying to do:-

a = the neck of the craw that goes into my mouth so I can suck
b = the other neck which goes to the gissar. Another pipe may be tied to this end and put into the vein of another living creature at the same time

d = a little crooked ivory pipe, fastened to a bladder
e = the capacity of the craw or bladder

Sir, I humbly present my service and best wishes unto you, and shall still be
Yours, in all true affection, to be commanded
Francis Potter
Kilmanton, Decemb. 7, 1652

Despite this lack of success, Potter didn't give up easily, and was encouraged to keep on trying when Aubrey sent him a surgeon's lancet. A year later he wrote again to Aubrey explaining that he had improved his technique and was using small bellows for collecting blood. He had also replaced the ivory pipes with 'windpipes of some small animals', suggesting that he had had marginal success in placing these into veins in two different animals and exchanging their blood. It seems unlikely,

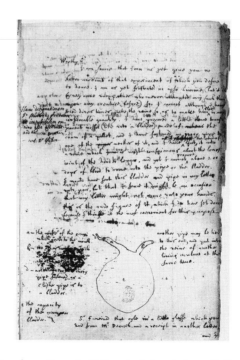

Plate 4   Letter from Francis Potter to John Aubrey, 7 December 1652, Bodleian Library, Oxford, Aubrey MS 6, F.61R, showing a diagram of a bladder. Reproduced by permission of the Bodleian Library, Oxford University.

though, that he would have had any real success, in that there would have been no pressure difference to drive the blood from one animal to the other. More probably, the connecting tube filled slowly and then clotted.

The methods described in Potter's letter also indicate that he was attempting to draw blood from veins, and was ignoring arteries. This is probably because veins tend to be more readily accessible, and didn't spurt blood when he cut them. Unfortunately for Potter, as veins take blood from capillary beds back to the heart, there is very little driving pressure. Consequently these vessels collapse easily. If they ran inside blocks of muscle, they would easily become compressed and block. Having them running on the surface, just beneath the skin, keeps them open. The ease with which they close would, however, have posed a problem for the early transfusion pioneers; if they attempted to use a syringe to draw blood out of the vessel too rapidly, they would suck the vessel closed. From this point of view, they would have had greater success trying to get blood from arteries, which are filled with blood at a much higher pressure and are consequently much less likely to flatten.

Potter's departure did not mean the end of experiments in Oxford — far from it. However, those who remained in Oxford followed a slightly different course of investigations. They initially began trying to infuse solutions into the bloodstream. One of the key mover-shakers was Boyle, who had arrived in Oxford around 1656 and had always been fascinated that a septic wound could disable a whole person. How, he asked, could an abscess in your hand or leg cause the whole body to suffer? Harvey's circulation could be the answer. Maybe the wound released toxins into the blood and the blood circulated them around the body. It was time for experiment.

Boyle first fed the head, tail and gall of a viper to a dog. These were the parts of the body that most people believed contained the poisonous venom of the snake. However, the dog was unaffected. This was a puzzle. Boyle was perfectly aware that one bite would kill. For him, the observation didn't make sense; if food was converted straight into blood, then feeding the poison to the dog should be just as effective as injecting it through the reptile's fangs. At this point, there was little or no concept of the processes of digestion. As far as anyone knew, the stomach simply dissolved food and mashed it up until it became a liquid paste. No one considered the possibility that the components of the food, what we would now call fats, proteins and carbohydrates, were taken to pieces, forming a soup of their constituent parts. In the case of the venom, this digestion had rendered it harmless.

Unaware of this, Boyle followed a different train of thought. There must be something intrinsic to the snake's anger that made its bite so deadly. After all, everyone knew that when mad dogs went into a rage and bit a person, they gave the victim a nasty illness. There was no sign that the dogs produced venom, so there must be something about the rage itself that transmitted the illness. (We now know that this occurs through disease-causing rabies bacteria stuck to the dog's teeth becoming injected into the victim as the jaws clamp onto the dog's prey. Or at any rate, this is our current understanding of what occurs!)

Writing in his 1663 book *Some Considerations Touching the Usefulness of Experimental Naturall Philosophy*, Boyle concluded that the best way to test this idea would be to dip a needle into some venom and then prick it into a dog's veins. This would transfer the venom, but not the anger. There is no record that Boyle ever carried out this particular experiment, though had he done so he would have discovered that the venom was capable of killing despite the lack of anger in the way it was inserted into the dog. Had he stabbed the needle into a blood vessel he would also have performed the first infusion experiment.

Instead, in the spring of 1656 Boyle had teamed up with members of the Oxford elite. One was the wonder youth, Christopher Wren, who had been driven out of Cambridge because of his Royalist background. This was the same man who was later to become famous when his sideline interest in architecture led to a chance in a lifetime – following the fire of London, he was asked to design a new St Paul's Cathedral. At this stage in his life, however, this short, neat young man with flowing black hair, was much more taken up by his lifelong passion for anatomy and astronomy. Another of the Oxford elite was the clergyman-scientist John Wilkins who had just married a widowed sister of Oliver Cromwell, and in a few years' time would be moved to Cambridge by Richard Cromwell to be Master of Trinity College.

For a few years, siding with Cromwell's family was a good route to success – King Charles I had been beheaded six years earlier, and a restoration of the monarchy seemed doubtful. In order to hedge their bets, the Boyle family had been careful to divide the allegiance of their members between the Royalist and Parliamentary camps.

So it was that Boyle, Wren and Wilkins met one day at Boyle's lodgings on the High Street in Oxford, overlooking Brasenose College and not much more than a stone's throw from the already famous Bodleian Library. The accommodation was over a chemist's shop, which was marked out from the others by the large mortar-and-pestle that hung from one of the criss-crossing oak beams making up the front wall. Wren and Wilkins opened the heavy oak door and were welcomed by the shop's owner, apothecary John Crosse, a portly man in his late fifties, who was dressed in the sort of drab-brown, but well cut coat that was common for successful merchants. His shop was a showcase of gleaming glass jars containing rocks and powders, herbs and spices; row upon row of them, all neatly arranged on immaculately polished cedar shelves.

Crosse beckoned the way, but the gesture was unnecessary: Wren and Wilkins knew where to go – this was far from their first visit. They crossed the polished oak floor, went through a door and climbed the stairs. Boyle was waiting, and was prepared, having bought a young dog in the market that morning. After the normal round of pleasantries the three set to work, placing aprons over their clothing to protect it from the inevitable splashes that were about to occur. The 24-year-old Wren and his helpers freed a large vessel in the hind leg of the dog and tied a piece of linen around it. This closed the vessel, but also allowed them to hold it firmly. Then, 'having surmounted the difficulties which the tortured dog's violent struggling imposed', they inserted a quill into the vein and infused opium that had been dissolved in red wine. Boyle recounts what happened next, saying that the circulation rapidly carried it to the dog's head and to the rest of its body. The transmission was so rapid that they only just had time to untie the animal before the 'opium began to disclose its narcotick quality, and almost as soon as he was on his feet he began to nod his head, and falter and reel in his pace'. The animal became so disorientated that Wren and Boyle started to lay bets on whether it was going to survive at all. It was the first recorded case of a narcotic overdose from injecting drugs.

Not only did the dog survive, it even grew fat, presumably because its celebrated status meant that people kept feeding it. 'But,' explained Boyle when writing about the experiment, 'I could not long observe how it fared him: For this experiment ... having made him famous, he was soon after stolen away from me.'[5]

41

Researchers are sometimes boastful, sometimes shy about their work. Wren was modest. He made few loud claims, but instead wrote to his former anatomy tutor Sir William Petty who had moved to Dublin. He gave the letter to colleague Robert Wood, who was heading out to that same city to seek his fortune. Petty had recently been appointed physician to the army in Ireland, and Wren was sure he would be thrilled to know of his pupil's various successes. In the letter, Wren describes the exciting work going on in Oxford, mentioning the microscopes and telescopes that were providing remarkable new insight into the workings of the entire Creation. He wrote about the anatomical dissections performed on fish and fowl, and the observations of kidneys, brains and nerves. None of this was as important in Wren's mind as the 'most considerable' experiment of injecting wine and ale directly into the veins of a dog. 'It will be too long to tell you the effects of opium, scammony and other things which I have tried in this way,' wrote Wren, 'I am in further pursuit of the experiment, which I take to be of great concernment, and what will give great light to the theory and practice of physic.'[6]

The main idea was that injection could be an effective way to get medical treatments into the blood. Opium was known to be an effective painkiller; scammony was a plant similar to bindweed, which when boiled with water yielded a potent laxative. It would not have taken long for the men to discover that not only were the effects quick, but that the effects would also have been induced by smaller quantities of the compound than would have been necessary if the person simply swallowed the medication.

Fuelled by their excitement, Wren and his friends performed further experiments, many being carried out at the home of an old friend of Harvey's, Henry Pierrepoint, first Marquis of Dorchester and the first person to be made an honorary fellow of the Royal College of Physicians. These experiments allowed the team to perfect their technique, and they were soon using a bladder fixed to a quill in place of a syringe. Experience taught them that the dog needed to be large and lean so that they could find the vessels they needed, and be able to get the quill inside them. Wren was fascinated that soon after they had injected a 'good quantity' of wine and ale into a dog's veins, the animal became 'extremely drunk, but soon after pisseth it out'. On other occasions, Wren noted the effect of injecting two ounces of an infusion of *crocus metallorum*, an impure form of antimony that acts as a powerful purgative and emetic combined. Shortly after receiving this emetic, the dog started to vomit violently, so much so that it spewed out its entire life and died.

Viewing these experiments in what we now think of as the moral and ethical light of the twenty-first century, one thing is immediately apparent – the issue of animal rights was not a major concern in seventeenth-century England. However, the researchers did have a tendency to keep any animals that survived the experiments as pets, and, believe it or not, Boyle was noted as being tender-hearted towards his animal subjects.

There was widespread fascination in scientific experiments, and on some occasions, people brought their sick pets so that the 'curious' could try out their latest ideas on them. If it worked, their beloved and valued pet might be given a new lease of life, and they would now own a valuable exhibit. If it failed, then at least they would have had the entertainment of seeing science in action. The advantage of this for science was that people could witness new endeavours at first hand, but it could all too easily have the unfortunate side-effect of reducing it to the level of a circus act. Three-hundred-and-fifty years later, little has changed. Most of the media coverage surrounding Dolly the sheep, and later discussions of technologies such as therapeutic cloning, have made little attempt to increase the level of scientific understanding in the public. Instead these scientific events have at times been treated as opportunities for entertainment of the 'weird and wonderful' genre, or as a tool to engender shock and horror. Either way, science was then and still is yet again a tool for supplying amusement and it was difficult to get anyone to look at underlying issues seriously.

Human rights in the seventeenth century were also viewed quite differently than they are today. The death penalty was widely used to eradicate murderers, following the Old Testament biblical edict. This gave human life an extremely high value, and meant that killing an innocent person was not only dangerous, but that any person who was deemed to have committed a serious crime, such as murder, had lost what we would now call their 'human rights'. This was particularly the case if they came from a lower class.

But murder wasn't the only action that could get you into serious trouble. This was a world where holding the wrong religious or political views could be interpreted as putting you outside of God's loving care, and victims of justice were on occasions burnt at the stake, or hung, drawn and quartered. Relative to this, participation in a scientific trial could seem positively lenient.

It should come as little surprise, therefore, that soon after they found a way of getting liquors into animals, they had a go at injecting into a human. The first subject was the servant of the duc de Bordeaux, the French ambassador who was living in London. Boyle comments that the man was an inferior domestic who 'deserved to have been hanged',[7] and in so doing deflects any criticism of malpractice. The experiment occurred in the autumn of 1657, a few months after Harvey had died and Wren had moved to London to take the post of Gresham Professor of Astronomy. Along with his associate and pioneering physician, Timothy Clarke, Wren infused some extract of *crocus metallorum* into the poor man. As soon as they started the injection, the fellow, either craftily or actually, passed out and flopped to the floor. Afraid of killing the servant, the scientists decided to stop the experiment. Few courts in the land would give them a hard time for simply carrying out an experiment on a mischievous man, but they would be in trouble for killing him. Unless a court had convicted the person, his death could easily be seen as murder, and that, of course, carried the death penalty.

Alongside the wonder at the powerful effects achieved by injecting narcotic or noxious compounds into the bloodstream, Wren had another idea. Would it be possible to inject nutrients directly into vessels, bypassing the need to eat and digest anything? He was aware that should this work, he would have created a major medical tool that could enable physicians to keep seriously ill people alive until they were well enough to eat once more. Working with Clarke, he tried injecting into dogs all sorts of nutrient-containing fluids, including broth, milk, whey, and even blood itself. Most of these had fairly damaging effects on the animals, but not serious enough to cause them to stop investigating the possibilities.

Wren's stay in London was brief, and three years later, in 1660, he returned to Oxford taking the post of the Savilian Professor of Astronomy. He would therefore have returned right in the middle of further developments in blood studies. Although history now records him as the 'first author of the noble anatomical experiment of injecting liquors into the veins of animals', most of his biological studies seem to have revolved around discovering and describing the anatomy of the nervous system.

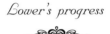

Lower's progress

While a few others were airing ideas of infusing fluids into blood, a young Cornishman, Richard Lower, was beginning to make serious progress. In a twentieth-century biography of Lower, American academics Ebbe and Phebe Hoff sum up his character as a prime example of the strength and stubbornness that could be expected in anyone who had grown up in Cornwall: 'It seems entirely fitting that a man of Lower's particular genius should have come out of Cornwall. The Cornish are an ancient people; and even today their dark, mysterious eyes and delicately moulded faces recall the many eerie legends which have sprung up about them from the time of the early Phoenicians and before, to the smugglers and wreckers of later years. Combined with a vivid imagination they have a sturdy perseverance, learned after years of struggle against the stony soil and a cruel sea. They are men of high courage, sly cunning and weird humour'.[8]

Lower had been born in 1631 into a time of change and uncertainty. Charles I was on the throne, and there was political and religious unrest around the country. Many people were voting with their feet and boarding ships for the hazardous trip across the Atlantic, hoping to find new lives and new freedoms in New England. At the age of 14 he followed his father to London and attended Westminster School. Located just a few hundred metres from Westminster Abbey and Westminster Hall, the seat of government, Lower would have grown up with a unique vantage point of history. Cromwell was at the same time building his New Model Army, Charles I was captured and had escaped, only to be recaptured a year later and beheaded on 30 January 1649, the year when Cromwell declared that Englishmen were no longer subjects of a Crown, but citizens of a Commonwealth.

In the same year, Lower had moved to Oxford to take up a studentship at Christ Church. There is no indication that this move was politically motivated, but Oxford still had a few prominent people who were bold enough to hold to a Royalist opinion.

Almost as soon as Lower arrived in Oxford, he met up with English doctor, anatomist and chemist Thomas Willis. The pair got on well and inspired each other's work. Willis generated ideas, while Lower developed skills in dissection that enabled him to put the ideas to the test. Indeed, Willis was one of the first to acknowledge that without Lower, few of his ideas would have come to anything. In his book *Cerebri Anatome*, Willis says:

> But for the more accomplishment of this task I had not sufficient leisure, and, perhaps, not sufficient ability, so I was not ashamed to summon the helping hand of others. I employed the assistance and co-operation of Richard Lower, a doctor of outstanding learning, and an anatomist of supreme skill. The sharpness of his scalpel and of his intellect, I readily acknowledge, enabled me to investigate better both the structure and the functions of bodies, whose secrets were previously concealed.

On 17 February 1653, Lower had taken the BA degree, and the following June took the MA degree. It was the year that Cromwell proclaimed himself to be the Lord Protector of England.

Intoxicated by learning, Lower eagerly took the opportunity of expanding the range of his knowledge by studying with the chemist Peter Sthael when he arrived in Oxford in 1659. Boyle had invited this former resident of Strasbourg in Royal Prussia to come to Oxford, despite the fact that many people felt that chemistry was a magical subject with little to offer true science. For many, the discipline was still closely associated with alchemy. Boyle thought differently, believing that if it was done properly, chemistry was a branch of natural philosophy, and if done well it could become the backbone of scientific endeavour. He would undoubtedly be very excited to see the way in which the subject has developed over the following century.

With Wren and Boyle to encourage him, Lower also started looking at infusion, and under Boyle's direction became enthusiastic about the possibility that infusions could remove the need to eat. In 1662 he repeated Boyle's earlier experiment by injecting two quarts of water from the spas at Tunbridge Wells into a dog. At the time, this spa water was greatly sought after for its healing properties. The animal soon 'discharged itself', and Lower became convinced that he would be able to keep a dog alive 'without meat, by syringing into a vein a due quantity of good broth, made pretty sharp with nitre, as usually the chyle tastes'.

Writing to Boyle on 18 January 1662, Lower suggested that it might be possible to implant a permanent pipe through which liquids could be fed into a patient, thereby removing the need to make a fresh incision each time more nutrients were needed. As such he had dreamt of the procedure that would eventually become an essential feature of intensive-care therapy – a process that has now been refined and goes by the name of total parenteral nutrition.

In 1664, Lower took his ideas one step further and injected two pints of warmed milk into a dog. The animal died within the hour. On further examination, Lower found that the vessels were blocked by 'blood mixed with milk, as if both had curdled together'. Lower's conclusion was that there was too much difference between blood and milk, and that for this sort of experiment to work, he needed to turn to a liquid more similar to blood.

No liquor was more similar to blood than blood itself. It is, however, not an easy fluid to handle. Any philosopher or scientist who had ever investigated it was immediately struck by the fact that its nature changed within minutes of removing it from the body – of a person or an animal. In the body it was always a fluid, but once outside it turned into a clotted red mass, sitting in a pool of straw-coloured, or pale pink, liquid.

According to Hippocrates, this was clear evidence that blood was inevitably corrupted when it was removed from the body, and most medics of the seventeenth century would have agreed with this sentiment. They would also have added that this corruption was due to a loss of heat and a loss of life. As keeping it warm over the flame of a candle or a small fire did nothing to prevent the clotting, it was clear that the heat required was something magically imparted by the living animal – the mysterious heat of the heart.

The combination of dissections, experiments and chemical learning kept Lower busy, and in 1665, as plague was devastating London and the south of England, he published his first book, *Diatribae de Febribus*. In this he reported an intriguing finding – blood changed colour when it passed through the lungs and heart. He next started to chip away at another of the critical problems left by Harvey – namely, how were the two different bloods, the blue venous blood and the red arterial blood, one and the same thing?

Plate 5   Richard Lower (1631–1691), anatomist. Oil painting by Jacob Huysmans. Reproduced by permission of the Wellcome Trust Medical Photographic Library.

It is interesting to see how often observations are guided by expectation. Since Harvey's famous publication, many had worked hard to explain the role of the heart. Most scientists still believed that its main task was to add vital heat to the blood, and this life-empowering heat was expected to be the explanation for the changes in the nature of the blood. This would have been etched into Lower's mind as he rummaged around inside animals' ribcages, trying to make sense of what was going on. It would not have been an easy task. To start with, the lungs are inflated as a partial vacuum develops in the space between the lungs and the inner surface of the ribcage, the pleura. This occurs with each breath as the muscles between the ribs contract and pull the ribcage out, and the flat sheet of muscle that makes up the diaphragm contracts and pulls itself down. As soon as Lower cut into the ribcage, he would have let air into that gap, destroyed this vacuum and consequently prevented the lungs from inflating.

With no air entering the lungs, the blood would have had only a limited ability to pick up fresh supplies of oxygen. There would therefore have been little colour change between that of the blood entering the lungs and that of the blood as it returned to the heart. Scientists are often faced with this challenge, in that as soon as they try to measure something they almost always end up disturbing it. This is not so bad if they are aware of the problem, because allowances can be made for it. But as Lower was unaware of the function of the lungs, he was not in a position to compensate. Getting true measurements is always very difficult, and it was only after he had started using bellows to pump air into the lungs during experiments that he began to get things right.

A further problem that Lower, and any other anatomist, had to overcome, was that the organs inside the chest are closely packed together, and the top of the heart is hidden beneath the lobes of the lung. This is the region where four large vessels plug into the heart. At this point the vessels are short and prone to tear if stretched or handled roughly. Lower would have had great difficulty seeing these vessels in a living animal, even though he was quite prepared to perform some gruesome dissections on the hapless dogs that had the misfortune of being handed to him.

He therefore approached the task with no notion of looking for a colour change as the blood passed through the lungs, and consequently it is little surprise that he failed to see it. Instead, he saw only that it had changed after leaving the heart's left ventricle. This just goes to show that, very often in science, the most obvious things can be invisible if you are not looking for them.

As it stood, Lower's careful observations now appeared to provide more evidence for the theory of the heart's involvement in the change of blood from its venous to its arterial state, though it still offered no scientific mechanism for the change in colour. Excited by his discovery, Lower had written to Boyle on 24 June 1664 explaining that he intended to find out 'the reason of the different colour of the blood, the one being florid and purple-red and the other dark and blackish'. It would take a few more years for Lower to unravel this mystery.

Little success in London

Back in London, others were dabbling with infusion and transfusion. A month earlier, the famous diarist Samuel Pepys recorded that he had witnessed a private demonstration in which Clarke and his colleagues at the Royal Society managed to kill a dog by letting opium into its hind leg. Pepys seems to be less than impressed by their technical prowess:

> May 16, 1664
> Forced to rise because of going to [see the Duke of York at] St James, where we did our usual business; and then by invitation to Mr Pierce's the surgeon, where I saw his wife, whom I had not seen in many months before ... By and by we were to see an experiment of killing a dog by letting opium into his hind leg. He and Dr Clarke did fail mightily in hitting the vein, and in effect did not do the business after many trials; but with the little they got in, the dog did presently fall asleep and so lay till he cut him up. And a little dog also, which they put it down his throate; he also staggered first, and then fell asleep and so continued; whether he recovered or no after I was gone, I know not – but it is a strange and sudden effect.

As an interested and intelligent observer, Pepys gives a valuable insight into how laypeople viewed this new pursuit of science. He was clearly excited by many of the experiments and thought that they provided some of the most entertaining moments in his week. Frequently, though, the various entries in his diary referring to scientific experiment show that Pepys is more taken by the spectacle than by the underlying principles. Like many observers of science from that point onward, he was also interested more by what science could deliver in terms of usable technologies, than by the minutiae of the underlying knowledge.

First steps

England's political and intellectual centre had moved around the country in the previous few decades, and in 1665 it was disrupted once again. Just as Charles II was establishing himself in London, plague hit the capital and people fled. Lower soon found that Oxford was filling with academics as well as numerous members of the royal court.

In mid-June, Boyle arrived, fresh from a meeting in the Royal Society when Wilkins had suggested the idea of injecting blood. It was a matter of days before he and Lower had teamed up to consider how to go about transfusing blood between animals.

The ideas of transfusion, Lower claimed, came to him while he was injecting various solutions into animals at meetings held in Oxford, and he recorded the chain of events that followed in chapter four of his book *Tractatus de Corde*, which was first published in 1671. 'Although one is not justified in drawing general conclusions from a single experiment,' he explained, 'nevertheless while I was pouring in various alimentary juices, I noticed that the blood of different animals mingled freely ... and the thought entered my mind. I wondered whether it would be possible to mix a much greater quantity of blood from different animals without altering it in any way.'

Lower was more aware than most of just how quickly blood coagulated once it had left the body: 'It seemed that a better idea might be to transfer the unaltered blood of one living, breathing, animal into another'. He was also well aware that if the right vessel was cut, an animal's entire supply of blood would rush out within moments. 'In my first attempt at transfusion I used a thin tube to connect the jugular vein of one dog with the same vein in another,' Lower explained. 'It didn't work. The blood flows very slowly from veins, and as a result it immediately coagulated in the tube, and blocked it.'[9]

And here the story of transfusion in England almost ended. Over the summer, Lower and his drinking pal, Anthony Wood, had been negotiating a possible marriage between Lower and Mrs H, a local widow. Mrs H lived in nearby Garsington, and on 8 August 1665 she wrote, declining Lower's offer. It's doubtful that Lower's heart was broken, but his hopes of resolving his bachelor status and finding a wife with wealth were certainly temporarily dashed. His solution was to head home, to Cornwall. Two days after receiving the rebuttal, Lower, Wood and various friends met at the Castle Tavern and toasted Lower's good health, wishing him success in his search.

For Boyle, this was a huge disappointment. Lower's expertise was vital to any work on injection or transfusion, so with his departure the experiments ceased. His frustration at not being able to pursue this work grew when, on 25 September 1665, the King and his court arrived in Oxford, bringing with them a copy of a recently published German text book. Johann Sigismund Elsholtz's *Clysmatica Nova* contained detailed descriptions of his work injecting various solutions into patients. Clearly others around the continent were busily investigating this area, and England was in danger of losing its status as world leader in blood research.

Still, in the short term, there was little Boyle could do about it. In addition, the King's arrival in Oxford brought with it a new problem – courtiers. They were everywhere, and worse still, for Boyle, they kept coming to visit. Courtiers might have had nothing to do all day, but Boyle had business to conduct. He had science to attend to. In the end he became so fed up with the disruption that in mid-November he fled the city and moved to Stanton St John, a village three miles northeast of Oxford. There he forgot all ideas of transfusing blood, and got on with performing and writing up his findings on a series of experiments, each trying to make sense of atmospheric pressure and hydrostatics.

CHAPTER FOUR

Scientific society

*A*rriving in Paris in 1664, Jean-Baptiste Denis had lost little time in becoming part of the fabric of academic life. By 1665 he had already set himself up as a self-proclaimed professor at the University and got to know the Cartesian circle of thinkers. He was young, intelligent, and eager to join in with the major centres of debate and make a name for himself in this thriving city.

'Location, location, location', are apparently the three driving influences behind setting up shop, and these must have been at the top of Denis' mind as he looked for a home. The choice of this ambitious young man was an apartment in a four-storey building on the Quai des Augustins (now the Quai des Grands Augustins), the road running along the edge of the River Seine, immediately opposite the Place du Dauphine on the Île de la Cité, with the impressive spire of Sainte Chapelle fingering the sky. It was easy to get to, being almost immediately at the end of Pont Neuf and just down the road from Pont Saint Michel. It also had prestige – looking left from the floor-to-ceiling windows revealed the magnificent riverside facade of Le Louvre, and looking right, Notre Dame filled the view.

The location was part of his plan to get known by giving lectures – and the plan worked well. His lectures were well attended, he rose rapidly from his previous obscurity, and it wasn't long before Montmor invited him to become a member of his society. The invitation was most welcome – not only did this bring him into contact with this group of thinkers, but Montmor was also known for giving money to those carrying out interesting work. Fame might have been Denis' long-term goal, but in the meantime, money would be a great help.

The Montmor group was itself the product of a quiet revolution in patterns of thought. While it is normally impossible to put your finger on the moment when an uprising begins, it would be true to say that the English philosopher and statesman Francis Bacon had set the wheels of change in motion. Denying centuries of precedent, Bacon had abandoned Aristotelian reasoning in favour of an approach that looked for physical evidence to support theories. He insisted on taking account of all the evidence from experiments, and not ignoring any data that might be inconvenient to a favourite theory.

This new approach to questioning ourselves, and the world that we live in, demanded a new approach to discussing ideas and disseminating knowledge. All around Europe, those interested in philosophy were in the process of gathering together in a variety of informal clubs. In 1603, Italian philosophers set up the Accademia dei Lincei in Rome, and the French soon established the Académie Florimontane d'Annecy in 1606. Not to be left out, the Dutch set up their Duytsche Academie in Amsterdam in 1617, and the same year the German Fruchtbringende Gesellschaft began to meet. Each academy tended, in reality, to be a grouping of local friends, some of whom took an interest in keeping in touch with members of other clubs. In 1635, the French set up a national academy, the Académie Française. Its founders hoped this would be the meeting point for all thinking people in France.

The problem was that these academies tended to be set up by the great and the good – that is to say, by people with wealth and position. While they *talked* of the need to break free, there was a great tendency to do just that – to talk. And talk. And talk. Hence there was very little attempt to perform any of the experiments that they dreamed up in spare moments and discussed at length in their presentations.

Within a decade, many of the younger members who were also interested in natural philosophy and science, split from the Académie Française when they became fed up with the time-wasting, long-winded rhetoric of their seniors who spent most of their time arguing over the fine detail of the language used, rather than the content at issue. All too often they would just stand and read out lengthy, formal papers, leaving little time for interaction. The nature of the growing dissent is wonderfully summed up in a letter from the celebrated astronomer and librarian Ismael Boulliau to the academic historians

Peiresc and Pierre Dupuys:

> October 14, 1645
> I should have liked to see these Moustachios you speak of around those
> manuscripts, for I would have given them a piece of my mind. This stupid
> rabble with its reformed dictionary aims to judge things it does not understand.
> You will see that this Academy will be a hot-bed of barbarisms, and so far as
> it can, it will stifle the knowledge of languages and letters, the more so
> because few men today will take the trouble to study. The learning and
> capacity of a wit will consist in rounding out a period and making a rondeau.
> They spend three weeks or a month over some little trifle that could be
> achieved with the blink of an eye, and love parading through the salons of the
> coquettes of Paris, who give credit according to the fancy. If the leader of this
> famous assembly, (Chancellor Séguier) had been well advised, he would have
> broken it up, and he would be justified, roused by a proper indignation, after
> having willingly made this outlay, and having sent a servant especially to bring
> back books that may be of more use to the public than anything that has ever
> come from the hands of these wits.

Having made the accusation that the academy was basically a collection of wind-bags spouting hot air, Boulliau evidently panics that he may have caused too much offence, and continues:

> But all this is under the seal of confession, and I make no exception of our
> friends of the Cabinet. I don't want them to see what I write to you, and I
> would be especially sorry that Monsieur de la Mothe whom I esteem, who is
> intelligent and who knows what literature is should see this part of my letter.
> It is not of him, nor of d'Ablancourt that I speak.[10]

One name soon rose to prominence among those who were disaffected by the current state of affairs, that of Henri Louis Habert de Montmor. He had all the essential ingredients of a seventeenth-century mover-shaker. He was rich, he moved in royal circles, enjoyed mixing with the curious and, to cap it all, had a large house in central Paris that served as a marvellous meeting place.

Montmor's generous hospitality gave him power, and this alone was enough to win him considerable praise, despite the fact that there seems to be some doubt over whether he had the sharpest brain on the planet. One commentator recorded that he had a 'taste for letters', and as such suggested that he shared the verbose faults of the people they were annoyed with. In addition he was accused of expressing himself with difficulty, was slow, timid, and cared little for his duties.

Another contemporary was slightly kinder, claiming that Montmor enjoyed spending time with people of literature and learning, was an intelligent person and had written a number of interesting Latin essays.[11] But there the compliments ended. The commentator went on to say that Montmor's work failed because he became confused by the subtleties of debate and allowed his arguments to fall into vagueness and uncertainty:

> We have seen nothing of his in print, although it is said he had many things begun of a philosophic nature. He professes Cartesian doctrine; and rumour has it that he has set up an academy in his house only to establish this novelty, and to destroy the doctrine of Aristotle, in which he has found serious contradictions.[12]

Rules, precedence and truth

Despite any personal weaknesses, Montmor found himself at the forefront of the intellectual revolution, and in many ways the Montmor group could be described as the birthplace of the sponsorship of science by institutions. Montmor's wealth enabled him to include people who were clever, even if they had few financial resources, rather than confine membership to those who were both interested *and* rich. It was in this way that the likes of Denis and Emmerey became enfolded into the club, with Montmor personally acting as their patron.

Through the years spanning 1653–64, the group met regularly, at first each Friday evening, and then as interest and excitement grew, Tuesday evenings as well. Denis was invited to join in 1664, and so got a taste of the group's activity, just before it started to wind down. The group's aim was clear: Montmor wanted to do business and he was keen to play a part in the efforts to discover how God's world worked. To do this he wanted to create an environment of structured debate, which would not be interrupted by those more interested in debating than in moving subjects forward. To prevent the group falling back into its old ways, a set of rules was created to govern the proceedings.

Rule 1

The meetings must not become empty parades of intelligence that wasted everyone's time by discussing useless subtleties. Instead the discussions should always aim to reveal the 'clearest understanding of the works of God'. This understanding should enhance the ability to perform arts and sciences, as well as leading to practical benefits.

Rule 2

The person presiding over any meeting should establish the topic for the next discussion. He will then ask two named people to present their opinions. These two should be chosen because they are knowledgeable in the area. The rest of the assembly can then express their thoughts.

Rule 3

The statements should be read out, but also recorded in writing. Reports should be as brief as possible, without unnecessary waffle or citing authorities. [By banning any mention of authorities, the rules were preventing people resting the unproved areas of their theories on some unchallengeable predecessor – it quietly slipped a dagger between Aristotle's shoulder blades. If you presented an idea, you needed evidence to support it.]

Rule 4

The two presenters will start by reading their papers without interruption.

Rule 5

Once each of the two speakers has read his contribution, each will make comments, criticisms or affirmations, about the other presentation. After that, the matter will be closed for that meeting, unless the president gives express permission for the discussion to continue.

Rule 6

Anyone unable to attend in person may submit his opinion on the proposed topic in writing.

Rule 7

The Assembly will encourage its members to correspond with learned men in France, and abroad, to learn from them about the work that is in progress, or about work that has been published in the arts and sciences. The Assembly will be informed of these matters at the close of its sessions.

Rule 8

Once the Assembly has been established, no new member can join unless two-thirds of those present agree when the proposal is put to them.

Rule 9

Only members of the Assembly will be allowed into the room where the discussion takes place. The Assembly shall be composed solely of people interested in natural science, medicine, mathematics, the liberal arts, and mechanics, unless there is a particular reason for allowing in some individual person of merit.

So by the mid-seventeenth century, Paris had two different sets of philosophers: those in the old society, who met under the auspices of the Venetian ambassador, were noted for their good behaviour and congenial atmosphere, while the Montmorians became known for the vigour of their debate. For the old set, prestige came with your position in life, for the Montmorians it came from recognition that you were the first to have a new idea. At times this clamour for recognition reduced the level of debate as one member would try to destroy another's argument for the simple reason that he feared his rival might be about to make a pronouncement on an area he was working on. Each person wanted to be the sole author of truth, and did not want to share the glory with any other.

Throughout this seventeenth-century story we see that the key players pursued their ideas based on what we now recognise as distinctly flawed reasoning. The rationale did, however, seem quite reasonable at the time. In Denis' situation, the misunderstanding of the nature of blood would prove to be distinctly dangerous for the people involved – at times the results were lethal.

Rivals, rivals everywhere

Rivalry was not limited to the salons of Paris. At the same time as Montmor, Denis and their friends were discussing their science, a similar activity was taking place in England. In fact it was so similar that the French claimed that the English club was modelled on the Montmor Académie. This was certainly the view of the French physician Samuel Sorbière, who in 1663 paid a visit to London:

> The Montmor assembly is the Mother of all those which have been formed since its foundation in the Kingdom, in England, and in the Netherlands, and which have the same desire as we to advance the science of natural things and to improve the liberal arts and Mechanics. It is on the plan that was drawn up here in 1657, or on a part of it, that work is done today elsewhere; it is certain that our illustrious Moderator was the first in Paris to encourage the studies we cultivate, the curiosity to know more intimately the works of God, and the desire to carry to a higher point the industry of men, two sorts of things, that many men of wit, most men of letters, and almost all men of rank had until then neglected.[13]

In a similar tone, the French poet and critic Jean Chapelain wrote to a friend, François Bernier, who later became a doctor to the infamous Indian Moghul emperor Aurangzeb. Chapelain commented that there were 'numerous Digbys, Morays, and other able milords', meeting in London in a manner that emulated the Montmor assembly. In addition to this, he noted that the King himself supported the English venture

and that its members were charged with the responsibility of performing experiments that would help discover the natural world and
understand the heavens more fully. He was referring to the newly
formed Royal Society.

When news of these sentiments wafted north across the Channel,
there was outright anger. One of the founding members of this English
group, Robert Hooke, caught wind of these statements and was furious
with the claim that the English had simply copied the French: '[This
writer] is in error concerning the beginnings and origin of the Royal
Society. Concerning which he might have been much better informed
if he had taken notice of what has been said concerning it, but that,
it seems, did not suit so well to his design of making the French to be
the first'.[14]

So from the outset of organised science, the competition to succeed
was not limited to bickering between individual members of a particular club or assembly, but became heightened when competing parties
were members of different groups, and taken to high altitude if the
groups were in different countries. When the countries concerned
were England and France, rivalry rose to its most extreme.

The exact history is more complex in that a central member of the
English community, Henry Oldenburg, spent time travelling in France
in the mid-1650s and certainly attended the Académie Montmor before
returning to England. As he then became a founding member of the
English science club, it seems reasonable that he contributed ideas for
ways of operating that drew from his experience on the continent.

A new view of power

Until now, power struggles around Europe had been dominated by the
church and organised religion. Establishing a basis of structured
science was a way of shaking off the past and moving forward. While
philosophy had previously been forced to bow before the altar of church
authority, people were now daring to think the unthinkable. Since
the days of the Italian scholar, philosopher and theologian Thomas
Aquinas, the Roman Catholic church had adopted Aristotle. Consequently, Aristotle's teachings were held to be almost as sacred as the

Bible itself. Challenging established ideas was still tantamount to questioning doctrine, and many people had been tied to stakes and incinerated for this heinous crime of heresy. This didn't prevent adventurous people stretching the boundaries of knowledge, but it did mean that they always needed to keep an eye on church authorities to make sure that they weren't stretching their patience too far.

This was not to say that early scientists intended to abolish religion and overthrow God – far from it. Many were passionate believers who were driven by a desire to convey their knowledge of God throughout the world. Rather, their belief was that God would be best served by them taking a serious look at his creation.

English intellect

One reason why Hooke had taken such umbrage at the suggestion that the English had simply copied the French was that English science had its own history. In 1645 a group of philosophers had started meeting in London. Among them were people like Wilkins, John Wallis and Jonathan Goddard. Having Goddard involved was particularly useful as he was one of Oliver Cromwell's physicians, and given Cromwell's power in the country, it never harmed to have one of his men on your side. The group met sometimes at Goddard's lodgings in Wood Street, London, sometimes in Cheapside, and on other occasions in Gresham College. Between 1648 and 1649 this group became divided as a mixture of national politics and personal promotion sent some of them to Oxford, Cambridge or Ireland.

Like the French equivalent, the team needed to work out their standing in relation to Aristotle. They were at pains to point out that they did not seek to slight or undervalue Aristotle, as his work had been taught in schools for ages with good effect. As one of the founding members, Willis stated that Aristotle was a great man and a superb enquirer of nature, but – and there had to be a 'but' – life had moved on. The members agreed that no one could be expected to exhaust the stock of all knowledge, not even Aristotle. Therefore they had work to do, and so would those who came after them.

Life in England at this time was distinctly complicated. As well as partaking in the Europe-wide intellectual revolution, anyone living on rticular island also had a physical revolution to contend with. nglish Civil War had broken out in August 1642 and ended with Charles I surrendering in the Royalist headquarters of Oxford; 1649 had seen Charles I executed and England declared a republic. A couple of years later, Cromwell had become Lord Protector and the English were at war with the Dutch, engaged in conflict with the Spanish, having alternate skirmishes and alliances with the French and using force to retain control over Ireland.

Work and war moved on side-by-side. On one occasion in 1657, Wren, a central member of the elite, turned up at his workplace one morning only to find himself locked out:

> Yesterday, being the first day of term, I resolv'd to make an experiment [at Gresham Hall]. But at the gate I was stop'd by a man with a gun, who told me that there was no admission upon that account, the College being reform'd into a garrison.[15]

In 1660, politics changed again, and King Charles II, son of the ill-fated Charles I – came to the throne. The English monarchy was restored. It was time for those who had given loyal support to the royal cause to breathe a sigh of relief and take all the advantage they could of the new situation, and those who had sided with Cromwell to change allegiance, and change it quickly. The Restoration court brought with it French fashion, and soon injected a new sense of colour and fun into what had become a drab and puritanical social scene. Charles soon became known for his love of entertainment and was almost as often found in the higher-class brothels as he was holding court.

With London now looking marginally more safe, a new group started to emerge. This group met on Wednesdays in Gresham College, and among the assembly were such people as Wren, who would soon become a household name. By 1660 the group was beginning to take on a formal shape, and the 40 members were asked to help finance this, everyone paying a ten-shilling joining fee, and then contributing one shilling a week to meet ongoing expenses.

On 28 November 1660, after one of Wren's regular Wednesday lectures at Gresham College, 14 men sat down and formed the inner core of a new organisation. Their big breakthrough occurred a few weeks later when Sir Robert Moray arrived on 5 December with the exciting news that the King had heard of the Society and wanted to help out.

However, it was not until 15 July 1662 that the King gave the group the title of the Royal Society. The list of dignitaries announced as officers seems impressive and hints at the nature of the Society. While it had firm intentions of pursuing discovery, it would be run in a very British way – by the gentry. If Chapelain had been wrong about the French

> May it please your Majesty,
> We your majesty's most loyal subjects, newly incorporated by your majesty's charter and honoured with the name of the Royal Society, do with all humility present ourselves before your majesty, the royal founder thereof, to offer you our most hearty thanks, as the only way we have at present to express our deep sense of your majesty's grace and favour to us, and to assure your majesty of our constant veneration for your sacred person, our devotion to your majesty's service, and our firm resolution to pursue sincerely and unanimously the end, for which your majesty hath founded this society, the advancement of the knowledge of natural things, and all useful arts, by experiments: A design Sir, that is deservedly accounted great and glorious, and is universally reputed to be of that advantage to mankind, that your majesty is highly admired and extolled for setting it on foot; and this society is already taken notice of, and famous throughout all the learned parts of Europe; and doubtless in time will be much more by the continuance of your majesty's grace and favour, and the happy success of their endeavours, to the great increase of the fame of your majesty's prudence, which hath justly entitled you to the honour of laying the first foundation of the greatest improvement of learning and arts, that they are capable of, and which hath never heretofore been attempted by any: so that men cannot now complain, that the favour and assistance of a potent monarch is wanting to this long-wished enterprise.
>
> And Sir, our assurance of this your majesty's favour and assistance is that, which gives vigour to our resolutions, and is the life of our hopes, that in due season we shall be able to make your majesty an acceptable present of choice and useful experiments, and accomplish your great design, being thereto engaged by so many powerful motives.
>
> And in the mean time we shall daily pray, that God will be eminently gracious to your majesty, and accumulate upon you all the blessings answerable to the largeness of your heart, the height of your condition, the weight of your charge, the multitude of your virtues, and the desires and wishes of all your faithful subjects.[17]

influence on the Society, he was right in identifying the aristocratic nature of its membership.

A single sheet of paper served as the registration form. This was headed by a simple agreement in standard legalese, spelling out each person's level of commitment. Exactly the same wording appears at the top of each page as new members are admitted even in the twenty-first century:

> We who have hereunto subscribed, do hereby promise, each for himself, that we will endeavour to promote the Good of the Royal Society of London, for Improving Natural Knowledge, and to pursue the Ends for which the same was founded: That we will be present at the Meetings of the Society, as often as conveniently we can, especially at the Anniversary Elections, & upon extraordinary occasions: And that we will observe the Statutes and Orders of the said Society: Provided, that whensoever any of us shall signify to the President, under his hand, that he desireth to withdraw from the Society, he shall be free from this Obligation for the future.[16]

A couple of months later, on 29 August, a formal petition was sent to King Charles II written in what would now be seen as grovelling language, but which was nothing more or less than he would have expected. While Charles was keen to have a scientific society in England, he was far too busy partying and seeking entertainment to attend any of their meetings.

A French Royal Society

While Denis was thrilled to be invited to join Montmor's group, this invitation soon lost much of its appeal. No sooner had he started attending the meetings than the meetings started to become erratic and infrequent. Montmor's academy was falling to pieces. It had come close to collapse once before in 1658 when Gilles Personne de Roberval had questioned Monsieur Descartes' intelligence, striking right at the heart of the academy's reason for existence. Roberval also appears to have been charged with saying that the reason for Montmor's prominence was his wealth and power, not because he had any intellect to offer.

The academy survived, but it now faced a new problem. In one of his *Letters Concerning the English Nation*, written in 1733, the French academic Voltaire took a retrospective look at this period of history. He explained that in 1666 French philosophers had become envious of the Royal Society – an organisation Voltaire refers to as 'this new glory'. They had wanted their own regally commissioned organisation, and persuaded Louis XIV to grant them permission to open an academy of sciences. Four years after the Royal Society set up shop, the Académie Royale des Sciences opened for business.

Regarding their origins, Voltaire made a few shrewd comments about the similarities and differences between the two organisations, saying that the French version was stronger because it had learnt from the mistakes of its English forebear. The Académie Royale des Sciences also had much more comprehensive rules governing its activities; it was regulated like a well-trained army, and consequently he believed its output was more glorious than the poorly disciplined English equivalent.

More importantly than this, though, Voltaire pointed out that being a member of the French academy brought distinct rewards. The position came with a salary, which meant that it could invite people to join on merit alone. In contrast, London's Royal Society charged people a membership fee, making it a club for those with time on their hands and cash in their pockets. Voltaire believed that anyone who could afford it would be welcomed into the Royal Society, while membership of the French academy was given only on the basis of skill and learning.

While this was a boon for French science, it sounded the death knell for Montmor's academy, as many of the key movers switched allegiance. Initially this was a source of annoyance for Montmor, but soon turned to anger. Although he had done more than almost anyone to foster Paris' new world of science, Montmor was not invited to join the King's club. This wasn't a passive oversight – it was active exclusion. The double-whammy also hit Denis. Like his patron, he too was not invited to join the new elite. His hopes of making a rapid rise to fame and fortune had taken a severe blow. Drastic action was needed, and quickly, if Denis was to prevent his plans from falling about his feet.

Licking his metaphorical wounds, one thing was clear – Denis needed to make a discovery, or to invent something. Quite what, didn't really matter, so long as it was useful, worked, and would grab attention. What he needed now was to embark on a series of experiments that would shake the world ... well, at least shake Paris.

English transfusions

$\mathcal{I}$f the Montmor group had been running at the time, Denis would almost certainly have heard of events occurring in England in 1665 and 1666. The few meetings that he did attend included talks on work currently occurring in England. With this group less active, his access to current scientific gossip was reduced, and with an inability to read English for himself, Denis had no idea that blood infusion and attempts at transfusion were raising great interest on the other side of the Channel. Besides, there is little reason to believe he would have been particularly interested in the developments anyway; after all, Denis' chief area of research was mathematics.

In England, investigations relating to blood were continuing apace. In fact, they had been given a jolt when Oldenburg reported to the Royal Society that Johann Daniel Major, a German physician, had published a book advocating injecting chemicals directly into blood vessels. The German clearly knew a considerable amount about the subject, and there was an apparent danger that he would come to be known as the world leader in the area. National pride dictated that action needed to be taken immediately. On hearing the news, several members decided to have a go themselves. The journal book of the Royal Society records the chain of events that followed:

May 17, 1665
It was suggested by Dr Wilkins that the experiment of injecting the blood of one dog into the vein of another might be made.

May 24, 1665
Dr Wilkins, Mr Daniel Coxe, Mr Thomas Coxe and Mr Hooke were appointed to take care of injecting the blood of one dog into the vein of another; and Mr Thomas Coxe was particularly desired to try the changing of dogs' skins.

Mr Thomas Coxe related, that he had made an experiment of injecting the blood of one pigeon into the vein of another, by opening the vein of one, and letting it bleed, till the pigeon was almost expiring; and then letting out the blood of another pigeon, and injecting it into the dying one, and thereby keeping it alive for half an hour, after which it died, as the other pigeon did, though a pretty while after.

May 31, 1665

It was ordered that the experiment of injecting the blood of one dog into another be tried at the next meeting; upon which occasion Dr Croune suggested that a common pipe might be used for both, in order to have thereby the blood of one dog sucked out by the other.

The comment that blood might be 'sucked out' by the receiving animal reveals the prevalent view at the time that blood was drawn to the body's extremities; later scientists would claim that is was pumped there by the heart.

June 7, 1665

Dr Wilkins made a report of an experiment committed to his care, viz. that a dog's belly had been opened, and out of the *vena cava* there was let blood to the quantity of 5 or 6 ounces into a bladder, having a small pipe of brass fastened to it in the manner of a [enema] pipe, the end of which being put into the [leg] vein of a bitch, there was, by pressing the said bladder, about two ounces of blood injected into that vein, but without any sensible alteration in the bitch.

It is difficult to see how this could be classified as an unmitigated success, but to those involved, it was at least progress. Little else happened in London that year – in 1665 plague swept through the city.

Another attempt

With another potential wife lined up, Lower returned to Oxford and tried to pick up where he had left off – meeting Wood for a drink, this time in the Blue Boar in central Oxford on 24 February 166⁵⁄₆.* His social life may have remained relatively unchanged, but work had become more difficult. While the court had returned to London in January, Boyle had not returned to Oxford from his country retreat, therefore Lower was forced to continue alone. In his *Tractatus de Corde*, he explains:

> My next attempt was more successful. In this, I decided to replicate nature more precisely. Nature forces blood from arteries into veins, so connecting the artery of one animal to the veins of another would simply extend the first animal's circulation.

Lower planned, got his equipment together and set the date for the end of February 166⁵⁄₆. Convinced that this would be a notable event, he sent out a series of invitations asking the likes of Wallis, Dr Thomas Millington and various other members of Oxford's medical elite to come to his 'party'. Few turned down the opportunity, and Lower found himself surrounded by an excited throng of intellectuals, academics and one or two gossips. He later wrote:

> The experiment I performed was spectacular. I had selected a medium sized dog and after securing it, I drained off most of its blood. At first the dog wailed loudly, but soon its strength was gone and it started to convulse and twitch. In order to resuscitate this animal from such an extreme blood loss, I tied a larger dog next to it, and fixed a tube running from the artery in the neck into the vein of the smaller dog.

---

* Tracking dates in this period of history is complicated by the fact that two different calendars were in use. For most of the seventeenth century, England retained the Julian (Old Style) calendar, while most of the continent had changed to the Gregorian (New Style) calendar. The two differ in where they place the New Year. In the Julian calendar the New Year came at the end of March, while in the Gregorian calendar it began on January first. Therefore an Englishman writing 'February 1665' would mean what we understand as February 1666. At this time, the English, slow as ever to adopt ideas coming from mainland Europe, were beginning to start the year in January rather than in March, and often used a system of double years to express the year. February 166⁵⁄₆ therefore signifies what was known on the continent as 1666.

The smaller dog regained its consciousness and resumed its struggle to get free. Maybe I had given it too much. Anyway, I tied the artery of the donor dog so that it stopped bleeding, and again drained the blood out of the receiving animal, before refilling it with the blood from another large dog.

Having completed the experiment, I tied off the jugular vein on the smaller dog, loosed the chains that held it down and watched to see what would happen. The dog jumped down from the table and appeared to be totally unaware of any injury. It ran to its master and then rolled in the grass to clean off the blood, apparently no more worried than if it had just been thrown in to a stream.

Communications between Oxford and London were rapid, for example a letter could be delivered to London within a day if it was taken to the Oxford post office. For that matter, a letter could get to Paris in five days. All the same, it appears that Lower was in no particular hurry to formally notify the Royal Society about the developments in his work. Quite probably, this reluctance to publish came from two drives. The first was that scientists were anxious not to make fools of themselves before their peers by publishing something based on a single experiment that proved to be unrepeatable. Second, publishing meant letting everyone know your secrets and tricks of the trade; any scientist in the world could then have a go and as a result win the race to future discoveries.

Even so, Lower naturally kept Boyle informed of progress. Almost immediately, Boyle wrote to two other scientists, John Beale and Hooke, asking for their opinions. Beale replied from his home in the West Country, stating his enthusiasm for the potential therapeutic benefit that this work might bring, while Hooke wrote from London with suggestions about new ways of making and arranging brass pipes so that the process might be more successful.

Integrity was important for Boyle, and when on 18 April 1666 he was asked at a meeting of the Society to give an update on transfusion experiments, he gave only the vaguest reply. He simply reported that as far as he was aware, the difficulties in the procedure were being tackled, and that Dr Lower in Oxford was the chap most likely to succeed first.

The gathering proceeded with Walter Charlton raising the possibility that blood's fluidity and vitality came from a fermentation that could only occur inside blood vessels. In this case, any experiment that made blood leave these vessels would surely fail – the blood would be ruined. If, on the other hand, the blood lost its vitality if it came into contact with air, then the experiment might work if the blood could be kept away from the air. The suggestion was bound to have been greeted with much muttering and nodding of long hair and the increasingly fashionable wigs sported by those who associated closely with the royal court.

In reality, the Royal Society wasn't kept in suspense for very long. Not all of those Lower allowed into his confidence were capable of keeping quiet, and four months after his February experiment Wallis seems to have let the cat out of the bag at a London meeting of the Society. According to Aubrey, Wallis was a renowned wheeler-dealer who had managed to manoeuvre his way into a senior position at Oxford University by seeding malicious gossip against the potential rival for the post. Aubrey claims that his basic ploy had been to suggest that the person most likely to get the job, Richard Zouche, had talked openly against Cromwell – a very dangerous thing to be accused of, and something the university would not want to be seen as condoning.

For Aubrey, this was not Wallis' only vice. Aubrey also accuses him of sitting in on discussions with Wren, Hooke and other Oxford academics, writing down the key ideas in his note book, and then publishing them as if his own. The practice may have got him into trouble, but at least it got the ideas published; if the world had waited for Wren to get around to writing them down, it would still be waiting. So, if Aubrey is to be believed, there is little surprise that it was Wallis who stood up in a June meeting of the Royal Society and gave details of Lower's work. Adding knowledge of his character to this action raises the possibility that he was trying to pass much of it off as his idea.

If this was the case, it was fortunate for Lower that Boyle was present at the Royal Society's meeting. At six-foot tall, and always walking with a very upright stance, everyone would have known when he attended meetings. He frequently travelled in his own coach to London and stayed with his sister, Lady Ranelagh, at her home in Pall Mall. The visits kept him up to date with life in the city, but also enabled him to drive forward the work in the laboratory he had set up in Lady Ranelagh's house, where he paid various servants and apprentices to keep his experiments running in his absence. As Wallace spoke, Boyle's knowledge of the goings-on in Oxford meant that he would instantly have thought of Lower. He hurriedly sent a letter to Oxford, politely but firmly asking for details. Lower must write, and write soon, if he was going to be recognised as the leading pioneer in this field:

> *London, June 26, 1666*
>
> *I was present last Wednesday (Honourable Sir) at the stated meeting of the Royal Society, held in Gresham's College. Here I heard from Dr Wallis that you had at last (in his presence) successfully accomplished that most difficult experiment on the transference of blood from one to the other of a pair of dogs. I judged the matter clearly worthy of being communicated to that very celebrated assembly. I therefore proposed that they should ask that distinguished gentleman for an account of the way in which it had been performed. His description of it was such as to increase not a little our opinion of your reputation. But, when asked for various details about so unusual and so unhoped-for an experiment, he voiced the opinion that it would be more profitable for you to reply in writing about the individual points than for him to attempt it orally. I therefore stated publicly that you had promised me, a little while before, that you would describe the matter to me … I have done so with less reluctance, because I thought it would be to your advantage, if this celebrated assembly became acquainted with you at this propitious moment. There are many among its members who esteem you at your right worth and are your friends, but none more so than.*
> *Yours affectionately*
> *Robert Boyle*
> *To be delivered to*
> *my most honourable friend*
> *Richard Lower, Doctor of Medicine, Oxford.*

Having kept his work under wraps for four months or more, Lower replied to Boyle with remarkable speed and detail. Whatever Wallis' motives for the disclosure, the chances are that Lower was thrilled to find that his work was being discussed at the centre of English science.

> *Oxford, July 6, 1666*
> *Dear friend:*
> *I received your letter and in accordance with your request I herewith briefly explain the whole method of blood transfusion. Select either a dog or whatever*

animal you wish to use as a donor to supply blood to another animal of like or diverse species, expose an artery in the neck, separate it from the eighth nerve and denude it almost a finger's length.

Lower replied, wasting no time with pleasantries and getting straight down to business. The vessel he described in his letter is the carotid artery, and the nerve that runs along it would now be called the vagus, now known as the tenth cranial nerve. He then went on to describe the method that countless experimental physiologists have used for centuries after in order to slip a fine tube into an artery or vein:

Tie a cord firmly around the artery end nearest the head – you won't need to untie this at any point in the operation. Place another cord under the vessel a half-finger's length below the first and secure by a slip-knot that can be tightened or loosened at will. Make a small cut in the vessel between the two cords with a sharp scalpel and insert a reed towards the heart, leaving one end projecting freely like a little wooden staff. Tie the cord tightly and add another one so made sure that it is held firmly.

This budding surgeon went on to give a similarly detailed description of the method he used to place reeds into the jugular vein of the animal intended to receive the blood. The difference this time was that he placed two reeds, one pointing towards the head and the other pointing to the heart. The idea is that he could drain blood from the head, but infuse the donated liquid into the heart. The two dogs were then lined with their necks close to each other, making as short a distance as possible between the reeds. He then described the draining and refilling experiment, concluding with the warning:

I have only one admonition, my dear friend, and that is that the reeds be secured in the vessels with tight ligatures before they are brought together, otherwise they will pull out as the animals struggle and you will have to start all over again.

It is clear that the occasions he records in detail are just a few of Lower's attempts, and that many others have ended in a messy disaster:

As I have become more experienced, I have lately constructed a silver tube, which does not tear the vessel where it is inserted and which has a projecting ring or ridge running around the outside near the end. This enables me to tie it in more securely. The two can then be joined using a section of artery taken from a cow or a horse. This intermediate artery has a number of advantages. Being elastic it is less prone to pull out when the animals struggle. Also, if it gets blocked with a clot, you can squeeze the clot into the recipient and start the blood flowing again. This letter furnishes you with the data for the Honorable Society and I trust it will not at any time be found wanting in any respect.

Yours most respectfully

Richard Lower

Written to the most honourable

Robert Boyle, in London.

Over the next few months, Lower repeated the experiment several times, each time transfusing blood between two dogs. His desire, however, was to expand the range of his experiments to see what would happen if he took blood from a number of dogs simultaneously, but he complained to his friends that he was thwarted by a lack of time and available dogs. This insufficiency, combined with his driving curiosity, led Lower to experiment between two sheep, and later, in a more extreme moment, he had a go at transferring sheep's blood to a dog. 'The experiments were attended with good success', he recorded.

A couple of months later, Boyle once again wrote to Lower, this time setting out a list of 16 suggestions for experiments he thought Lower should carry out. He was fond of sending these sorts of lists to people, as it appears he could always think of more experiments to perform than he had time to perform himself:

1. Would transfusing blood change the nature of the animal. For example, what would happen if you transfused blood from a timid dog into a fierce one, or vice versa?

2. Will a dog that has recently received blood still recognise its master, and behave as before?

3. Would a gun-dog that could point to the scent of game, lose that ability if transfused with blood from a dog that did not share that ability?

4. What would happen to a dog that had been trained to perform tricks like fetching a stick? Would transfusion cause it to lose its training?

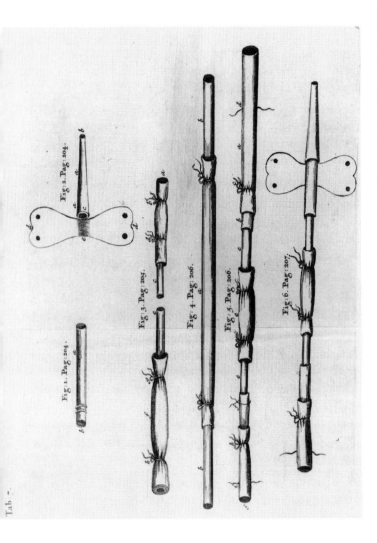

Plate 6 Illustrations of cannulae in *Tractatus de Corde* (Richard Lower). Reproduced by permission of Lane Medical Library Special Collections. Stanford University.

5. Are there any signs that transfusion alters the animal's pulse, urine or other excrements?

6. If blood is taken from a dog that has recently been given a good meal and given to a hungry dog, will that hungry dog lose its appetite? [The reasoning here was that if the animal had just eaten, its blood should be packed with chyle. Even though he had accepted Harvey's concept of the circulation, Boyle was still working on the idea that blood was formed directly from food.]

7. Is it possible to keep a dog alive by frequently injecting chyle from another dog?

8. Can a sick dog be cured by replacing its blood with blood from a healthy animal? Or for that matter, can a healthy animal be given a non-infectious disease by giving it blood from a sick animal?

9. What will happen if you give an old dog blood from a young one? Will it affect its liveliness, dullness, squeamishness etc.? Or how about the other way around – giving old blood to a young animal?

10. If you give a small dog blood from a large one, will it suddenly start to grow?

11. Could you inject medicated liquors along with the blood? Is the effect different from giving an injection of the liquor on its own, or from taking the medication by mouth?

12. There could be a whole series of experiments to see what happens if you give a purgative to an animal and then transfuse its blood into a second animal.

13. Could you swap blood between animals of different species, such as a dog and a calf? What would happen if you took the blood from a cold-blooded fish, frog or tortoise and gave it to a hot-blooded animal?

14. Would transfusion change the colour of an animal's hair or feathers so that it becomes the same as the donor's?

15. If you repeatedly transfuse blood from a different species, will the animal slowly change species? For example, could an Irish greyhound become an ordinary greyhound?

16. Could you transfuse blood into pregnant bitches, and what would be the effect on their pups?

Boyle also recommended weighing donors and recipients before and after the transfusion as a way of trying to determine exactly how much blood had been successfully transfused.

In addition, he made a further point, stressing that negative results were just as important as positive ones. All too often when something doesn't work, scientists forget about it and move on, and publishers are less than keen to include it in their journals as negative findings are not normally desperately exciting. Boyle had an implicit confidence in the credibility of the scientists he worked with. Apart from anything, their negative findings would let the scientific community know that further research in a particular area was unlikely to be a fruitful.

Philosophical Transactions

A year earlier, in 1665, Oldenburg had begun a new venture that would inadvertently link the work in England with Denis' efforts in Paris. At this point he was paid nothing by the Royal Society for his secretarial services, and was keen to develop sources of income. His chief asset was his ability to read and write all of the major languages used in scientific Europe; in particular he was fluent in German, French and Italian. He also had a wide circle of European pen-pals. Always keen to glean ideas from other countries, and having the wealth to pay handsomely for this information, Boyle became a valuable source of income, frequently employing Oldenburg as a translator and as a source of scientific news and views.

However, Oldenburg needed more. What better than to record all of these wonderful ideas, publish them in a journal and then post the journal to paying readers? Geographically he was well positioned, as the book trade was growing fast, and London was one of the prime centres for publishing in Europe.

As secretary to the Royal Society, Oldenburg was in an ideal position to keep up to date with all of the latest work. Such a journal, he hoped, would gather together all the important thoughts and concepts that were being generated but were in danger of getting lost. His dream was that the journal would achieve worldwide recognition if the publishers would distribute it throughout Europe, and this dream slowly turned into reality. His publication enabled researchers in distant countries to benefit from English discoveries. He also hoped that, as its reputation grew, it would be recognised as the publication where scientists could stake their claim to be the first to perform some experiment or develop some theory. Unlike Wallis and his publishing ventures, Oldenburg was keen to give credit where credit was due.

Oldenburg's vision was that the journal was his, not that of the Royal Society, and that it would publish work carried out by non-members, as well as members of the Society. Being secretary to the Royal Society meant that he had day-to-day responsibility not only for recording what was said at meetings, but also for receiving letters and comments from around the world. He also wrote letters on a near-industrial scale, claiming to never open a letter without having a pen in his hand ready to write the reply. Oldenburg was supported in this role of international correspondent by the fact that the Royal Society's charter made such international communication one of the organisation's key features. His linguistic skills made it relatively easy for him to translate foreign letters and journals, and place the most exciting bits in his own publication.

The purpose of the journal was spelt out in its subtitle: *Philosophical transactions: Giving some account of the present undertakings, studies, and labours of the ingenious in many considerable parts of the world.* Even so, some still thought of it as the Royal Society's publication, thus at the end of Number 12, published on 7 May 1666, Oldenburg made explicit his claim on the journal:

> Whereas 'tis taken notice of, that several persons persuade themselves, that these Philosophical Transactions are published by the Royal society ... the writer thereof hath thought fit expressly here to declare that that persuasion, if there be such indeed, is a mere mistake; and that he, upon his private account ... hath begun and continues both the composure and publication thereof ...

It is in issue Number 1 of the journal that we find Lower's description of his method for transfusing blood recorded for all time. The published account is a mixture of Lower's letter to Boyle, along with additional material indicating that Boyle had seen Lower's work at first-hand.

Writing this letter to Boyle stood as a landmark in history and brought Lower to the attention of the esteemed Royal Society. In it,

Lower summarises his ideas so far with the thought that the most probable use of his experiment may be 'that one animal may live with the blood of another'. The consequence of this would be that fresh blood could be donated to any animal in need of extra blood, and that replacing their 'corrupt blood' with healthy blood could possibly cure many sick animals.

Not only did publication mean that Lower's method was recorded in the learned journal, it also meant that the details of how to perform a successful experiment were distributed around England, as well as being sent to various notable dignitaries and scientists around Europe. Anyone who was interested could have a go, as long as they could read English. This would soon include Denis and friend Emmerey.

At times, seeing others repeat your work can be frustrating, particularly if they then use your information to get to the next stage of discovery first. But checking that work is repeatable is a fundamental plank of science. A chance, one-off observation might be fascinating, but is of little value unless it can be repeated. Consequently, a main requirement of scientists is that they present their methods and results in a way that is clear enough to enable others to test to see if the results are the same. Comparing different findings can reveal whether a particular result was a fluke, and can also eliminate possible exaggeration or even fraud.

Fire and fervour

Within weeks of Lower's work being made public, researchers in London were also trying out transfusion for themselves and calling their friends to witness the spectacle. At this point, Willis accepted a job from Gilbert Sheldon, the Archbishop of Canterbury, and set himself up in St Martin's Lane, only a short walk from Boyle's London residence in Pall Mall. Remembering the person whose skills had enabled his work to be so successful, Willis immediately pressed the Royal Society to invite Lower to move to London and work as its Anatomical Curator. Excited by this new opportunity, Lower accepted the offer and found somewhere to live in Hatton Garden, before moving into Covent Garden, right in the heart of the bustling city.

The year was 1666, and many were bracing themselves for bad fortune – 666 being the biblical number denoting the beast, the number that had so concerned Potter. Others were consoling themselves; they had just lived through one of the worst plagues on record, and those who were still around were obviously born survivors. What could be worse than that? But when fire broke out on 2 September and raged until the seventh, they found their answer. It seemed to many as proof-positive that the devil himself was pouring his wrath on the city.

On the evening of 1 September, Londoners had gone to bed as usual. Their great city had grown with little control, and despite a ruling that new buildings should be made of stone with slate roofs, every conceivable inch was packed with wood-beamed, thatched houses. The desire to put the largest house on the smallest plot of land had led ingenious craftsmen to develop a method in which each floor stepped out a foot or more beyond the storey below. This created large upper floors and dark, festering streets. In many places, if you climbed a stairway in a house to the third or in some places fourth floor, you could open a window and shake hands with your neighbour. This might have provided a way of using all the available space, but it was also a sure way of letting the inferno jump from house to house.

As Pepys recorded, the fire had started at night, at the end of a long, hot, dry spell:

> September, 2, 1666
> Some of our maids sitting up late last night to get things ready against our feast today, Jane called us up, about 3 in the morning, to tell us of a great fire they saw in the City. So I rose, and slipped on my nightgown and went to her window, and thought it to be on the back side of Markelane at the furthest; but being unused to such fires as followed, I thought it far enough off, and so went to bed again and to sleep.

His complacency turned to amazement when his maid told him at 7 o'clock in the morning that 300 houses had been burned during the night. Pepys' mood darkened further when he took a boat on the River Thames and discovered the extent of the inferno. Meeting his friend, the Lieutenant of the Tower of London, Pepys discovered that the fire had started in the house of the King's baker in Pudding Lane. By mid-afternoon the army had begun blowing up houses to create firebreaks, and had succeeded in preventing the fire from reaching the Tower. After five smoke-filled days and flamelit nights, the fire was brought under control, but not before the great St Paul's church, along with more than 13,000 buildings, including 97 parish churches and goods valued at the time at £3.5 million, had been destroyed. Remarkably, the fire stopped just short of Pepys' house.

While only six people died as a direct result of the fire, a wave of xenophobia ran through the population – almost an early version of ethnic cleansing. Rumour had it that the fire had been the result of a dastardly plot, and many foreigners, particularly the Dutch, were summarily murdered.

Lower had missed this devastation, as he had had other business to attend to – namely pursuing his quest to find a wife – which demanded another trip to Cornwall. During his absence, the Royal Society voted, on 17 October, to admit him as a Fellow, and on 17 November he married Elizabeth Billings, a woman who came with land. Now he had an academic reputation and the financial support of estates near Tremeer, Cornwall. It was, therefore, with a sense of considerable triumph that he returned to what was left of London late that year.

With up to six out of every seven houses eradicated from inside the city walls, the Great Fire had created an accommodation crisis. Gresham College, which stood on a site now occupied by Tower 42 (formerly known as the NatWest Tower), had escaped the fire and so had become a valuable resource – too valuable for so much of its space to be occupied by the Royal Society. With the Great Exchange in ruins, this financial heart of the city moved in, and threw the scientists out, overnight. Another benefactor, Henry Howard, who later became the sixth Duke of Norfolk, stood in. His London property had also been unscathed by the fire, and he invited the Royal Society to move into Arundel House, just off the Strand, the site where King's College now stands.

Though Arundel House provided the Society with a good place for meetings and discussion, it had nowhere suitable for routine anatomical work. The Society therefore hired a small room nearby, next to the River Thames, a convenient place for Lower to conduct his anatomical experiments.

Always looking for entertainment, the London elite demanded experiments, and soon transfusion became the talk of the town. It wasn't long before Pepys was once again writing about developments,

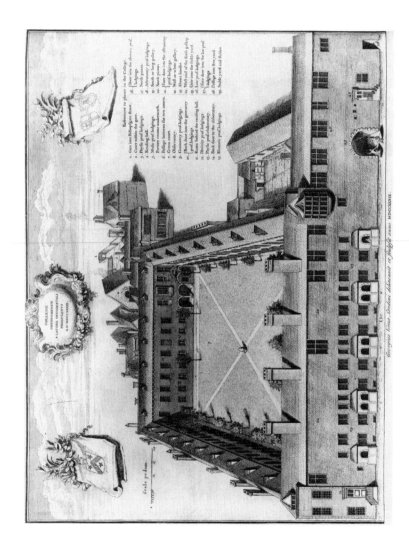

Plate 7 Gresham College. © The Royal Society.

Aula Domus Arrundelianæ Londini, Meridiem versus, &

Plate 8 Arundel House. © The Royal Society.

as once more science stepped out from behind its veil and entered the public domain:

November 14, 1666.
Here [at the Popehead public house] Dr Croone told me, that, at the meeting at Gresham College[18] to-night (which it seems, they now have every Wednesday again) there was a pretty experiment of the blood of one Dogg let out (till he died) into the body of another on one side, while all his own run out on the other side. The first died upon the place, and the other very well, and likely to do well. This did give occasion to many pretty wishes, as of the blood of a Quaker to be let into an Archbishop, and such like; but, as Dr Croone says, may, if it takes be of mighty use to man's health, for the amending of bad blood by borrowing from a better body.

A trip to the theatre

For its core members, the Royal Society was a place of serious learning. It was an organisation where the light of new discoveries could be brought to a focal point, where novel ideas could be aired and challenged, and intriguing experiments demonstrated. For the public it was more of a puzzle, or a source of outright amusement – they would have understood the contemporary view that scientists are mildly crazed individuals who wander around in white coats getting desperately excited about details that fail to arouse any interest in 'normal' human beings. Contemporary scientists complain that they are seldom taken seriously and seem to think that their lack of status within the public realm is something new. This poor esteem is as old as the subject itself. On one occasion Pepys recorded that on 1 February 166¾ he had spent an amusing hour or two laughing at Sir William Petty as he tried to present some new thoughts about boats. Pepys also noted that the King had joined in the merriment, poking fun at the fact that since the Society had been formed its members had spent most of their time weighing air – a task that he clearly thought was a waste of time!

Ten years later, the playwright Thomas Shadwell parodied blood transfusions in his play *The Virtuoso*. King Charles II attended one of the Duke's Company's first performances when it came to His Royall Highnesse

Theatre on 25 May 1676, and thoroughly enjoyed the way that the play poked fun at the Royal Society in general, and a few specific experiments in particular. The names of the play's characters – Sir Formal Trifle, Sir Samuel Hearty, old Snarl and the central character of Sir Nicholas Grimcrack – give a clue as to how Shadwell viewed the Society. The name Grimcrack relates closely to gimcrack, a cheap showey gadget and knick-knack, this character being a dabbler who messes around with useless ideas and artefacts. The character most probably draws inspiration from Boyle, and spends much of the first part of the play concerned with weighing air. Shadwell satirises this by giving Grimcrack a cellar of wine bottles, each containing air from different locations – if Grimcrack wants to experience a change of scenery he merely pulls a cork and pours it out.

Keeping his text firmly focused on the work that was going on within the Royal Society, Shadwell moves the play on to look at transfusion, and introduces an experiment performed by Thomas Coxe on 4 March 1667, and read to the Society a month later.

Sir Nicholas Grimcrack: ... Besides, though I confess I did not invent it, I have perform'd admirable effects by transfusion of blood: to wit, by putting the blood of one animal into another.

Sir Formal Trifle: Upon my integrity, he had advance'd transfusion to the acme of perfection and has ascended over all the virtuosos in point of that operation. I saw him do the modest admirable effects in the world upon two animals: one a domestic animal commonly called a sound bulldog. Be pleas'd sir, to impart it.

Sir Nicholas Grimcrack: Why I made, sir, both the animals to be emittent and recipient at the same time. After I had made liga-tures as hard as I could (for fear of strangling the animals) to render the jugular veins turgid, I open'd the carotid arteries and jugular veins of both at one time, and so caused them to change blood one with another.

Sir Formal Trifle: Indeed that which ensu'd upon the operation was miraculous, for the mangy spaniel became sound and the bulldog mangy.

Sir Nicholas Grimcrack: Not only so, gentlemen, but the spaniel became a bulldog and the bulldog a spaniel.

Sir Formal Trifle: Which considering the civil and ingenious temper and education of the spaniel with the rough and untaught

savageness and ill-breeding of the bulldog, may not undeservedly
challenge the name of a wonder.

Bruce: 'Tis an experiment you'll deserve a statue for.[19]

At this point, the audience would not have known whether to laugh or
cry: whether to be amused by the fantastic outcome or terrified that
anyone would contemplate such an experiment. Many would have been
aware of the Royal Society's exploits, but hazy on the details. Spotting
the point where reality stretched into parody would not have been easy.
Coxe had in fact reported that the healthy dog had been unaffected by
this transfusion, and that the dog with mange was cured within 10 days
of the operation.

Edmund King's experiments

On 18 April 1667, physician Edmund King read a report to the Royal
Society. In it he detailed his latest developments in transfusing blood,
claiming that he had found a safer method of doing so. King was a
budding physician, aged 38 and recently married. He was rising in the
esteem of many, and soon became one of the King's band of personal
physicians. In fact, his chief claim to fame came a few years later when
he dashed to the King's bedside and took a decision to bleed the mon-
arch before any other physicians arrived to give second opinions.
Charles II survived and Edmund King was hailed as a hero and awarded
£1,000 from the Privy Council. Given Charles' finances it is little
surprise that Edmund never saw the money.

The experiment, King explained to the gathered members, had been
performed on 29 March 1667. Having paid 50 shillings for a reasonably
sized calf, and 33 shillings four pence for the largest sheep he could
find, King had taken them to his own house. His idea had been to go
back to using vein-to-vein transfusion. This had two main advantages.
Firstly, the veins were easy to get to without the need for extensive surgery. Secondly, in contrast to working with arteries, blood didn't spurt
everywhere if you got it wrong.

King had started by draining 49 ounces of blood from the sheep. At
this point, all of the observers had reckoned the poor animal was faint.

Creating the deficit would, King hoped, cause the sheep to suck blood from the calf once their veins were connected. With the tube in place he had waited for five minutes, in the hope that this would be enough time to transfer more than the 49 ounces the sheep had lost. The sheep had walked around and appeared to be healthy.

The experiment may have pointed to a safer way of transfusing blood, but it didn't help the sheep. With this phase of the experiment over, King decided to see what would happen if he let out all of the poor sheep's blood. Unsurprisingly, the sheep died. 'But,' King told the Royal Society, 'the whole sheep looked of a lovely white, and the mutton was more than ordinarily sweet, according to the opinion of many that ate of it.'

Having disposed of the sheep, King turned to the calf. It was in a less than stable state as half of its blood had been let out or transfused into the sheep. The low blood pressure made it hard for King to get any more blood from the vein. 'I then opened the carotid artery … ,' he explained. The resulting mess would have been extraordinary, as blood would have shot out across the room. Even if the calf had been tied securely, it would have struggled, sending each pulse of red fluid to a different location. All the same, King claimed to have caught 25 ounces of blood before the calf died. Again, the calf meat was incredibly pale and white, just as had been found in the lamb, and those who gathered to examine the corpse were sure that it was much whiter than usually occurred as a result of standard butchering techniques.

The next experiment King described involved only one unfortunate mastiff dog. On 4 April 1667, King had drained 18 ounces of blood from the dog, and hoped now to infuse the same volume of warm milk in which he had dissolved a little sugar. Clearly, King was working from the premise that the role of blood was to distribute nutrients around the body – a very reasonable idea, and indeed at least partly true. However, the experiment didn't go quite as planned. To start with, the milk began to go into the animal more rapidly than King had hoped. The animal had then become agitated, and struggled to get free of his restraints. A few minutes passed, and the dog calmed down, probably running low on energy and thus rapidly exhausted, enabling King to infuse the remaining milk.

The experiment over, King untied the dog, which, remarkably, jumped down from the table and 'went briskly about my side'. This success was shortlived, as the dog soon became 'very sick and short winded, in so much that I feared he would die. But after a vomit or two, in which there was a little blood, he revived again'. Taking a sample of blood from the dog to see what was going on inside, King had found that the milk and blood had not mixed, though he was convinced that they would have done so over time. Seven hours later, he was surprised to find that the dog had lost the use of its limbs, but responded when it was spoken kindly to. After three more hours the dog was in a coma, its only movement being its breathing. King opened its mouth and poured in a beer glass of good liquid food. The animal was released from its misery and died.

By now it was 10 in the evening, and it was too dark for King to open up the animal to see what had gone on. He resolved to rest, sleep, and then perform a post-mortem in the morning. But by the time morning gilded the skies, he faced a new problem – a violent stench. Human excrement and all other forms of waste sat in festering pools in the streets of London, and flowed in swirling masses in open sewers. But this smell was more extreme than this. King's porter, a man who by now was more used than many to bad smells and sights, ran from the room, being violently sick as he went. King decided to knuckle down and complete his inspection. He concluded that blood and milk did not mix well, and that if milk was injected, the heart filled with clotted blood and the blood failed to properly get into the lungs. The bladder was empty, though extremely contracted. A twenty-first-century pathologist would simply say that the mixture had created large blood clots, which had blocked all of the fine capillaries, giving the dog a massive stroke and heart attack.

As the members of the Royal Society listened to this graphic retelling of events, many would have been convinced – infusion of food was going to be difficult, but infusion of blood might well be the way forward. It seems clear that King certainly believed this, as nine days later, on 14 April, he was at it again.

This time he returned to transfusion, his subjects being another sheep and calf. Again in his own house, he started by bleeding the sheep. The bleeding went so well that King had soon removed 45 ounces. The spectators were convinced that the animal was beyond recovery. Not so. Like a magician, King revived the animal by transfusing blood from the calf, before letting the sheep down from the table.

At this point chaos broke out. One of the spectators had brought his dog along to the experiment; the sheep had decided to attack it and 'struck at the dog three or four times, not seeming to be at all concerned at what she had suffered in the experiment'. This was a rare animal for King, as he kept it alive, pleased to see it live and grow well.

On 30 May 1667, King was ready again, this time with a sheep and a dog. However, all did not go well on this occasion. When the dog's blood was transfused into the sheep, the animal simply lay down in agony, so much so that King and the friends who had turned up to watch thought it was about to die. Their conclusion was that they had given too much blood and had over-stocked the beast. They watched, waited, and then most of them went home. By the next day the sheep had recovered and was eating hay, though she seemed uninterested in spending time with the other sheep in the pen. Three days later she died. And the explanation for the death? Obviously, said King, she must have been unwell before the experiment began, though he also thought that the dog may have been less than well due to an experiment he had performed on it the day before!

Despite the lack of success, King was gripped by the concept, and anxious to have another go at the earliest opportunity. This came on 9 June 1667. There appears to be little sense of direction to King's studies, because rather than working to perfect his technique he this time introduced a new species to the study – a fox. The concept of moving blood from a lamb into a fox was so intriguing that Boyle showed up for the spectacle. The fox was weak from the start, so King removed only a little blood before starting the transfusion. This new blood did little to improve the fox's health, and when released it sat miserably on the ground, only raising its head to growl and snap at sticks that were placed near to it. A day later the fox died, and 'had some blood come out of his nose when dead'.

The post-mortem showed that the animal's thorax and abdomen were awash with bloody fluid, causing King to question whether the difference between lambs' blood and that of foxes was so extreme that it had reacted, causing the blood to become very thin. This watery blood was then incapable of retaining the foxes 'spirits', and therefore his life had simply flown away. The curious in England may not have been swamped by their own success, but they were certain that these experiments clearly placed them as the world leaders in this area of research.

At the same time, King hoped that his work would establish him as one of the leading lights of research in England, and presumably dreamed that this would give him entry into the prestigious Royal Society. Alas, despite his frantic efforts, he got no further, and was never elected as a Fellow.

CHAPTER SIX

Denis' route to the top

Communication between England and France was good, and there is every reason to believe that French scientists would have known about the transfusion experiments Lower and his friends were performing. In the spirit of good science, the French scientists decided that if this technique was as good as it seemed, they ought to have a go at doing it themselves.

Their first attempt was in the last week of December 1666, when Parisian physician and researcher Claude Perrault headed a small team and tried to transfuse blood between two dogs. On 22 January 1667 they tried again. This was a few years after Potter and Lower had begun their research in and around Oxford, but a couple of months before King's work in London. On this occasion a group of members of the new Académie Royale des Sciences gathered in the King's library, bringing with them two dogs. The dogs were duly strapped to tables and an attempt was made to transfuse blood from an artery in the leg of one animal, into a leg vein of the other. After messing around for a while, and getting thoroughly spattered with blood, the investigators abandoned the procedure, blaming their tools. The cannulae, they complained, were not made exactly as described to the artisan, and consequently they had no idea whether blood was flowing through them or not.

Not to be put off, however, they reconvened on the 24th, this time meeting in the home of Louis Gayant, a renowned Parisian surgeon. Their newly crafted pipes were much better, and they successfully connected the carotid artery in the neck of one dog to the jugular vein in the neck of another. This time it was clear that a connection had been made, as they could now see the jugular vein pulsing as arterial blood pumped in. The dog receiving the blood died almost instantly, and when its chest was opened to investigate the cause, the heart and large veins were found to be packed with blood clots.

The enquiring minds met up again two days later, again in the French King's library, for another attempt. Their conclusion was that the receiving dog fared much worse than the donor, even though the donor had lost a lot of blood through an 'accident' during the procedure – it takes little imagination to conjure up a mental picture of the mess. Given that the majority of Paris' physicians had spent their working careers bleeding people and making them well, it is probably not surprising that they were inclined to believe that the donor was better off than the recipient. In reality, both animals would probably have been in less than good health by the end – one from an adverse reaction to foreign blood, the other from acute blood loss.

The last four trial transfusions were performed at Gayant's house on 28 February, and 3, 15 and 21 March. Again the experimenters were unimpressed. The blood had a grave tendency to clot in the recipients' veins, and the only animals that seemed to be well after the procedure were those that had probably received little if any blood.

In the final experiment a nice touch of science was added to the proceedings. The animals were weighed before and after the transfusion, and any excrement that came out was collected and also weighed. Consequently, it was confirmed that the transfusion had passed two ounces of blood from one dog to the other. The trial was repeated, transfusing a further two ounces, but this time also bleeding three ounces out for fear of over-filling the animal. The recipient died the next day.

Given these poor results, it is little surprise that the members of the Académie were not desperately enthusiastic about transfusion. Even so, they hadn't given up totally, and they wondered whether it would be possible to use two tubes and transfuse in both directions simultaneously. The idea would be to allow the blood of each animal to mix and unite, however it was decided that the technical problems of doing this on small animals like dogs were formidable.

The conclusion was that transfusion held little hope, though it was possible that there might still be some use for remedies based on using blood in potions. A concluding remark in their report stated that:

> These arguments, nevertheless, when they were examined, could
> not support the belief that there was much foundation to the hopes

that had been conceived for such a substitution of blood, and the method that Medea employed to rejuvenate her father-in-law has seemed less fabulous and more probable, since this judicious operator did not claim to renew the blood of [Aeson] solely by infusing medicinal fluids into his veins from which she has withdrawn the old blood, but she made the principal part of her cure consist in the virtue of a remedy which she made him take by mouth.

Denis makes his move

So what makes a person have a good idea? Occasionally, people can record the moment, but more often it is a slow-dawning process. Even stories such as that of Isaac Newton being hit by a falling apple and conceiving of the theory of gravity are believed to be apocryphal. Certainly there is no record of why Denis left his numbers behind for a while and turned his attention to transfusion. Clearly he had caught wind that others were trying it out, and having teamed up with Emmerey he saw this as a way of furthering his career. The first person to successfully cure a patient by using transfusion was going to be important. There was no time to lose.

Thus it was that on an evening early in March 1667, Denis sat down to write his first publication revealing his work on transfusion. His aim was to get it published in the *Journal des Sçavans*. This relatively young journal had already gained a wide readership within Paris, and readers around the world were beginning to subscribe to it as well. Founded by the Paris magistrate Denis de Sallo, its first edition had come out on 5 January 1665. It was primarily a reviewing journal, but occasionally published papers on science, medicine and technology.

Much to Denis' excitement, the article was published in the 14 March 1667 edition of the journal, and included details of his initial attempts, explaining that the first experiment had occurred on 3 March that year, the same day as Gayant's fifth attempt. This had involved transfusing blood between a small fox-like dog, and a spaniel bitch. Flicking through a copy of the journal, he smiled as he read his report of the second transfusion that he and Emmerey had performed on 8 March. This was particularly satisfying as they had successfully transfused blood from the previous recipient and given it to a third dog. It included the important detail that they had ensured the room was kept warm. The last thing they had wanted to do was to let the blood run cold as it passed through the connecting tubes – that would surely make it lose its vital heat. His excitement about the procedure was demonstrated in his description that the operation had been less dangerous than they had feared. The blood used had served three dogs in only a couple of weeks, and all three seemed perfectly fit, strong and friendly. A physician who had witnessed the event had been impressed, saying that he would never have thought it possible had he not seen it for himself.

Any modern scientist would be jealous of the fact that these experiments were apparently published in a journal within a week. It is easy to fall into the trap of believing that technology inevitably makes things happen faster. But with all the additional requirements for protocol and scrutiny that are these days imposed, publication in an academic journal normally occurs at least six months to a year from the time an experiment is completed.

Once again, Denis was composing a letter in his study. This time the letter was addressed to his patron Montmor, setting out his work on blood transfusion to date. As was customary for the times, Denis began by giving Montmor considerable credit for the success of the work, based on the fact that the ideas were first discussed in his house and at his academy. Denis was clearly anxious to flatter his benefactor, and at the same time to defend himself against the claims of rashness that were flying around in the public sphere:

> You have heard of the trial we made about four months ago upon dogs, to transmit the blood of the crural artery [in the leg] of one into the jugular vein of another. And being this operation even at the first attempt succeeded as happily as we could wish … we were encouraged to repeat the same several times both in public and private, and we added so many circumstances to the manner of performing it, that its easiness seemed to invite us not to neglect it, but to make abundance of observations which might be of some benefit in practice.[20]

Denis went on to explain how he and Emmerey had tried various techniques. Sometimes they took blood from the artery of a donor and transfused it into a recipient's vein, and on other occasions they tried vein-to-vein transfusions. They had used weak dogs and strong dogs, big dogs and small dogs. In fact, being a dog in central Paris was indeed a dangerous position to be in that summer!

> And not finding one in nineteen to die, but on the contrary always observing some surprising effect in all such as had received new blood, we were strongly persuaded that the transfusion would have no such dangerous consequences, as some people endeavoured to suggest.[21]

Spurred on by their success, Denis explained that he wanted to stretch the issue and perform trials in which they would transfuse blood from one species into another. Without pausing, they pressed ahead. The first attempt involved taking blood from a calf and placing it in a dog. This had been a good evening. Not only had the experiment worked, but Montmor had been there to witness it:

> In your presence we transmitted a calf's blood, into a dog's veins on the 28th of March; since which time we have also done the same upon other occasions, always acting somewhat towards the facility of the operation.

This became the first of three occasions when Denis transfused blood from calves into dogs. His main concern in each case was to see what happened when the strong blood of a large animal was mixed with the necessarily weaker blood of a small dog. In all these experiments, claimed Denis, they had never seen any problems in the dogs. The dogs had always seemed as healthy at the end as they had been at the beginning. Denis was also excited that he and Emmerey had developed a simpler method of transfusion that entailed simply pushing the pipes through the skin and into the vessels. This sounds very similar to today's hypodermic needles, and obviously saved making a large incision. If they had known about air-borne disease they would have realised that keeping the skin closed also massively reduces the risk of infection.

First human

Then came the big world first, the critical step in the history of blood. On 15 June, Denis and Emmerey were introduced to a 15- or 16-year-old boy – no one seems to be sure of his age, and it was anyway quite usual for people not to know their own age. This poor fellow had spent the past two months suffering from a severe and debilitating fever. His relatives had called in the physicians and inevitably they had bled him. Fever was seen as an indication that a person's humours had become unbalanced and that the body now contained too much heat-generating blood. Releasing a pint or so of the person's blood should solve the problem.

However, bleeding had not cured this particular youth's fever, hence the physicians had returned and repeated the treatment. Over two months he had been bled 20 times. Not surprisingly, the unfortunate boy was now weak and dull-minded, his memory was poor, his body felt heavy, and he was constantly falling asleep. He slept for 12 hours each night, and it took considerable effort to rouse him in the morning – he even slept at the breakfast table. This was in marked contrast to the reports that before the fever had started he had been fit and nimble.

Calling in a physician was expensive, and also dangerous. The youth's problems were now more the result of the treatment he was receiving than the original illness. It is very probable that over the two-month period, the initial cause of the fever had passed away, and that the boy's fatigue was a result of the anaemia he was suffering due to the extreme use of bleeding – twenty severe haemorrhages in two months is enough to make anybody distinctly weak.

When Denis arrived, the situation had the potential of going from bad to worse. Denis looked the patient over and listened to the story. He discussed it with Emmerey and the two came to the conclusion that the boy had too little blood inside him, and that what little was left was clearly packed with a concentrated mass of fever. Having so little blood in his body, the fever was not being diluted. In addition, the small amount of blood now meant that there was not enough intrinsic heat left in the patient's body to boil off the fever-causing agents. Rather than flowing around the body, they believed that the blood was probably lying in stagnant pools in the vessels, and not carrying the life-giving power that it possessed into the nerves and muscles.

There was one way to check their theory, and that was to open a vein to see what came out. Once again, the boy lost some of his precious blood. Using standard blood-letting instruments, the pair sliced a vein and watched a little blood come out, noting that it was so black and thick that it could hardly leave the vessel. Clearly this person was very unwell.

Their solution was obvious to themselves, but radical to the observers. Give him more blood. It was time to send someone out to find a donor, and a sheep seemed as good a bet as any other animal.

The transition from concept, through initial animal experiment to the first human trial was therefore incredibly rapid. This is not something that would be allowed to occur today, as regulatory safeguards and ethical committees stand to protect patients from the actions of overzealous practitioners. A Western ethical committee might allow a scientist to try out an idea on an animal, knowing that the animal will not survive the experiment, but will insist that nothing is carried out on a human being unless there is strong evidence that the individual will benefit from the procedure. This leads to the distinction whereby scientists perform 'experiments' on animals, but doctors carry out 'trials' on humans. The 1964 Helsinki Declaration now sets out the framework for the way that doctors and patients should interact, with the insistence that the patient's interests are the principal goal of any therapy. In medical research, the wellbeing of each human subject should take precedence over the interests of science or society. In this regard, Denis appears to have performed with remarkable integrity, even by twenty-first-century standards. It wasn't always the case that physicians were primarily concerned about the health and wellbeing of their clients.

By 5 o'clock in the morning, everything was ready. Denis incised a vein in the youth's arm and let out three ounces of blood. He wanted to let some out to be sure that there would be room for the new blood – after all, Denis had no argument with the acquired wisdom that too much blood was dangerous. Then to the lamb. By this point Denis and Emmerey had inserted a thin tube into the lamb's carotid artery, the artery in the neck that carries blood from the heart to the brain. This artery would have had a number of advantages in that it was relatively easy to locate in the side of the sheep's neck, and once they had found it, there would be a 10-centimetre stretch of vessel that could be readily exposed.

Quickly, Emmerey slipped a tube into a vein in the young man's arm and connected it to the tube in the sheep. They waited and counted. Their aim was to transfuse about three times as much blood as they had taken out. This would restore the loss, dilute the fever, and also give sufficient blood to restore the vital heat. At the point when they felt the transfusion ought to be complete, they withdrew the pipes, and stemmed any loss of blood by tying a small pack of material tightly against the wound on the patient's arm.

Now all they could do was sit and observe. Denis plied the patient with questions and discovered that during the operation he had felt a great heat in his arm. Other than that there appears to have been little to report in terms of immediate effects. The youth did, however, remark that the evening before he had fallen down a flight of 10 stairs hurting his side, and that since the transfusion this pain had gone. It raised the intriguing possibility that transfusion may not just cure fevers, but may also be a treatment for all sorts of physical aches and pains.

By 10 o'clock in the morning, just five hours after the operation had begun, the youth was feeling cheerful, and asked if he could get up. Denis could see no reason why not, and was thrilled to see the patient spending the rest of the day eating, drinking and leading an altogether normal existence. In the afternoon, around 4 o'clock, he had a mild nose-bleed, and Denis thought that he had lost three or four drops of blood. This, he felt, was curious, but was perhaps they had given him a little too much and the reaction was like an overflow pipe in a water tank.

The afternoon had gone well, so Denis encouraged his patient to eat a hearty supper and go to bed. By 9 o'clock he was in bed, and by 10 o'clock he was asleep. In marked contrast to the previous days when he had been unable to wake up, the youth found it difficult to sleep and woke at two in the morning. By four he was bored and decided to start the day. It was the start of the rest of his life. Denis commented:

> The next day he slept a little more, and from that time he easily got the victory over his drowsiness, which before he had often attempted without success; for now he never fails to rise very early without needing to be wakened. He executes nimbly whatever is appointed him, and he has no longer that slowness of spirit nor heaviness of body, which before rendered him unfit for any thing. He grows fat visibly, and in brief, is a subject of amazement to all those that know him, and dwell with him.

The apparent success of this trial fuelled Denis' enthusiasm for the technique. As far as he could see, transfusion was here to stay.

Whether it was out of a sense of charity or curiosity, Denis invited the boy to come to his house as his valet. Looking at the incident with the benefit of more than 300 additional years of medical science, it appears that the most likely explanation for the youth's recovery was not the introduction of the transfused blood, but the cessation of

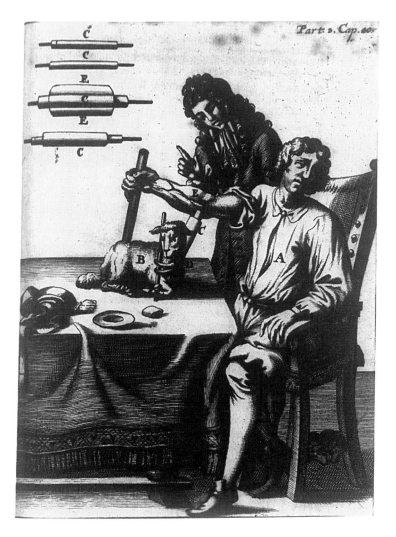

Plate 9 'Sheep to Man' (Purmann, 1705). Reproduced by permission of the United States National Library of Medicine.

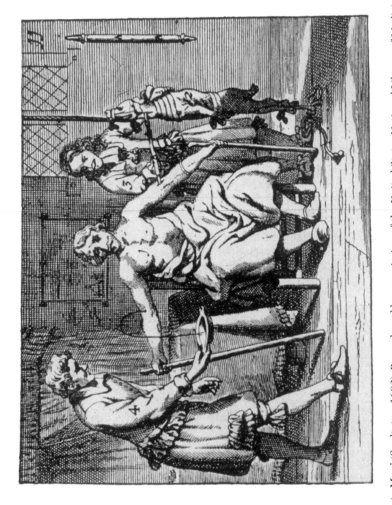

Plate 10 'Dog to Man' (Sculetus, 1693). Reproduced by permission of the United States National Library of Medicine.

bleeding. Indeed, the nasal haemorrhage indicates that he may have had an adverse reaction to the lamb's blood, but not one of sufficient power to cause him lasting damage.

Transfusion realisation

It took 200 years before doctors began to unravel some of the complications involved in transfusing blood, and at that point they revealed just how dangerous the process really was. Blood turned out not to be a simple red liquid, but a living organ composed of many different types of cells, each of which performs different duties around the body. Red blood cells transport oxygen from the lungs to tissues, and actively enable blood to transport carbon dioxide in the reverse direction. White cells fight infections, and platelets play a vital role in enabling blood to clot. These solid lumps float in a liquid plasma. Soon scientists found that if blood was allowed to clot, the liquid had slightly different properties to plasma, and they called this fluid serum.

In 1875, the German physiologist Leonard Landois, working in Greifswald, took red cells from lambs' blood, mixed these with sera taken from the blood of another animal, such as a dog, and kept the mixture at body temperature. Watching through a microscope, he saw the blood cells burst within about two minutes. It was obvious that a similar process would not be good if it occurred inside a human body. The loss of red cells would make it hard for a person to move gases around the body. Landois was also aware that this destruction of red cells had another implication. Red cells are packed with potassium and this ion would flood into the bloodstream. While potassium is one of the body's vital ingredients, high concentrations of potassium in the blood are lethal and can prevent the muscles in the heart from contracting. The person would feel pains in their arm and chest, and effectively experience heart failure.

Given this knowledge, it seems amazing that anyone survived a transfusion from another species, although when Landois examined all the documented occasions of animal blood being given to humans, he found that in about one-third of cases the person suffered no long-lasting damage. The most likely explanation is that they did not receive very much of the blood, and therefore the body was able to absorb the impact. Even so, a few doctors were still advocating animal-to-human transfusions right up until 1928.

A quarter of a century after Landois' discovery, Austrian Karl Landsteiner took the science one step further. Landsteiner began looking at the way blood from different people responded when mixed in different combinations. His first samples came from the 22 people who worked alongside him in his laboratory. In some instances he found that the red cells would clump when he mixed sera from one person with whole blood taken from another. In other combinations, this agglutination did not occur. In time, this tall, lean man made a discovery that set the foundations for what would become the blood transfusion industry. He believed that people could be placed into one of three groups according to their type of blood – he called the groups A, B and C. Mixing blood from people within the same group was harmless, while mixing between groups was damaging. Serum from A clumped B blood, and serum of B clumped A blood. C was different in that its serum clumped both A and B. A year later, a pupil of Landsteiner discovered a fourth group – a rare set of people whose serum didn't clump either A or B. He had discovered the 'ABO blood groups' system.

In 1919, Landsteiner was head-hunted and offered a top position in the Rockefeller Institute for Medical Research in New York, where he went on to show that life was more complex and that there were many other blood groups. For example, he discovered groups M, N and P by injecting human blood into rabbits, where crossing the species created a more violent reaction. Sorting out this set of blood reactions and the concept of blood groups won Landsteiner the 1930 Nobel Prize for Physiology or Medicine.

Incompatible transfusions

One of three things can happen when inappropriate blood is transfused. Occasionally, nothing occurs. The body doesn't recognise this invading mass of foreign cells and fails to mount a defensive response.

A second response is an immediate and life-threatening breakdown of the transfused red blood cells. This occurs because the patient's ABO system spots the foreign blood and invokes what is known as the 'complement' system. Complement is a molecule that binds to the red blood cells and causes holes to be knocked in their membranes. Because there is a higher concentration of chemicals inside the cells than in the plasma, water rushes in through the holes, the cells swell and burst, releasing their contents into the bloodstream. The body is then faced with the enormous task of clearing all of this debris away. On top of this, the body's clotting mechanism can be put out of order, leading to severe haemorrhaging from any weak areas. This situation is called disseminated intravenous coagulation, or DIC for short. The bleeding may be internal and go unnoticed, or from old wounds or in the nasal passages, result in a bleeding nose. The total shock to the system can be overwhelming. However, in less severe cases, the complement system is not fully stimulated and the body will lose only a third of its red cells over the first 24 hours. The affected person should in this case stabilise and slowly recover.

The third main possibility is that foreign red cells are slowly removed from the bloodstream. This process does not involve the ABO recognition system, but instead uses white blood cells specially designed for spotting invading cells and removing them. In this case, destruction of the donated cells occurs outside the bloodstream, in the liver and spleen. The affected person may feel unwell, but the situation is not life-threatening.

In a modern medical environment these mismatches do occur very occasionally, but only where there has been a clerical error and a person is given the wrong blood.

Clinical signs

The most common sign of a mismatch transfusion is fever, as the body reacts to all of the chemicals pouring into the bloodstream. This can be made worse if the transfused blood happens to be carrying a bacterial infection, or if the equipment used is not sterile and so introduces bacteria to the recipient. Denis and his contemporaries might have cleaned the tubes they used, but given that they had no idea that bacteria existed, there is little hope that the quills that were poked into vessels would have been sterile. Consequently, there was a high chance that along with the blood, they placed disease-causing microbes into the circulation.

People can also experience chest pain as the heart starts to suffer from the high levels of potassium floating around. In Denis' experiment, the resulting heart failure could have been one of the causes of the youth's comment that his arm was aching as the blood went in, although much of that fiery pain was probably due to an extreme allergic reaction as the two bloods mixed within the vein.

With the heart struggling to work, a patient's blood pressure drops, he or she starts to feel very sick, and some vomit. A combination of the low blood pressure and millions of small clumps of red blood cells can easily cripple the kidneys, compounding the problems. With the kidneys not working, the body finds it difficult to clean its blood, and if the problem cannot be resolved, the person is likely to die of the consequent internal poisoning.

Chemical messengers released into the blood make fine arteries relax, and this allows fluid to leak out into the surrounding tissue. The combined effect is that blood pressure drops further. In an attempt to restore blood pressure, other hormones cut in, making some blood vessels clamp shut. One group of vessels particularly affected are those in the kidney. Blood pressure is low, so the kidney then finds it difficult to filter the blood and clear out the junk. On top of this, its filter mechanism becomes blocked with mini clots floating in the blood, and the vessels supplying it with blood begin to close. If this situation continues, the kidney not only fails to perform its task, but the cells within it start to die as they run out of life-giving oxygen.

In Denis' patient, the kidneys appear to have managed to keep going. In later patients he recorded that they produced copious quantities of black urine – black because it contained all the breakdown products from the destroyed red blood cells. The patients also complained of severe back pain, a symptom that may be associated with the chaos occurring in the kidneys.

Denis' patient also had clear signs of DIC. Far from triggering a sense of anxiety, Denis' medical training told him that bleeding was so much part and parcel of normal treatment that he took this as a healthy sign – after all, menstrual bleeding was seen as a female body's way of naturally restoring its internal balance once a month. For Denis, this response to the transfusion was a sign that the body was obviously sorting itself out. Indeed, rather than worrying about such nose-bleeds when they occurred in future patients, Denis decided to encourage the process by cutting a vein and removing further blood.

Moving on

As far as he could see, Denis' transfusions had been a success – but where next? There were plenty of sick people in Paris, but experimenting on the sick was fraught with problems. If the person died after blood had been transfused into them, how would it be possible to tell whether this was the natural course of the disease, or whether the infusion was to blame? To investigate the technique more fully, he needed to try it on a healthy person. Medical history has many examples of scientists trying new techniques on themselves, but on this occasion, Denis decided to seek a volunteer, and thus instigated the world's second human transfusion.

Just as there were plenty of sick people, there was also an ample supply of the poor, and a few days later Denis had enrolled a 45-year-old labourer. He was large, fit and strong, and Denis calculated that he would need to infuse a greater volume of blood into him to see any reaction.

The trial started badly, with Denis and Emmerey finding it difficult to bleed the labourer from his veins. Eventually they had managed to extract a meagre 10 ounces. Using a similar technique as they had employed with the youth, they connected the labourer to a lamb, but this time, rather than employing the carotid artery in the lamb, they took blood from the larger crural artery in the lamb's leg. Again they counted, on this occasion waiting until they believed they had transferred 20 ounces of blood into him.

Apparently, the man retained his good sense of humour throughout the trial, which is just as well, as the tubes used would undoubtedly have leaked, spraying blood around the room and covering all involved. The lamb is also unlikely to have joined in the event with anything like a resigned spirit. Even if it was tied so tightly that it had no chance of moving or making more than a muffled cry of protest, it would have at the very least sprayed the place with urine from time to time.

Once again, the recipient of the blood commented on the extreme heat in his arm as the blood flowed in. Denis explains what happened next, saying that when the operation was ended, they advised him to lie down to rest, but as the man felt perfectly well he ignored their commands. Instead, he decided to butcher the lamb, explaining that as a youth he had been trained as a butcher. In fact, it appears that he did a very good job of cutting the animal's throat and removing its fleece. He then announced that he was going home, and promised to cook a rich broth, lie down and rest for the remainder of the day.

For Denis, this was disappointing because it meant that he couldn't take minute-by-minute notes of the labourer's response to the transfusion, but in the end he had no choice. Still, Denis insisted that the man rest. The labourer left, and Denis and Emmerey also went off to rest, while their house servants cleaned up the mess. Later, they went to the labourer's house, but found that he had never made it home. It wasn't until Denis bumped into him in the street the following day that he discovered what the man had done.

It is clear that the man had been paid for his services, though there is no record of how much he received. While this would have been common practice at the time, it would now be deeply frowned upon. Paying a person in this way means that he or she is no longer a volunteer, but is using his or her body as a means of earning money. The person could almost be said to be selling his or her body – a short step away from slavery.

As soon as the labourer had left Denis' home, he had bumped into a group of friends. Armed with the money that he had just been given as payment for taking part in the trial, and exhilarated by the day's events, the man and his friends had gone for a drink in the nearest tavern. He had soon forgotten any notion of going home to rest:

> At noon finding himself more hearty (whether by the new blood he had received six hours before, or by the quantity of wine he had drunk) he fell upon a sort of work so laborious to his whole body that it might almost tire a horse; thus he spent all the afternoon.

Hearing this angered Denis – the man's behaviour had put his trial in danger and, he explained, worse than this, it meant that he had not been able to make vital observations. The man had after all been paid for his services, and the period of observation was as important to the

106

trial as the infusion itself. It is a graphic reminder that one of the problems with conducting trials involving human beings is that they have
a tendency to get up and walk out halfway through. Again, this is at
present enshrined in the Helsinki Declaration – the idea that 'the
health of my patient will be my first consideration', and it is to Denis'
credit that he chose to give the labourer his freedom as opposed to
finding ways of restraining him while he conducted his work.

In his defence, the man claimed that it had been impossible for him
to contemplate resting when he felt so full of energy. He explained that
he had felt no pain, that he had eaten, drunk and slept well, and that he
had more strength than ever before. Indeed, he was so excited by the
results of the transfusion that he offered to have the procedure repeated
any time they wished him to – adding that this time he would behave
better and lie down if Denis so commanded him to.

There is no record that Denis ever did offer this service to this
unnamed man again, but this is not the last we will hear of him.

Precedence and prison

or Denis, the end of July 1667 had brought with it the warm glow of recognition. It was one thing to write up his work and publish it in his own pamphlets, as Denis had been doing over the summer, and to have some of them published in the new, but increasingly influential *Journal des Sçavans*, the editor of which was a personal friend. However, seeing his work translated into English and published in Oldenburg's *Philosophical Transactions* was the icing on the cake.

There it was, in Issue Number 27, page after page of his work and ideas, printed and distributed to all the centres of learning in Europe. This indeed was recognition. This would make his critics sit up and think. England was, after all, the place where circulation had been discovered. If they thought his work worthy of note, then who was to complain.

Unable to read English, Denis was prevented from analysing it fully to check that his ideas had survived translation, but even a casual scrutiny showed that many of the key features were there. For example, right at the beginning was the statement pointing out that Denis had been considering the possibilities of transfusion for 10 years since hearing it mentioned at a meeting at Montmor's academy. It was great to have this in writing, because now his precedence in this area was assured. When transfusion became widely used throughout the world, his name would be on everyone's lips and fortune should pour into his pockets.

The paper clearly mentioned his first transfusion into the youth and the second into the labourer. No one in the world had attempted anything so bold. Surely with this international recognition, the French Académie Royale des Sciences would now offer him a place within its esteemed membership? How could it refuse? All he needed

(489)　　　　Numb. 27.

A LETTER

Concerning a new way of curing sundry diseases by Transfusion of Blood, Written to Monsieur de MONTMOR, *Counsellor to the* French King, *and Master of* Requests.

By J: DENIS *Professor of* Philosophy, *and the* Mathematicks.

Munday July 22. 1667.

SIR,

THE project of causing the Blood of a healthy animal to passe into the veins of one diseased, having been conceived a-*bout ten years agoe*, in the illustrious Society of *Virtuosi* which assembles at your house, and your goodness having received M. *Emmeriz*, & my self, very favorably at such times as we have presum'd to entertain you either with discourse concerning it, or the sight of some not inconsiderable effects of it : You will not think it strange that I now take the liberty of troubling you with this Letter, and design to inform you fully of what pursuances and successes we have made in this Operation ; wherein you are justly intitled to a greater share than any other, considering that it was first spoken of in your *Academy*, & that the Publick is beholding to you for this as well as for many other discoveries, for the benefits & advantages it shall reap from the same. But that I may give you the reasons of our procedure & con-

C c c　　　　　　　vince

Plate 11　Philosophical Transactions, Issue Number 27 (Oldenburg, 1st edn).
© The Royal Society.

now were a few more successful operations and further high-profile coverage.

This high point in Denis' career lasted a month, maybe a few days more. But the blow came in August. Oldenburg had rebutted the said issue of his journal and replaced it with a new version. The grudging praise that Denis had managed to gain in recent weeks turned rapidly into sniggers and direct guffaws of laughter. As far as Denis was concerned, the chief difference between the two versions was that his lengthy letter had been removed, and replaced by a short article pouring vitriol on his claim to precedence.

Denis called in a friend to translate the new version, and sat with his head in his hands as he heard the full frontal attack on his claims and credibility:

An advertisement concerning the invention of the transfusion of blood

The author of these papers returning now to his former exercises, which by an extraordinary accident he was necessitated to interrupt for some months past, thought fit to comprise the Transactions of all the months omitted in one Tract; In the very beginning of which he must inform the reader, that if himself had published that letter, which came abroad in July last 'Concerning a new way of curing sundry diseases by transfusion of blood', written to Monsieur de Montmor, &c. by J Denis Prof of Philosophy, &c. he should then have taken notice, as he doth now, of what is affirmed in that letter about the time and place of the conception of that Transfusing design.

This was a marked difference in tone – without reading further it was clear that Denis had gone from hero to usurper. His friend read on. The article was short, but clearly stated that the English, not the French, had thought of the idea first, announcing that the winners of this particular race were Lower and King. To add insult to injury, the article was now followed immediately by an account of an Italian researcher who was also looking into the possibility of manipulating the bloodstream.

A month later, Denis' despondency turned to despair. In late October, Issue 28 of the *Philosophical Transactions* arrived, and in it was a

(489)   *Numb.* 27.

PHILOSOPHICAL
TRANSACTIONS.

For the Months of *July*, *Auguſt*, and *September*.
Munday, Septem. 23. 1667.

The Contents.

An Advertiſement concerning the Invention of the Transfuſion of
bloud. *An Account of ſome Experiments of* Infuſing *Liquors*
into the Veins of Animals ; *As alſo, of ſome new diſcoveries pre-*
tended to be made in the ſtruĉture of the Brain *and the* Tongue.
An Experiment upon bloud *grown cold. Some Obſervations of*
Quickſilver *found at the roots of Plants* ; *and of* Shells *found*
upon in-land *mountains* ; *Other Obſervations made by a curious*
perſon in his Voyage from England *to the* Caribes, *concerning*
the ruſting of Iron *by the Sea-air* ; *the* Changes of Thames-
water *carried by ſea* ; *The* Variety of ·the Colours of the
Sea ; *The* burning *of the ſame* ; *the* Night-winds *in the* Indies ; *The Relations of the* Seaſons of the year *rectified* ; *Ob-*
ſervables about Tortoiſes ; *The condition of* Engliſh *bodies*
firſt coming to Jamaica ; *A way of preſerving* Ale, *as far as to*
the ſame Iſland. An Extract of a Letter concerning ſome Mag-
netical *Experiments* ; *and an Excellent Liquor made of Cyder-*
Apples and Mulberries. *An Account of two or three Books* ;
One, The HISTORY of the ROYAL SOCIE-
TY: *The other,* DISQUISITIO DE FÆTU
FORMATO, *The third,* MUSCULI DESCRI-
PTIO GEOMETRICA.

An Advertiſement concerning the Invention of the
Transfuſion of Bloud:

THE Author of theſe Papers, returning now to his former Exerciſes, which by an extraordinary Accident he
was neceſſitated to interrupt for ſome months laſt paſt,
                              C c c   thought

Plate 12   Philosophical Transactions, Issue Number 27 (Oldenburg, 2nd edn).
© The Royal Society.

lengthy article.[22] He slowly made sense of the title:

An account

Of more trials of transfusion, accompanied with some considerations thereon, chiefly in reference to its circumspect practise on man; together with a farther vindication of this invention from usurpers.

This experiment, as it hath raised disputes among the curious both here and abroad ...

It was time to call on the services of his translator again. This article was no longer a simple transcript of his article, but drew from a number of different sources. It mentioned the ideas of others on the likelihood of successful transfusion, and had stern warnings that if performed, it should be done only with great caution and by the right people. There was an implicit undertone that neither of these two provisos had been met.

Denis realised that his dreams of fame and rapid fortune had been hit hard. Not only was the article decrying Denis' work, it was also pouring doubt over this whole area of research.

Whereas the first part of the article had only implied criticism of Denis, the middle section had no such restraint. Here the author turned directly to Denis' claims of precedence:

Before we dismiss this subject, something should be said of the reason why the Curious in England are cautious about practising this experiment upon men. The above-mentioned ingenious Monsieur Denis has acquainted the world with his Parisian experiments, and told us just how successful they were. He has even published his work in the Journal des Sçavans and rejoices that the French have advanced this invention so far, as to try it upon Men, before any English did it.

While we readily grant they were the first we know of that actually took the step and performed transfusion on a human, we must take leave to inform the world that the philosophers in England would have practised it long ago upon Man, if they had not been so tender in hazarding the Life of Man. Their intention is always to preserve life and relieve suffering. In addition they have a legitimate fear that if the experiment went wrong and the patient died, they could be punished by the law. Bear in mind that the penalties of the law in England are more strict than are those of many other Nations.

But this does not mean that the English haven't thought about it. The publisher can assert bona fide that several months ago he saw with his own eyes the instruments ready, and heard the method agreed on, thought proper to execute this operation upon man. And, for further proof thereof, he shall here insert the full methods that the ingenious Dr Edmund King has devised for this purpose, by Dr Edmund King, and by him communicated in a Letter. This genuine precedence, because Monsieur Denis has not thought fit to describe the manner they used in France for Men; nor any body else come to our knowledge.

Denis sat in shocked silence while his friend continued to read the description of a method for transfusing blood between animals much like those that had been published before. He could not fault the method, but he had no reason to fault it − it was the method he had used himself.

We would have said no more of this argument at this time were we not obliged to remove a mistake found in one of the late French journals, affirming with confidence, that 'tis certain that French have given the English the first thoughts of notion of this experiment. And why? Because (say they) they are witnesses, that a Benedictine Friar, one Dom Robert de Gabets, discussed it at Monsieur Montmor's ten years ago. Surely, all ingenious men will acknowledge that the certain way of deciding such controversies as these is a Public Record either written or printed. That record should declare the time and place that an Invention was first proposed, an explanation of the method, and the instances of success. All this appears from England.

'First to publish. I was first to publish,' shouted Denis, jumping from his seat and beginning to pace around the room brandishing a copy of the old version of *Philosophical Transactions*. 'Here, look here, this is it in print. A physical record for all time. I was first until they tore it up in an attempt to revise history,' he yelled, his voice breaking in his fury. 'Do I have to start my own journal to get my ideas read?' His friend beckoned Denis to sit down and let him continue reading. Denis refused and instead stood staring out of his window at the law courts on the other side of the Seine. 'Where is the justice?' were the only thoughts tumbling around his mind. His friend continued:

> Number seven of these Transactions (printed in 1665, December) acquaints the world how many years since Dr Christopher Wren proposed the experiment of infusion into veins. And this was hint enough for the Royal Society to see that you could move from infusion to transfusion at some point in the future. In fact when they held a public meeting on May 17, 1665 they gave an order for this trial. If you doubt this, you can find it recorded in the appropriate volume of their Journal, where 'twas registered by the care of the secretaries obliged by oath to fidelity.
>
> At that point the trials did not get far because the equipment was not very good and there was no agreed method. But then came the learned physician and expert anatomist, Dr Lower. He has perfected a method and published it in number 20 of these tracts. Prior to publishing he had used the method in Oxford and several others had used it in London.
>
> It seems strange, that so surprising an invention should have been conceived in France, as they will have it, ten years ago, and lain there so long in the womb, till the way of midwiving it into the world was sent thither from London. To say nothing of the disagreement, there seems to be about the French Parent of this foetus, Monsieur de Gurye says it is Abbot Bourdelot, but the author of the letters in the Journal des Scavans claims it was a Benedictine Friar.
>
> But whoever this parent be, that is not so material, as that all that lay claim to the child, should join together their endeavours and care to breed it up for the service and relief of human life, if it be capable of it. And this is the main thing aimed at and solicited in this discourse. It was not written to offend or injure any, but to give every one his due, as near as can be discerned by the publisher.

By this point Denis' rage had reached a peak. He stared into the distance while his friend quietly let himself out of the room, and informed the house servants that it would probably be best if they didn't let visitors in that afternoon. Denis had had a bit of a shock, was all he said to their questions.

To deny the French claim that it was they who had thought of transfusion first opened a deep sore, and the final paragraphs had simply rubbed salt into the wound. Oldenburg had stated that, because the English had thought of infusion, they had in effect laid claim to any further work that related to placing material in the blood. He had then defended this by referring to the ideas being written down by himself in note books housed only at the Royal Society. What else were they going to claim as their ideas by citing a brief entry in these note books as evidence?

Still, of one thing Denis was sure – though the fact brought him surprisingly little comfort. He alone had transfused blood from an animal to a human – if the English had done so, their worthy servant Oldenburg would surely have mentioned it, and claimed that the English had precedence there as well.

Tales of towers

But there was another question in the back of Denis' mind. Why had Oldenburg gone to all the trouble and expense of tearing up an edition of his journal and producing a new one? If he had wanted to trounce the French, why hadn't he done it initially? To Denis, the answer was simple. The publication had obviously caused a hue and cry among the scientists in England who wanted to stamp their own authority on this area of research. They must have forced Oldenburg to retract and reprint his journal.

This seems to be the most likely explanation, but it in fact turns out to be quite wrong. As is so often the case, truth is stranger than fiction.

The morning of 20 June 1667 had begun just like any other. Oldenburg had spent the previous couple of days working at the Royal Society's offices, writing a couple of letters to people in the East Indies, and this morning was preparing to go to work as usual. Then there was a knock at the door. Instead of presenting a calling card, the official who

Plate 13   Henry Oldenburg. © The Royal Society.

stepped though swiftly as the door was opened handed over an arrest warrant:

> *Warrant to seize the person of Henry Oldenbourg for dangerous designs & practices, & to convey him to ye tower.*
>
> By &c Arlington[23]

With little ceremony, Oldenburg was bundled into a carriage, and found himself whisked across London escorted by half-a-dozen soldiers. Arriving at the notorious Tower of London, the nameless official drew a second warrant from his pocket and handed it to the gatekeepers:

> *Warr^t to ye L^t of ye Tower to take him into his Custody & keep him close prisoner. June 20th 1667*
>
> By &c Arlington[24]

The experience was terrifying. While the Tower was currently playing less of a role as a state prison than it had done a century before, it was no holiday camp, and there had been plenty of instances of people who went in on their feet, and came out in a box. The loss of the Tower, and London as a whole, by Charles I, had been a crucial factor in his defeat, and as his son was not about to repeat the error, he had turned it into a heavily fortified garrison. It had a frightening array of guns set in place along the walls and supplied by a vast arsenal.

Along with fear came confusion. Why me? What have I done? What is the charge against me? Oldenburg asked frequently as they travelled along, though he soon realised no one was about to respond. These were men carrying out instructions, they were not the decision-makers and probably had no idea who he was, nor why he was being detained. He became even more anxious, however, when no one in the Tower knew either, and he was banned from having access to pen or paper. He had no way of communicating with friends outside. The prospect looked bleak.

While the scientists were going about their lives inventing and investigating, England in 1667 was at war, and at this point all was not going well. The war with Holland had in effect begun in the summer of 1664, although it had not been declared officially until spring 1665. The root of the problem was international trade, with Holland and England literally fighting for dominance and for the right to bring goods from foreign lands into Europe. The English parliament had, in 1660, passed a Navigation Act requiring any English merchant to register his foreign-built vessels in London, and had thrown up trade barriers in naming goods that could be imported from the continent only in English ships. Another act passed in 1663 had gone a step further. The Staple Act forced English colonists to import goods only from England, and even then, the goods had to be transported in English ships. To cap it all, in March 1664, Charles gave New Amsterdam, the city that later became New York, to his brother, James Duke of York. Holland was not impressed. War was inevitable.

This was England's second war with Holland. The first had gone in England's favour, and few expected anything different this time around. Pepys recorded the first great naval battle off Lowestoft on 3 June 1665 with great relish:

> This day they engaged – the Dutch neglecting greatly the opportunity of the wind they had of us – by which they lost the benefit of their fireships. The Earl of Falmouth, Muskery, and Mr Rd. Boyle killed on board the Dukes ship, the Royall Charles, with one shot. Their blood and brains flying in the Duke's face – and the head of Mr Boyle striking down the Duke, as some say.

All the same, Pepys says that at the end of the day the English had killed or captured between 8,000 and 10,000 men, with a loss of only 700 – 'A greater victory, never known in the world'. Then the rot set in, and in a disastrous battle from 1 to 4 June 1666, 20 English ships were lost along with 8,000 men. With the plague and the fire destroying much of London's trade, finances were short, and by January 1667 Charles was ready to start peace talks with the Dutch. Lulled into a false sense of security, the Navy did little to defend its fleet while it tied up in Chatham harbour, and left it easy prey to a lightning attack. On 11 June the Dutch sailed in, set fire to houses and barns on Canvey Island, and attacked Sheerness and the Isle of Sheppey – Sheerness was taken. The following day the Dutch forced their way through the Medway's defences and sailed up the river. They burnt some of the finest vessels in the English fleet and captured the Navy's largest ship, the *Royal Charles*. Though the Dutch got no further, they had inflicted considerable damage and great humiliation.

Fear and panic spread throughout the land in the aftermath of the attack. Rumours spread that Chatham, Queenborough, Harwich, Gravesend, Colchester and Dover had been burnt. Some suggested that the King himself had disappeared, and there were loud whispers of treason plots. Anxieties spread throughout the land when an enemy fleet of 50 to 60 ships was sighted off Lands End, the western tip of Cornwall. The authorities looked for spies and scapegoats. It would appear that Oldenburg's name appeared on one of the lists of suspects.

But as often as Oldenburg asked someone to tell him with what he was charged, he was met with silence. Either no one would tell him, or no one knew. It's incredibly difficult to demonstrate your innocence if you don't know what you are accused of. In times of war, however, it is very tempting for authorities to seek powers that allow them to arrest a person without making a formal charge, and take prisoners indefinitely. The warrant against Oldenburg had been issued under an earlier form of what is now named 'Regulation 18b' of the Emergency Powers (Defence) Act 1939, an act that in more recent times was used to detain Sir Oswald Mosley and eight of his close associates.

Oldenburg was an easy target. He had been born in Bremen, Germany, in about 1618, and like many academics had begun by studying theology. Through the 1640s and 1650s he had been the official envoy from Bremen to Cromwell, and had also worked extensively in Germany and Holland. It was when visiting Cromwell that he had got to know the Boyle family, probably via an introduction from the poet John Milton. In parti-cular he became acquainted with Lady Ranelagh and her brother Robert Boyle. This friendship turned into patronage, when in 1657 Oldenburg was asked to act as tutor to Richard Jones, Lady Ranelagh's son, and spent the next four years wandering the continent, introducing the young Richard to the finer points of European life.

While Oldenburg had started life as something of a wanderer, with few roots to keep him in one place, he settled in England at the Restora-tion of the monarchy, and his 1663 marriage to Dorothy West grounded the link. This link had grown a little stronger when the couple found themselves in partial charge of an 11-year-old orphan, Dora Katherina, an heiress with land in Kent. Sadly Dorothy died two years later.

Throughout his European travels, Oldenburg had acquired a valu-able list of contacts and associates, and had become increasingly fascinated with the emerging world of science. His knowledge of the international science scene, along with his association with Boyle, made him an obvious choice as first secretary to the Royal Society when it was formally established.

Part of the Society's charter was a statement expressly encouraging foreign correspondence, and Oldenburg made full use of this privilege. The Society paid him nothing, and the Great Fire had ruined the London book trade, so his journal was not generating the income he had hoped for. To fill his time – and his purse – Oldenburg had also started to use his language skills in working for Joseph Williamson, a fellow of the Royal Society and Assistant to the Secretary of State, Lord Arlington – the same Arlington whose signature was on the warrant for Oldenburg's arrest.

Reading between the lines of history, Arlington had become suspicious that this foreigner, who had a history of wheeling and dealing, had buried his way into the heart of English government and, if he hadn't done any harm so far, was not to be trusted. These suspicions were most probably stimulated by Oldenburg's frequent correspondence with France and Holland, combined with his use of the post box in Arlington's office. Having incoming mail delivered there, the office met the postal charge and saved Oldenburg a lot of money. To make this less obvious, he got his correspondents to address their envelopes to Mr Grubenol – a crude anagram of his name. Most of these letters were handed over to Oldenburg unopened, and in return for this liberty, Oldenburg passed any politically sensitive intelligence in the letters back to Williamson.

For example, on 24 March 166⅚ he had received a letter from Parisian correspondent Henri Justel:

> I have received all of your letters. From that last that you were good enough to write me I have learnt of the warlike spirit in England. Here, it seems the same sentiments prevail. The English have taken a few of our ships. I have been told that the King said to the Queen Mother of England that it would end by his being compelled to declare war on England.

And later that year Justel wrote again:

> I have never doubted that the Parliament would provide the means for continuing the war; but also I am sure England will suffer much by it. Some troublesome occurrence that one can't foresee may still happen, and the enemies are very uncertain; however brave one is, when one meets a strong and stubborn resistance one is bound to suffer from it. We have lost a fine vessel I admit; but by mischance, and it could not resist seven of yours which attacked it; that was no decisive stroke – we must wait for the end of the War.[25]

A letter written by Oldenburg while on a trip to Paris shows how active he was in sending news to the highest offices in the land. It was addressed to Williamson, and written in French, presumably to keep down the number of people in England who would be able to read it:

> The Tartars have entered Poland, and have put everything to fire and sword. They have reached as far as Lemberg, The Diet is to reassemble in three months. 'Michael Abassi plans to make war on young Ragotzki. The Turks are to give him troops. This war will serve as a diversion and by preventing the Emperor's sending troops to Flanders will facilitate the conquest of that province.
>
> 'here the only talk is of peace and everyone believes it will be made.
>
> 'your affairs in America are in bad shape, and whatever you may say, peace will assist you. No one believes you can make your reckoning with Isola'.[26]

This postal system was a cosy arrangement, but it is easy to see how it could have raised grounds for suspicion that Oldenburg might be passing news in the other direction as well. In the fevered times of this war, however, Arlington started to have his post seized and read. It appears that Oldenburg had said something 'sensitive' in one of his letters.

Those who knew Oldenburg had their own opinions as to whether he was treated unjustly. Hooke, the scientific collaborator of Boyle, and fellow of the Royal Society, was known for his sharp tongue and ability to make and break friendships. For him the situation was clear: Oldenburg dealt in the murky world of intelligence-gathering and his imprisonment was his comeuppance.

Even if Oldenburg had overstepped the mark, Pepys was troubled at the idea that a man who spent his time living at the centre of government and recording details of history and science, should be sent to the Tower. The situation would have been even more real to him as he lived only a few hundred yards away from the celebrated landmark. On 25 June he commented:

> I was told, yesterday, that Mr Oldenburg, our Secretary at Gresham College, is put in the Tower, for writing news to a virtuoso in France, with whom he constantly corresponds in philosophical matters; which makes it very unsafe at this time to write, or almost do any thing.

One day early in July, Oldenburg had his first glimmer of hope – a letter from his friend and colleague, Williamson. Maybe he would now discover why their joint boss Arlington had signed the warrant. Things were looking up:

> S^r
>
> *In this misfortune that hath befallen y^u I know little I am yet able to serve y^u in besides seconding y^r own reason & philosophy, wch is to persuade patience. A little time I hope may recover all I shall be most glad of it for y^r sake and on any occasion contribute what I may to serve y^u.*
>
> *If y^u desire I should send y^u w^t comes for ye from any part I shall, those from France I presume to open & keep by me. The Code Louis I see is coming for y^u 2. packets being already arrived. I wish y^u content & short confinement & am wth much truth,*
>
> > *Sir*
> > Υ^r *most humble Servt*
> > *Joseph Williamson*[27]

Oldenburg would have been forgiven for reading this time and again, trying to work out what exactly Williamson was trying to say. But the implications were there. Williamson felt sorry for him, but had no power to do anything. There is no hint that he even knew why Oldenburg had been incarcerated, and the suggestion that he could forward his international correspondence seems bizarre.

Officially, Oldenburg was to be held a 'close prisoner', a term that would have told the jailer that he should have few privileges, and certainly no access to pen and paper. If he was a conspirator, the last thing the authorities wanted was for him to be able to carry on his operation from within their prison. Still, Oldenburg seems to have used his diplomatic skills of negotiation and managed to write a short note in pencil on the back of Williamson's letter.

> S^r
>
> *I thank you for y^r friendly letter: I pray, continue y^r kindness, as far as you may, and, when you see it seasonable, present my very humble service to My Ld Arlington, telling him, that I hope his Lord^{p} will experience in time, when this present misunderstanding shall be rectified, of my integrity and of my zeal to serve his Maj^{ty}, the English nation, and himself to the utmost of my power. Mean while, I beseech you, be pleased, when you find it seasonable, to cast in a word of the narrowness of my fortune for to lie long in so charge*

able a place, as the Tower is. What you shall think fit to send to me of the
papers that are come to yʳ hand for me, will be a welcome diversion too.

Sir

Υʳ obliged and humble

Servant

H. Oldenburg

Ps

Procure me, I pray, if it may be, the liberty of seeing now and then a friend. I
have not the use of pen and ink, but only this I had by the particular favour
of the Lieutenant.[28]

Oldenburg's comment about lying long in so chargeable a place was a
mild way of stating what everyone at the time knew. The only way one
could have a remotely pleasant existence in prison was to pay for it.
Food and washing had to be paid for, and even then the wheels needed
to be oiled with cash hand-outs to the turnkeys.

Oldenburg's letter seems to have achieved little. What is worse, he
began to hear that former friends had visited the prison, but on seeing
the warrant book statement that he was being held 'for dangerous
designs & practices', had left rapidly. Even if he was innocent, he was
clearly too hot to handle. Moreover, he had no power of authority, so
there was no reason for anyone to go out of their way to help him. He
would be in no position to return the favour. Worse still, many of the
acquaintances seem to have gone away and spread the rumour that
Oldenburg was a spy. The trickle of visitors soon dried up.

However, Oldenburg did in fact receive one further visitor, though
the man was not keen to reveal his identity. Oldenburg was able to dic-
tate a letter, which the anonymous visitor wrote down after he had left,
before posting it to Seth Ward, a fellow of the Royal Society and now
Bishop of Salisbury. The letter explained that he was not allowed access
to pen and ink, but that he was hoping this long-standing friend might
be able to establish his innocence. Clearly by now he had some idea of
the accusation against him, but because of the nature of his arrest he
had been afforded no opportunity to present his defence:

My case is this. I am committed for dangerous designs and practices; and I
understand, that that is inferred from some letters and discourses of mine, said
to contain expressions of yt nature. This is all, I can learn to be yᵘ ground for

my accusation. To wch I shall now answer wth all ye candor and truth, y^t can be desired, as in ye presence of ye all seeing God, what follows.[29]

He went on to explain that if it looked as if he was critical of the English in the war, this was only because he wanted to see them do better. This should in no way have been seen as a slur against the King or his nation. Moreover, he emphasised that his letter-writing had been a distinct advantage to the King in gaining useful intelligence from the various countries with which he corresponded. He finished his defence with a cry that he was more than ready to suffer the full force of punishment if any offence could be found against him. He pleaded with the reader to do all that he could to seek the favour of Arlington and the King so that he wouldn't be left in prison to go to rot and ruin.

All the indications are that this letter never left the confines of the Tower. It was probably discovered in the hands of the visitor and confiscated, and it now rests in the State Papers Office. (It is reasonable to assume that if Oldenburg had had the chance he would have also written to Boyle, and that if Boyle had received the letter he would have burnt it to remove any evidence of the communication.)

On 20 July, Oldenburg managed to get another letter through the Tower's supposedly impregnable walls. This time his plea was direct – he wrote to Lord Arlington asking him to petition the King:

> *Right Honble*
> *Since by ye obliging Application of his Maj^ies Lieutenant of ye Tower to y^r Lord^tp, I have obtain'd ye use of Pen, Ink and Paper, so far as to present my Humble Petition to his Maj^ty, and wth all to recommend ye same to y^r Lord^tps favor for good success, I cannot but at ye beginning render humble thanks to y^r Lord^tp for allowing me this freedom, and at ye same time make it my request, that this Petition may be so happy, as to come to his Maj^ies view by ye favor of y^r Lord^tps hands, and ye advantage of y^r charity, to ye end, that I may be so represented to his Maj^ty, as I hope some of those, that know me well, may possibly have represented me to y^r Lord^tp.*[30]

Even locking him up for a month had done nothing to reduce Oldenburg's power in writing florid and grovelling opening sentences. There is, however, no indication that anyone took the risk of standing in his defence and representing his cause. Not even Boyle seems to have been prepared to step in and use his influence.

Little did Oldenburg know, but while he was writing letters in an attempt to regain his freedom, someone, probably Wilkins, was publishing the next edition of his journal, the first version of the controversial *Philosophical Transactions* Number 27. It could be that the motivation behind this was to keep Oldenburg's journal alive and therefore preserve it – and its income – so that when its creator was released he would have a job to go back to. Alternatively, whoever stepped in may have been looking to take over the publication and either claim ownership of it or make it more firmly part of the Royal Society. It's difficult to know, but without Oldenburg's knowledge or consent, the edition was published and distributed to the list of fee-paying subscribers.

On 5 August, Oldenburg wrote again to Arlington. His note had changed and the letter was short and to the point. If he wasn't released soon, he would be bankrupt and would be sent straight to a debtors' prison. Maybe this letter had some effect, or more likely the next move came as a result of the end of the war between England and Holland, a peace treaty being signed in Breda on 31 July. Whatever the reason, on 26 August the Lieutenant at the Tower received a simple message:

Oldenburg. Discharge for Oldenburg Prison^r in ye Tower. Aug 26th 67.[31]

Being confined to a cell must have been frustrating beyond belief. But being released brought further dangers. Whom could he trust? Was it safe to go back to his London home, or would he be lynched by a mob who failed to recognise an innocent man when they saw one? Plenty of foreigners had been summarily dispatched in the streets in the aftermath of the fire, and Londoners were known for rapidly taking their suspicions to a gruesome conclusion. Oldenburg knew little of the current mood in London now that the war was over.

He might have been quaking at the knees as he went, but Oldenburg was no coward. He wanted to appear before the person whose signature had put him away, if only to prove that he had nothing to fear. He set off by foot and walked the mile or so from the Tower to Arlington's home in the middle of the city, and as he later told Boyle, he 'waited on my Lord Arlington, kissing the rod'. He had expressed his sincere loyalty to King and country and made peace with his accuser.

He might have kissed and made up, but few on the streets would have known this. The safest move now was to keep a low profile and get out of London – at least for a few days. It would take little time for word to get out that he was free, and hopefully the same chattering rumours would spread the message that he was innocent. His lodgings in Pall Mall would offer little security, so with as much haste as could be expected from a man with little or no money, he headed for the country, to Crayford in Kent, probably to the home of Dora, his ward.

The country air was wonderful, but he had no means of creating money this far away from London. Having regained his strength and got a few good meals inside him, Oldenburg resolved to return to London to see if it was possible to pick up where he had left off. It took no time at all before he realised that this was not going to be easy. On 3 September 1667 he wrote to Boyle, who at the time was living in Oxford, wishing him well, and apologising for his absence. He wrote to many other former friends and was frustrated that with the exception of Boyle and Beale, there were no replies – this was certainly no welcome home party.

> London Sept 12, 1667
>
> Sir,
>
> Though it be above a fortnight since I gave notice to some of my corresponding friends that I was returned to my former station, yet have I received as yet no answer from any but yourself and Dr Beale, (for which I am the more obliged to you) which makes me conjecture that foreigners especially in the neighbouring parts, may be grown shy to resume that commerce they were wont to entertain with me, out of some tenderness and concern for my safety, which they may judge may be endangered as well by their freeness of writing to me, as by mine of writing to them. But I intend to take them off such apprehensions, if I find really they are possessed with them, by confining our communications to matters of a philosophical nature; or, if there be a mixture of civil things, to such of them as cannot be misinterpreted, or suspected of any ill design.[32]

Oldenburg had been away for a couple of months, and ought to have expected to find a few surprises in the pile of mail awaiting him. He must have been intrigued to open a copy of what purported to be his journal. Most likely, he thumbed through it and put it to one side. He would find out who had kept the press running once he had opened the rest of his mail.

An Account
Of what hath lately passed at Paris in the
matter of Transfusion etc:

1. Monsieur Denis, the Learned Author of ye Letter, which was lately written to Monsieur de Montmor, concerning ye Usefulnes of the Transfusion of Blood, acquainteth the Publisher, not only of this, that they have very lately transmitted the Blood of 4 Weathers into a Horse of 26 years old, with so good successe, that the horse thereupon was found to have more strength and vigour, and a greater ... than before: Besides, he mentions, that they wish, shortly to try this Experiment upon Phrenetick persons, and such other subjects, as Competent Judges shall think proper, to try this operation upon: Taking notice, that, notwithstanding the good effects, that have followed upon these Experiments, yet many prejudiced doe oppose it, and doe what they can to hinder the making Tryals thereof: but from what motive, he saith, may easily be Judged.

2. The same Author was pleased to transmit to the Publisher another printed Letter, written to the Abbot Bourdelot by one Monsieur Gadroys (in answer to a certain Paper of one Mr Lamy) vindicating this Experiment from objections, and confirming it at the same time with new Tryals. The chief Contents whereof are, as followeth.

First, That Mr Lamy undertakes to refute the Experiments of Mr Denis by simple ratiocinations; Whereas 'tis returning, that the Quodlibetical Learning of ye Scholes is capable to furnish Arguments both for and against all sorts of Opinions; and that there is nothing, but Experience alone, that was able to give ye last decisive, ... Sophistries principally in matters of Natural Philosophy and Physick: That an hundred years ago, there were no Arguments wanting to prove, that Antimony or the Emetique Vinum Emeticum was Poison, the use of it being then forbidden by a Decree of ye Faculty of

Plate 14 Oldenburg's translation of a letter from Denis. © The Royal Society.

127

Among the letters were a number complaining about the said edition of his journal, suggesting that he had given the oxygen of publicity to scurrilous claims of precedence to a French nobody. He might have walked away from accusations of treason against the Crown, but he was now facing cries of treachery from within the scientific community. Oldenburg leafed through the copy of the journal once again, this time with more care. There it was – the translated version of the French article. He remembered translating it only a day or so before his arrest, and had placed the translation in a pile of papers ready for the next journal. Clearly the claims of precedence in the article were excessive, and he had always planned to take his editor's liberty to insert appropriately balancing information. Instead, it had been published in full, without editorial comments.

By 23 September, Oldenburg had rewritten and reprinted the new edition, and 500 new versions were being distributed around Europe. Given the fact that only a dozen of the original version still exist, it appears that most people simply binned the first and filed the second. For most, the difference would have been immaterial, if they noted it at all. For the few who were passionately involved in transfusion, and for whom prestige in the area was imperative for their careers, the episode had been a calamity.

It was time for some more fire-fighting. On 24 September, he wrote again to Boyle, pointing out that the new issue of Number 27 was currently at the publishers, and that it contained his denial of responsibility for the previous version. He also mentioned that Lower had called in to see him, and that he had taken the opportunity to explain what had occurred. Oldenburg closed the letter with a complaint that his publisher, Mr John Martin, had altered the rates of payment, and that the journal was now likely to earn him only fl30 this year. This was a stark lesson in the harsh world of business – it is difficult to make money from selling scientific knowledge at the best of times.

A turbulent autumn

All in all, the autumn had been a setback for Denis, and a disaster for Oldenburg. The next few months, however, were about to be eventful for both men. Within the year, Oldenburg had married his ward of court, the now 14-year-old Dora. As a result he became the proud possessor of the Kent estates, improving his position considerably, though this did not give him financial independence. For Denis, the following months continued to be difficult, the problems beginning in early autumn with his next patient, Baron Bond. In fact, news of the case had travelled so fast that Oldenburg had been able to comment on it in his October article that questioned Denis' claims.

Baron Bond was the son of the first minister of state to the King of Sweden. He would have spent time in close contact with the former Queen Christina, a colourful woman who in 1655 announced her conversion from the Protestant faith to Catholicism, and abdicated her throne. Christina's parents had wanted a boy; the astrologers had predicted that the baby would be a boy, and the physicians initially announced that Christina was indeed male. When her mother realised that she was, in fact, a girl with some form of pelvic abnormality, she rejected her. Her father had decided to raise her as a prince – hardly a good start in life. Things improved a little when her father was killed in battle in 1632, and the five-year-old Christina was crowned Queen of Sweden in his place.

Immediately, Christina was launched into a punishing training schedule of 12 hours of sports and study, six days a week. By the age of 15 she was fluent in five languages and had already started to run the country, taking only about three to four hours' sleep a night. Relaxation came in the form of riding and bear-hunting. Her enthusiasm for early rising seems to have been the death of Descartes. Christina had employed Descartes to teach her philosophy, but he became exhausted by the constant demands of being ready to lead tutorials at 5 o'clock each morning, preferring the more leisurely Parisian approach of rising around 11. In 1650, he contracted pneumonia, died and was buried in Stockholm.

It is little surprise, then, that a year after Descartes' death, Christina too was exhausted. Her physicians had recommended numerous potions, but Christina had instead called in a friend of Descartes, Paris physician Pierre Bourdelot. On his arrival, Bourdelot dismissed all the physicians and threw out their potions. In place, he recommended frivolity and play – rest and recreation. This must have been a shocking concept for this exceptionally driven woman, but she soon recovered and thrived in this new-found freedom. Using this new sense of independence, she abdicated and moved to Rome.

Bourdelot returned to Paris laden with gifts, though he and Christina remained in contact by letter. It was via their correspondence that Christina heard of the idea of transfusing blood. Clearly she was impressed by the concept, but in replying to Bourdelot, she said:

> I think the invention of injecting blood is all very fine, but I should not like to try it myself, for fear that I might turn into a sheep. If I were to experience a metamorphosis, I should prefer to become a female lion, so that no one could devour me; I am feeling quite well ... but if I should need this cure, I have decided to be injected with the blood of a German, for the German animal is less like a human being than is any other animal I know.[33]

Life in Rome failed to live up to Christina's expectations, and she soon made enemies within the upper echelons of society. After a failed attempt at conquering Naples and wresting it from the Spanish, she decided to return to her native Sweden in 1666. In the autumn of 1667, she heard that her former advisor, Baron Bond, was seriously ill. As luck would have it, the Baron was in Paris, home of the latest medical technology – transfusion. It is most likely that Christina contacted Bourdelot, and that as a result Denis and Emmerey were called in.

Baron Bond was so sick that the two physicians were at first unwilling to have anything to do with him. Treating a person just before he died was a very good way of becoming accused of malpractice. For three weeks he had been afflicted with what Denis described as a diseased liver and spleen, bilious diarrhoea and a violent fever. By the time Denis and Emmerey had arrived, he had been visited by four other physicians, each of whom had bled the Baron in the hope of removing the diseased blood. The patient was now so weak that he could not stir, he couldn't speak, and he was virtually unconscious – the main sign of life was that he vomited violently as soon as any food or water was given.

Bond's relations had called in the pioneers as a last resort, but Denis was less than enthusiastic. Transfusion, he explained, was not designed to restore the solid parts of a person's body, and it was clear from the symptoms that the patient had gangrene in his intestines. He was convinced that if the relatives had called them earlier, then all would have been different. If they had transfused blood instead of just letting it out, then he felt sure the technique would have been of great benefit.

Still, the relatives argued that to give up now would be to throw away the man's last hope, and in the end Denis relented. Even so, he was keen to cover his back, and insisted that the physicians who had previously treated the man should first agree that their treatments had not worked, and that it was reasonable to try this experimental therapy.

The next morning, with the formalities over, Denis and Emmerey returned with a calf. The patient was lethargic and had convulsions. His pulse was slow and feeble. As soon as a small quantity of blood was transfused into Bond's veins, his pulse quickened and strengthened, his convulsions ceased and he began to talk in many different languages. A few minutes later he dropped off to sleep. Denis and the relatives waited to see what would happen next.

After three-quarters of an hour, Bond awoke and managed to eat a few bowls of broth through the course of the day. Better still, he kept it all down. His diarrhoea ceased for the first time in weeks. Sadly, 24 hours later, his strength ebbed away, his pulse weakened and he became physically floppy. Urged on by Baron's friends, Emmerey linked the patient to the calf and they quickly gave him another shot of blood. Once again the patient showed some mild recovery, but died at 5 o'clock that afternoon.

At a gruesome post-mortem, a dozen physicians gathered around to witness the examination and give their comments. They discovered that the poor man's guts were rotten. His pancreas was hard, and the pancreatic duct, which carries digestive juices into the gut, was blocked. His spleen was very thick and his liver enlarged, in some places showing distinct signs of disease. Denis was particularly intrigued by the state of the man's heart. It was 'very dry, and, as 'twere burnt'. He was also intrigued that the vein into which they had transfused the blood was no more full than the rest of the veins. Indeed, all the vessels seemed particularly empty.

In a sentiment much loved by surgeons, Denis concluded that the transfusion had been a success, but that the patient had been so ill that the transfusion was not capable of restoring health. Denis was undaunted – the technique was fine, and what he needed now was a patient who was physically well, but had some other disease. This would be the perfect case to demonstrate the benefits of his new treatment.

CHAPTER EIGHT

Playing catch-up

hile life was looking grim for Denis, Lower was having a better time. He appears to have been satisfied with what he considered slow but steady progress on transfusions in animals, and more keen to understand the intricacies of blood and blood transfusion than to rush into turning it into a medical therapy. But once again, London was goaded into action by reports of developments on the continent. This time it was Denis' letter. Oldenburg might have written an editorial complaining that Denis had ignored the English superiority in this matter, but couldn't deny the fact that Denis had stolen a march by taking it from the laboratory into the medical work place. According to Denis, the transfusions had been a success, and there was every indication that he would go on and do this again. England was clearly in danger of falling behind in the medical success race.

Action was needed – and quickly. The manhunt began. The fellows of the Royal Society needed someone poor enough to find a small payment sufficient inducement to take part in their experiment, but not so poor that he had no education. Someone with no learning would be less likely to give them an accurate account of what it felt like receiving the blood, and would be unlikely to keep an accurate record of any of the effects. They needed someone who was not physically sick, as this infirmity might in itself jeopardise the experiment, but then again, any beneficial effects would not be seen in a completely healthy person.

In the end they found a slightly mad, 22-year-old Bachelor of Theology from Cambridge, whose brain was considered to be 'a little too warm'. His name was Arthur Coga, and the fee was set at 20 shillings. Again the chattering classes were chattering and Pepys' pen was recording:

> November 21, 1667
> I out and took coach to Arundell House, where the meeting of
> Gresham College [The Royal Society] was broke up; but there
> meeting [Mr] Creed, I went with him to the tavern in St Clements
> churchyard ...
>
> Among the rest they discourse of a man that is a little frantic,
> that has been a kind of minister, Dr Wilkins saying that he hath
> read for him in his church, that is poor and a debauched man, that
> the College have hired for 20s. to have some of the blood of a sheep
> let into his body; and it is to be done on Saturday next. They pur-
> pose to let in about twelve ounces; which they compute, is what
> will be let in in a minute's time by a watch. They differ in opinion
> they had of the effects of it; some think it may have a good effect
> upon him as a frantic man by cooling his blood; others, that it will
> not have any effect at all. But the man is a healthy man, and by
> this means will be able to give an account what alteration, if any
> he do find in himself, and so may be useful ...

Without pausing, Pepys then moved on to another set of circumstances
which had also been the subject of discussion whilst they sat in the
tavern. The juxtaposition reveals their train of thought. The questions
in their minds were less associated with any scientific measurements of
what blood was, but rather their interest lay in more spiritual and mys-
tical matters. The general expectation was that any fluid originating
from a person must be tainted by that person's spirit. If it entered a
second person, they expected to see an effect on the recipient's spirit:

> ... On this occasion Dr Whistler told a pretty story related by Muf-
> fett, a good author, of Dr. Cayus that built Key's College: that being
> very old and lived only at that time upon woman's milk, he, while
> he fed upon the milk of a angry fretful woman, was so himself;
> and then being advise to take of a good-natured, patient woman,
> he did become so, beyond the common temper of his age. Thus
> much nutriment, they observed, might do.

Thus on 23 November 1667, Lower and King met before selected
members of the Royal Society at Arundel House. Their aim was to catch
up with Denis and transfuse blood to a human. Oldenburg described the

experiment, publishing the details in the 6 December 1667 edition of the *Philosophical Transactions*:

Of the experiment of transfusion, practised upon a man in London

This was performed November 23 1667 upon one Mr Arthur Coga, at Arundel-House, in the presence of many considerable and intelligent persons by the management of those two learned physicians and dextrous anatomists Dr Richard Lower and Dr Edmund King, the latter of whom communicated a relation of it as follows.

The experiment of transfusion of blood into a human vein was made by us in this manner. Having prepared the carotid artery in a young sheep we inserted a silver pipe into the quills to let the blood run through it into a porringer. In the space of almost a minute, about 12 ounces of the sheep's blood ran through the pipe into the porringer; which was some what to direct us in the quantity of blood now to be transfused into the Man. Which done, when we came to prepare the vein in the man's arm, the vein seemed too small for that pipe, which we intended to insert into it; so that we employed another, about one third part less, at the end. Then we made an incision in the vein, after the method formerly published, Number 28; which method we observed without any other alteration, but in the shape of one of the pipes; which we found more convenient for our purpose. And having opened the vein in the man's arm, with as much ease as in the common way of venaesection, we let thence run out 6 or 7 ounces of blood. Then we planted our silver pipe into the said incision, and inserted the quills between the two pipes already advanced into the two subjects, to convey the arterial blood from the sheep into the vein of the man. But this blood was near a minute before it had passed through the pipes and quills into the arm; and then it ran freely into the man's vein for the space of 2 minutes at least; so that we should feel a pulse in the said vein just beyond the end of the silver pipe; though the patient said, he did not feel the blood but, (as we reported of the subject in the French experiment) which may very well be imputed to the length of the pipes, through which the blood passed, losing thereby so much of its heat, as to come in a temper very agreeable to venal blood. And as the quantity of blood received into the Man's vein, we judged there was about 9 or 10 ounces: for, allowing this Pipe is less than that, through which 12 ounces passed in one minute before, we may very well suppose, it might in 2 minutes convey as much blood into the vein, as the other did in the Porringer in one minute; granting with all, that the Blood did not run so vigorously the second minute, as did the first, not the third, as the second etc. But, that the Blood did run all the time of those two minutes we conclude from thence; first, because we felt a pulse during that time. Secondly, because when upon the Man's saying, he thought he had enough, we drew the Pipe out of his vein, the sheep's blood ran through it with a full stream; which it had not done, if there had been any stop before, in the space of those two minutes; the blood being so very apt to coagulate in the pipes upon the least stop, especially the pipes being so long as three quills.

The man after this operation, as well as in it, found himself very well, and hath given in his own narrative under his own hand, enlarging more upon the benefit, he thinks, he hath received by it, than we think fit to own as yet. He urged us to have the experiment repeated upon him within 3 or 4 days after this. But it was thought advisable to put it off somewhat longer. And the next time, we hope to be more exact, especially in weighing the emittent animal before and after the operation, to have a more just account of the quantity of blood it shall have lost.

From Oldenburg's point of view, this experiment appears to have been a success, if a little unexciting. The man survived, but was unaltered. Whether in fact Coga received very much blood is questionable, given their concern about the length of the pipe connecting him to the sheep and the initial signs that the blood was sluggish in passing through the tube before it was even inserted into Coga's arm. On top of this, there is Coga's lack of comment about any sensation of heat – a repeated observation in the French experiments, and a symptom that is likely to occur as foreign blood stimulates an intense allergic reaction within the recipient's blood as it enters the vessel.

Quite what effect the transfusions really had on Coga is difficult to determine. Pepys certainly seems to have been fairly positive, though he does mention that Coga was possibly a little mad and as such it would have been difficult to be sure of any outcome:

> I was pleased to see the person who had his blood taken out. He speaks well, and did thus give the Society a relation thereof in Latin, saying that he finds himself better since, and as a new man, but he is cracked a little in his head, though he speaks very reasonably, and very well, He had but 20s for suffering it, and is to have the same again tried upon him; the first sound man that ever had it tried upon in England, but one we hear of in France.

So, the virtuosi, being impressed by their first performance, agreed that the experiment should be repeated. Confident that their first attempt had shown that they would not be presiding over a disaster, they threw open the doors to a wider group of spectators. Less than a month later, on 14 December 1667, Lower and King performed a second transfusion before the entire Society, augmented, as Oldenburg reported to Boyle, by a 'strange crowd of Forrainers and domesticks'.

This time the transfusion was not reported in the *Philosophical Transactions*. But why not? Well, quite possibly because it was so unremarkable. In fact, Sir Philip Skippon wrote to the pioneering environmentalist and theologian John Ray at the time, saying 'the effects of the transfusion are not seen, the coffee-houses having endeavoured to debauch the fellow, and so consequently discredit the Royal Society and make the experiment ridiculous'.[34] Clearly, the chattering classes were disappointed that they had neither a cure nor a freak, and had consequently kicked out the mildly demented man.

Almost the final word on this attempted cure comes in a letter to the Royal Society from Agnus Coga, either the subject's mother or wife. She is less than upbeat about the whole affair. Reading between the lines, it seems that Arthur is now very poor, somewhat despised, and unable to get a job. This could be seen as a classic 'sob-letter' appealing for money, but given the poor state of the Society's coffers there is no reason to expect that any was sent:

> *To the Royal Society The Virtuosi, and all the Honourable members of it, the Humble Address of Agnus Coga*
> *Your creature (for he was his own man til your Experiment transform'd him into another species) amongst those many alterations he finds in his condition,*

which he thinks himself oblig'd to represent them, finds decay in his purse as well as his body, and to recruit his spirits is force'd to forfeit his nerves, for so is money as well in peace as warre. 'Tis very miserable, that the want of natural heat should rob him of his artificial too: But such is his case; to repair his own ruines (your, because made by you) he pawns his clothes, and dearly purchases your sheep's blood with the loss of his own wool in this sheep-wrack't vessel of his, like that of Argos, he addresses himself to you for the Golden Fleece. For he thinks it requisite to your Honours, as perfect metaplasts, to transform him without as well as within. If you oblige him in this, he hath more blood still at your service, provided it may be his own, that it may be the nobler sacrifice.

The meanest of your flock

Agnus Coga.[35]

As is often the case, the physician had the final word, and writing in his book *Tractatus De Corde*, Lower gives the impression that he is disappointed with Coga. From Lower's point of view, Coga had been generously remunerated for his services, particularly considering the fact that he had been paid to receive a pioneering therapeutic treatment. Lower clearly wanted to repeat the infusion on many occasions, hoping to gradually cure Coga of his mild insanity, but Coga, on the other hand, had 'consulted his instinct rather than the interests of health, and completely eluded our expectations'. With this, Coga quietly stepped off the stage of history, and nothing more is recorded of his life.

At this point, blood transfusion in England died a quiet death as well. In fact, the next serious effort did not occur until English physician James Blundell began experiments involving the transfusion of blood between dogs in 1817–18, before moving on to transfuse blood into 10 patients who had suffered severe haemorrhages. The gap between the seventeenth and nineteenth centuries was, however, due mainly to the furore about to erupt in Paris.

European claims

The way Denis wrote about his work implied that no one else had ever thought about transfusion, but it is difficult to believe that he really imagined this was strictly the case. He and Emmerey were indeed excited to be challenging ancient beliefs about the way the body functioned, but their medical education would have almost inevitably brought them in touch with a few books from which they would have learnt that others in Europe had put similar ideas down in writing. In addition, contrary to the claims in England, it seems surprising that the highly travelled Boyle, along with his companions Wren and Lower, had failed to grasp the significance of some of the texts dating back to the beginning of their century. This said, however, there were no official ways of distributing knowledge around Europe at the time, and many found themselves working in isolation. It is only with the benefit of hindsight that we can get a better picture of who really did what first.

To start with, there had been a rather bizarre attempt at transfusion in Rome. Pope Innocent VIII was ill – he had suffered a stroke, and although he had made a partial recovery, he never regained his full health. In fact, his health soon began to deteriorate, and at one point in 1490 his aides thought that he had died. However, he had struggled on, and over the next two years a Jewish physician (some reports name him as Abraham Myere of Balmes) had taken up his case and proposed a remedy. How about transferring all of the ancient blood in the old man into a youth, and in exchange move the youth's blood to the 58-year-old Pope? This manoeuvre should restore his health by literally giving him a shot of young blood.

Quite possibly this physician was basing his ideas on work published in 1489 by the Italian philosopher and head of the Platonic Academy in Florence, Marsilio Ficino. Ficino was one of the key figures in driving the Renaissance, and had also suggested that drinking the blood of healthy young men would be a good way of dispelling the weakness and diseases associated with old age.

Exactly what happened next is lost in the sands of time, but there is strong evidence that three 10-year-old boys were summoned, given a ducat each, and then deprived of a considerable quantity of their blood. None of the contemporary accounts indicate whether any attempt was made to transfer this into the Pope, either by incorporating it within a potion or by force into his veins, but the outcome was clear. The three boys died, as did the Pope, and the Jewish physician fled for his life. The incident did not go down well in the local vicinity, and triggered riots and disturbances as rumours of the boys' deaths began to circulate.

The incident may have had a less than successful outcome, however it did not abolish all such thinking.

Before we throw our hands up in horror, it is worth reminding ourselves of the contemporary understanding of blood. If venous blood was simply a nourishing fluid built by the liver, then it is rational to believe that it could be drained out of a young man or boy and that he would quickly build more. The boy would be fit and full of health, he would be given a good meal and possibly a short period of rest so that he didn't overexert himself while the food was digested, passed to the liver and from there to the heart, where it could be transformed into blood. Draining a person's arterial blood would be more cavalier, as this would severely deplete his vital spirits, and this could endanger his life. All of this was of course happening more than a century before anyone had produced evidence that venous and arterial blood were one and the same thing, and almost two centuries before the notion that blood distributed not only nutrients, but also oxygen, throughout the body. In fact, at this point in history, no one knew that oxygen even existed.

As if the papal event were not gruesome enough, history records worse. Hungary in 1560 saw the birth of a girl who, on 8 May 1575, married Count Ferencz Nadasdy and became known as Countess Elizabeth of Bathroy. Legend has it that one day a servant girl accidentally pulled her hair – Elizabeth's response was to slap her so hard that she drew blood. When the incident was over, the countess became convinced that the skin where the servant's blood had landed had softened – it was smoother and more supple. To her mind, the magical properties of this fluid were apparently very potent.

This conclusion sadly led to a grisly chain of events. Over the next few years, Elizabeth systematically enticed young peasant girls to Castle Csejthe on the pretence of employment and money. Three of the countess's accomplices – Dorottya Szentes and Darvula, and her nurse Iilona Joo – drained these girls' blood, using the gory fluid to create baths for their mistress. It appears that one potential victim managed to escape, and ran to the Hungarian King, Mathias II, who ordered an enquiry. On 30 December 1610, soldiers raided the castle, and in the trial that followed, Elizabeth confessed to having murdered some 650 girls for her 'beauty baths'.

In a manner characteristic of the period, the punishments were as revolting as the crimes. The assistants were tortured, beheaded and cremated. The countess herself was considered to be too eminent for such treatment, and was instead walled-up within her bedchamber, with only a small hole through which food could be passed. She died three years later.

The first serious suggestion of transfusion came from the celebrated German-born chemist Andreas Libavius, who in 1615 published a detailed description of how he thought it should be carried out. In his book *Appendix Necessaria Syntagmatis Arcanorum Chymicorum*, he wrote:

> *Adsit juvenis robustus, sanus, sanguine spirituso plenus. Adstet exhaustus viribus tenuis macilentis, vix animam trahens. Magister artis habeat tubulos argenteos inter se congruentes. Aperiat arteriam robusti, et tubulum inserat, muniatque; mox et aegroti arteriam findat et tubulum foemineum infigat. Jam duos tubulos sibi mutuo applicet, et ex sano sanguis arterialis, calens et spirituosus, saliet in aegrotum, unaque vitae fontem afferet, omnemque languorem pellet.*[36]

This roughly translates as:

> Take one strong, healthy, youth who is rich in spirited blood and a powerless, debilitated old man scarcely capable of breathing. Now, if the physician wishes to practise the rejuvenating art on the latter, he should make silver tubes which fit into each other, open the artery of the healthy person, introduce one of the tubes into it and fasten it to the artery. He could then open the artery of the ill person and fasten the other, female tube into it. These two tubes could then be fitted into each other. At this point he will see that the arterial blood of the healthy one, warm and full of spirit, will leap into the sick person and immediately will bring to him the fountain of life and will drive away the fatigue.

On careful examination of this statement, there are clear reminders that Libavius was writing this prior to there being any widespread knowledge of Harvey's ideas of the circulation. After all, he was writing more than a decade before Harvey published his idea of blood circulating around the body in *De Motu Cordis*. All the same, this was a time when Harvey had begun to discuss his ideas with many people, and the theory would have been circulating within European circles.

Libavius' idea was to connect two arteries together. But why arteries? He was working on the theory that there were two different types of blood – venous and arterial. Obviously he wasn't interested in giving the old man nutritional support, but rather wanted to transmit the youth's vital spirit to this geriatric patient. Ancient theory maintained that the spirit was present in arterial blood. (Presumably Libavius would have recommended linking the veins of two people if he had wanted to donate nutrients.) There is no evidence that Libavius ever tried the procedure, and there is no reason to suppose that it would have worked even if he had. The pressure in the arterial system of both patients would have balanced out each other, preventing blood from flowing through the tube. Libavius would not have been aware of this potential problem – he would have anticipated the impoverished body of the older person to draw blood across from the more abundantly supplied youth.

Despite Boyle's interest in chemistry, and the relatively advanced state of communications around Europe, no one in England owned up to being aware of Libavius' ideas until an Italian correspondent, Pauli Manfredi, wrote to Oldenburg bringing the book to his attention in 1668. However, it might also have been that they dismissed anything that was pre-Harvey as irrelevant on the basis that any ideas that did not draw on the idea of circulation were inevitably fundamentally flawed.

Working in Padua, Italy, Professor Johannes Colle wrote a book suggesting novel methods for prolonging life. Published a few years after Manfredi's work, Colle's *Methodus Facile Parandi Tuta et Nova Medicamenta* did mention the idea of transfusion, though it gave no indication that he had actually tried to perform this technique.

Both French and English scientists also claimed to be blissfully unaware of the claims also being made by the Italian physician Francesco Folli. Folli's assertion was that on 13 August 1654, and in the presence of Grand Duke Ferdinand II, he used a device made from silver tube, a section of artery and a pipe made from a piece of bone to transfuse blood between two animals.

In 1680, Folli published a small book in which he set out his claim as the originator of blood transfusion:

This I pointed out in my pamphlet on life culture which was published for no other reason but to make known to all that blood transfusion had been invented by me at the end of 1654 and demonstrated to his Serene Highness Ferdinand II, Grand Duke of Tuscany, of undying memory. The novelty of it had pleased him, or the fascinating ingenuity or the considerable experimental elaboration. [37]

Unlike Libavius, Folli had the benefit of having read Harvey's work, and he based his claim for fame on the premise that when he read *De Motu Cordis* in 1652, he had immediately thought of the potential power of transfusion. The idea had been further strengthened by his observation of a pair of conjoined twins who shared a liver and were linked at the abdomen. As is often the case, one of the twins was seriously deformed and unable to eat or drink, and was consequently dependent on the sibling for nourishment and fluids. To Folli's enquiring mind, this was an example 'natural' blood transfusion.

His enthusiasm led him to suggest that physicians should collect lists of 20 young men who could act as a chain of donors, giving a daily supply of blood to a recipient. His book illustrated equipment built from silver and gold tubes, and funnels made from less expensive metals, connected by arteries taken from a goat. The question is why, if the experiment had been so exciting and successful, did no one know about it? What seems more likely is that Folli discussed the possibility of such a procedure with his honoured guest, but never performed it, as there is no mention of the event in any court records. Folli himself provides an alternative explanation:

> To no one else did I impart my idea, believing that if such an invention were successful, Monarchs alone were worthy of it.

Even in this explanation of his desire for secrecy, there is more than a hint that he had not managed to get the process working fully, as he looked forward to a time that 'such an invention were successful'. At the end of the book, however, he comes clean.

> Finally, I know that I have said too much concerning the manner of carrying out the operation, not having made the experiment ... but I have done it solely so that every one, however simple and ignorant, could understand, be inspired, and even make the experiment with the least possible expense, and to this end only I have written in the vulgar tongue.

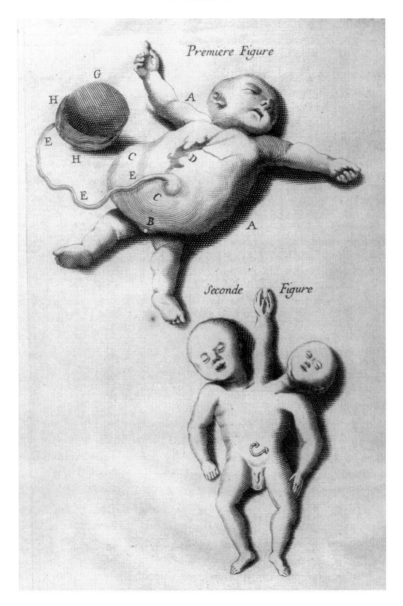

Plate 15   Folli's fascination with conjoined twins seems to have been shared by Denis, as can be seen from this illustration in the 1672 publication of reports from his Parisian conferences. Reproduced courtesy of the Clendening History of Medicine Library, University of Kansas Medical Center.

In addition to these books that attempted to claim some form of precedence, the late 1600s saw the arrival of a couple of medical text books that talked about blood transfusion as if it were a normal part of advanced medicine. Johann Sigismund Elsholtz, the German physician to the Baron of Brandenburg, recorded his experiments in his little book *Clysmatica Nova*. In it he used graphic anatomical images to supplement the description in the text, so that his readers would be able to go away and transfuse blood from a sheep's leg into a man's arm, or alternatively transfer blood between two human arms.

According to Elsholtz, transfusion held out the best hope for curing illnesses that resulted from unbalanced humours. If a person had a melancholic disease, then a doctor should give him or her blood from a person who is excessively sanguine. Similarly, receiving phlegmatic blood would presumably cure a choleric person. Elsholtz also maintained that blood transfusion should be able to solve marital disputes. The problem in marriages that were breaking down, he said, was that the two people had incompatible natures. Given that a person's nature was contained in his or her blood, the answer was obvious – mix their bloods. Elsholtz wanted to perform reciprocal transfusions between husbands and wives, but there is no evidence that he ever got the chance to try this revolutionary form of marriage counselling.

Elsholtz's book was published in 1667, the year of Denis' trial, was much more concerned with injecting medicinal liquors than transfusion, and can claim to contain the first illustration of an injection using a syringe. His comments on transfusion were based more on hope and prophetic insight than practical reality, although he did claim to have performed at least one transfusion.

Another German physician followed similar lines of thought, and in 1679 Georg Abraham Mercklino published his text book, *Tractatio Med. Curiosa de Ortu & Occasu Transfusionis Sanguis*, which contained illustrations showing just how simple it was to transfer blood from a dog to a person, or between two people.[38]

Scultetus published his textbook *Armamentarium Chirurgicum* 26 years later. Again, this demonstrated how to transfuse blood, this time fixing the donating animal to a rope that was stretched taut between the floor and the ceiling. The book makes little or no mention of the mess that would be involved in this procedure. Neither does Gottfried Purmann's surgical textbook of 1705, *Lorbeer Krantz, oder Wund Artznei*.

Plate 16   First illustration of a syringe injection. Reproduced courtesy of
the United States National Library of Medicine.

145

Published in Frankfurt, this included a drawing of a lamb sitting calmly on a table while generously donating its life-blood to an equally passive recipient – a person sitting at ease on a chair. Purmann claims to have got his ideas after seeing a transfusion of blood from a lamb to a young man in Frankfurt in 1668, but makes no mention of who performed this operation, nor its outcome.

Working with Balthasar Kaufmann, Purmann claims to have cured a Herr Welslein of leprosy by transfusing him with healthy lamb's blood, but failed to cure two 'scorbutic soldiers' and a fisherman suffering from 'devouring eruption'. In general, though, Purmann concluded that transfusion normally had very little effect on the recipient – presumably because the apparatus was so ineffective that he or she did not receive very much blood.

The lack of tangible benefit meant that by the early 1700s no one in Europe was continuing to perform blood transfusions. However, this didn't deter people describing how to do it in their texts. For example, in 1763 the German surgeon Lorenz Heister, who hadn't even been born when the seventeenth-century transfusions had been occurring, included a series of diagrams in his book entitled *Surgery*.

In Holland, in 1668, two physicians, Regnier de Graaf and van Horne, performed transfusion experiments using animals, but the assumption is that they were unimpressed with the technique and soon gave up.

Further afield, reports came in from Spain suggesting that Dr Fabritius, a physician of Dantzick, was looking into the possibility of injecting medicated liquors into people's veins. In a report translated into English by Oldenburg and published in his *Philosophical Transactions* on 9 December 1667, Fabritius described three trials on three different people. One was a 'lusty soldier' who was seriously infected with venereal disease, with 'many grievous protuberancings of the bones in his arms'. On injecting a laxative into the veins in his arms, the soldier complained of severe pain and the veins in his arm became extremely swollen. After four hours of careful massaging, the swelling in his arm had been removed, and the following day he produced five good stools – always seen as a sign of good health. Furthermore, the venereal disease and the lumps in the man's arm had disappeared without further treatment.

The remaining injections were given to two women – one married and aged 35, the other a 20-year-old serving maid. Both had suffered from severe epileptic fits the whole of their lives, and had given up hope of finding a cure. Fabritius injected a laxative dissolved in an 'anti-epileptical spirit'. The 35-year-old woman had gentle stools soon after the injection, and from then on her fits had become less extreme and less frequent. Eventually they disappeared altogether – she had been cured. For the maid, the treatment had been less successful. She had produced four stools after the operation, which allowed Fabritius to intimate that the process had had a measure of success. However, she had then gone outside, caught a cold and failed to keep to her diet. The sum total of these actions killed her.

In concluding his report, Fabritus said: ' 'Tis remarkable, that it was common to all three to vomit soon after the injection, and that extremely and frequently; the reason whereof we leave to intelligent Physicians to assign'. We now know that injecting many poisons into the bloodstream will make a person extremely sick.

Back in Italy, Signor Fracassati, the professor of anatomy at Pisa, carried out a series of experiments in 1667, injecting liquors into veins. In the first he injected aqua fortis (nitric acid) into a dog. It died, and a post-mortem revealed that many of the vessels in the lungs were broken. Fracassati found that the blood was coagulated, and concluded that something that dissolved clots might provide a cure for particular diseases.

Injecting spirit of vitriol (sulphuric acid) into another animal triggered epileptic fits and caused great suffering before the poor dog died. Looking inside, Fracassati discovered that the blood was 'fixed in the veins, and grumous, resembling soot'. Oil of sulphur (similar to sulphuric acid) had no distinct effect, though oil of tartar (an ingredient of baking powders) created pain before killing the dog.

A publication in *Giornale dei Letterati*, the Italian equivalent of Oldenburg's journal, showed that blood transfusions were being attempted at the far south of the continent. On 8 May 1667, Signor Cassini transfused blood from the carotid artery of one lamb into the right jugular vein of another. He had previously drained the receiving lamb of enough blood to make space for the arrival of the new blood. After finishing the transfusion, he had tied off the jugular vein, sewn up the wound, and let the animal down from the table. The lamb was healthy and grew well for eight months when it suddenly died on 5 January 1668. It had obviously survived the transfusion, and it seems unlikely that the death was directly due to the experiment.

As in England, news of transfusions raised interest, and Cassini was soon called to cure one Signor Griffoni's 13-year-old deaf spaniel. This medium-sized dog had been deaf for three years and was almost lame. When untied after the transfusion, the dog leapt from the table and ran out of the room to find its master. Two days later the dog was able to go for walks, and within a month was no longer deaf. There seems no reasonable explanation for this incredible recovery.

Altogether, there seems no doubt that Denis and Emmerey were the earliest people to transfuse blood into a human being, and that the English were the first to perform the operation between animals. In addition, German and Italian scientists were the first to think seriously of the idea. It's often said, no good experiment is ever done for the first time!

French opposition

There also appears to be a basic historical rule that many people are either reluctant to accept, or are actively opposed to, new technology. Very often the validity and accuracy of claims and counterclaims of 'pro-change' or 'maintain status quo' groups can only be determined by looking back on the event with the well-worn benefit of hindsight.

While a few book-writing medics were tinkering with the idea of blood transfusion, the majority of the medical profession held its collective hands in the air in horror of the idea. Unfortunately for Denis, one of the most vocal sets of opponents turned out to be the Faculty of Medicine in Paris. The attack came in the form of letters and printed pamphlets that started to appear over Christmas 1667. Supporters of Denis responded, but the Parisian physicians had mighty political clout – even though their arguments were largely ill-informed and misjudged, life for Denis was becoming difficult. At one point he had been grateful to Montmor and his friends for their patronage, now he needed them for protection.

CHAPTER NINE

Mauroy mystery

And so we arrive back in Montmor's library on the night of 19 December 1667. To the pleasure of some, and the extreme consternation of others, the two physicians, Denis and Emmerey, announced that as far as they could see, Mauroy, their prospective patient, was stable and in good basic health. He was a perfect candidate for their revolutionary therapy. Yes, he would be the next patient to receive some transfused blood. To avoid any possible deterioration, the operation should be carried out at the earliest possible time. This, they stated, was a trial of an idea. They weren't about to look too confident in claiming any sense of certainty that the procedure would cure the poor man's condition, though they certainly hoped to perform a wonder. Looking cautious and then claiming stunning success in a few days' time was definitely their preferred course of action.

Their hesitation was justified on practical grounds. They had never performed the operation on a man who was physically well, but had deranged behaviour. Their best guess was that they should use blood from a calf as 'its mildness and strengths might possibly allay the heat and ebullition of his blood'. A time was set for the operation – 6 o'clock that evening – and with much fuss and elaborate bowing the assembly dissipated.

Soon the room was empty save for the two scientists, their host and patron Montmor, and the unfortunate Mauroy. His continued presence was less than voluntary as he was still tied to his chair, and he had once again started to complain bitterly. As usual, Montmor was in charge. He summoned a troupe of servants and began to make arrangements to have the 'patient' transferred to another house, as the thought of listening to his shouting for the rest of the day was too much to be contemplated. Besides, his residence was in a fashionable part of Paris, and

Montmor had no intention of bringing bad repute to his name and his house by having the neighbours make accusations that a riot was about to break out.

It is most likely that as Montmor and Denis planned the rest of the day's details, discussing where they would obtain a suitable blood donor and agreeing the level of fees involved for all the participants, they saw this as their opportunity to stun the world and gain entry to the newly formed Académie Royale des Sciences. Becoming the first people in the world to cure mental illness would certainly do their applications for membership no harm whatsoever.

Recording the events that followed in a letter sent initially to Montmor, a copy of which then went to Oldenburg in London, Denis said that they had transported Mauroy to a 'private house', most probably Denis' residence on the Quai des Augustins. Montmor and Denis had also sent for a burly labourer to act as their 'porter'. They needed to contain Mauroy, but Denis also wanted to reassure him. Working with calm patients was always easier, and more likely to bring about good outcomes. Who better to employ as this guardian-cum-gaoler than someone who had benefited personally from trans-fusion? Their choice was no muscle-man picked at random, but the man into whom Denis had transfused lamb's blood eight months ear-lier; the man who Denis claimed had been so eager to receive a second dose.

Throughout the day, a stream of people began to arrive, and Denis was pleased that among them were both physicians and churchgoers. These witnesses were people who understood what he was doing, as well as members of the public who were held in good repute. As evening came, so too did the two scientists and a calf. In Oldenburg's translation of Denis' words: 'We used what art we could to dispose the fancy of our patient to suffer the transfusion'. It is a nice turn of phrase that can quite probably be translated as: 'we strapped and bound the patient firmly to a solid table in the middle of the room'. He might even have been gagged to lessen his wails of protest.

Denis and Emmerey were determined not to run out of blood halfway though the trial, so a calf was a good choice as it would be fairly large. It would also be relatively docile. Even so, it is a fair assumption that the calf in this particular episode would have been securely tied to a table, in such a way that it was incapable of moving.

Conversation dimmed to a dull murmur as, working under the light of several lanterns, Emmerey cut into the inner thigh of the calf's leg and revealed a bulging crimson artery. The spectators jostled gently for position, each wanting to get close, but at the same time anxious to keep out of the line of fire because, with the possible exception of Mauroy, everyone in the room would have been well aware that a minor slip of Emmerey's knife would send a pulsing fountain of blood across the room.

With the calf's vessel exposed and ready to deliver its elixir, it was time to turn to the patient. Standing over him, Emmerey cut into his right arm and revealed a vein just above the elbow joint. His work was hampered by the patient's struggles, and by the time the incision was complete, Mauroy had managed to curl himself into something resembling a foetal position, a primal act of self-protection. However, his arm was still tied firmly to a table leg and the incision and vein were neatly exposed.

Following instruction, the tables bearing the calf and Mauroy were brought close together ready for the transfusion, but Emmerey first wanted to make room in the patient's body for the influx of blood. This meant that some needed to be let out before the transfusion could begin. He snicked the exposed vein and watched while blood streamed into a bowl. He waited until Denis calculated that some 10 ounces of blood had escaped, and then inserted the end of a hollow quill into the vein. Quickly he cut the calf's artery, pushed a second quill into it and watched blood spurt out of the end. With surprising dexterity, he and Denis joined these two together with a series of quills, forming a complete pipe. Emmerey was excited and stretched out his fingers to relieve the tension – things were going well.

Denis began counting in order to establish the time that would be needed to let in 10 ounces of blood and replace the full volume lost in the enforced haemorrhage. It was soon clear, though, that all was not going quite so smoothly. In their enthusiasm to witness the event, the spectators surged forward to get a better view. For a few moments it was impossible for either Emmerey or Denis to get near to their patient. Etiquette also made it difficult for these experts who came from the middle ranks of society to order their superiors back, but necessity called and they elbowed their way back to the centre of proceedings.

Mauroy's struggles meant that he was no longer lying in a convenient position, and that the blood was no longer flowing through the tube. By the time the two technicians had got back to their charge, this lack of flow had allowed the blood to congeal in the tubes so that it was no longer transfusing from calf to human. The occasional plume of blood shot across the room while they frantically tried to change to new quills, and attempted to restore some of the flow.

By now the patient was complaining that his arm was feeling very hot, right up under his armpit. 'Perceiving that he was falling into a swoon we presently stopped the blood running in, and closed up the wound', comments Denis. The transfusion was over and Denis calculated that Mauroy had received something in the order of five or six ounces.

Denis was relieved. The transfusion had worked, but now the critical part was to keep a close watch on the patient to see what happened next. Some of the guests decided this was the time to move on and seek more lively entertainment elsewhere for the rest of the evening. Others took to their seats and waited, staring at the man as if wondering whether he was about to bellow like a calf or grow horns or hooves.

The next few hours were marked by a lack of events. Mauroy dozed in his chair for a couple of hours and then asked for some food – a good sign. Under Denis' watchful eye he was then helped to a room with a bed where they kept vigil. The night was much like any other for Mauroy. He hadn't slept for weeks, and this was no different: 'He passed the night singing, and whistling, and other extravagances usual to him', recorded Denis.

As Tuesday morning dawned, Mauroy was calmer, even subdued. While twentieth-century science would show that he was suffering from severe anaemia, Denis could only detect that the patient was much less violent. Clearly the transfusion had had some effect. The obvious thing was to repeat the transfusion, and plans were set in motion for a repeat performance the following day. Once again the time was set for 6 o'clock in the evening, a time when most of the businessmen and court officials who wanted to attend would be free.

News of the first transfusion had spread through the scientific fraternity, and this time everyone who was anyone came along. The crowd, said Denis, included several physicians such as Bourdelot, Denis Dodart, physicist Pierre de Bourger and churchman Guillaume-Hugues Vaillant.

This time Mauroy was not in a fit state to put up a struggle. On top of this he was aware that his behaviour was beginning to resume to normality, and so was more inclined to permit this second transfusion. Consequently he lay in a 'convenient position', which greatly assisted the process. Owing to his weak state, Denis decided that it was wise only to draw off two or three ounces of blood before commencing the transfusion.

Emmerey prepared the patient's left arm this time, and the two physicians estimated that they transferred a pound of blood to Mauroy. As the transfusion was larger, so were the effects, both in terms of duration and strength. As soon as the blood started to enter his body, Mauroy reported a great heat in his arm. His pulse rose and he started to sweat profusely. Then his pulse became erratic, he complained of great pains in his lower back and said that his stomach was feeling unwell. He started to panic. He felt as if he was about to choke and pleaded with them to stop.

As they were removing the pipe from his arm he vomited violently, bringing up the bacon and fat that he had eaten an hour earlier, leading to a great debate among the spectators as to whether the bacon was bad. Soon he needed to urinate and defecate. The shock was that his urine was now black – as black as chimney soot. He strained and vomited for the best part of two hours and eventually fell asleep at about 10 o'clock at night and slept until 8 o'clock the following morning. It was his first sleep in weeks, greatly encouraging Denis that the technique had been a success.

When he awoke, the results were even more pleasing. Mauroy was sleepy, but calm and remarkably clear-headed. Apart from the fact that he still had extreme pains in his stomach and arm, was physically weak and continued to produce jet-black urine, Denis judged that he looked much better!

Thursday came and went, and Mauroy lay in bed saying little and asking to be left alone whenever Denis tried to interrogate him demanding descriptions of any symptoms. Aware, however, that Christmas was only two days away, Mauroy thought it would be a good time to set himself right before God his maker, and asked if a priest could be found to come and hear his confession. Monsieur de Veau duly arrived and listened to what the former madman had to say. He was impressed and stated that his confession had been sufficiently lucid for him to receive the sacrament, but only if his progress continued.

On Friday, 23 December 1667, Mauroy haemorrhaged badly from his nose, all the time producing copious quantities of black urine. Another day passed and the calendar moved to Christmas Eve, bringing with it another priest, this time a Monsieur Bonnet. The priest listened to Mauroy's confession, and this time pronounced him sane. He was welcome to take communion, and the priest administered the sacrament without further delay.

If Denis needed confirmation that the transfusion had worked, he need look no further. The priest, the respected man of church and God, had pronounced that the madman was now well – this was an independent witness of the highest calibre and public trust.

It was at this point that Perrine Mauroy arrived at the house. No one had thought to tell her where her husband was, and she had spent the previous few days searching in vain. It is interesting to surmise whether this was indeed an oversight on Denis' part, or deliberate secrecy – the last thing he wanted was for some meddling relative to turn up and demand to take their loved-one home. It would ruin the experiment.

Antoine was thrilled to be reunited with his wife, and immediately began to recount the story of the previous week, from the point where he was running naked through Paris, to the current situation where he had just received communion from a priest. Perrine was equally pleased, and told the physicians who were coming and going how much he had changed from a 'full moon lunatic' to this calm man before them.

Denis and Emmerey were walking tall. Little did they know that this was merely the lull before the storm.

Current comparisons

It doesn't take long for tongues to start wagging. Soon every man, woman and child in Paris seemed to be airing their opinion about this incredible cure. Some insisted that it was a miracle, others that it had all the hallmarks of the devil himself, masquerading as an angel of light. It certainly brought a novel topic to the yuletide conversations.

As people discussed Mauroy and his renewed spirit of calm, they began to ask questions, which revealed a few surprises. This was not the first blood transfusion that Denis had performed; it was simply the first that had got this level of interest and attention from the public. It appeared that the scientists had been working away behind closed doors, operating some clandestine conspiracy, and were now forcing their findings on society – a society that felt it had not been given the chance to debate the issues, or give an opinion as to whether they felt favourable to this new development.

In contrast, those at the centre of the scientific community were aware that the 'curious' had been tinkering away on the subject for at least a few years. They had discussed their ideas in meetings, and a few of the curious had even published some of their methods and findings in the newly appearing learned journals. They would have argued that there had never been any deliberate attempt to hide this from the public – until now there was little interest in the work, and consequently it had never before become a public issue.

A similar situation occurred in the twentieth century with the July 1996 birth of Dolly the cloned sheep. Ask most people and they will tell you that Dolly was the world's first clone. She wasn't. Far from it. Cloning had been going on for decades in laboratories around the world. The first cloned animal, a northern leopard frog, leapt around its Philadelphia laboratory in 1952, and in 1977 a German scientist claimed to have cloned mice, though the claim was disputed at the time. The first definite reports of a cloned mammal came in 1984 when Danish scientist Steen Willadsen succeeded in cloning a sheep from embryo cells while working at the British Agricultural Research Council. Soon others tried, and in 1986 a team of scientists led by Neil First at the University of Wisconsin in the US, cloned a cow. Each fascinated the scientific community but raised few eyebrows among the public. Over the next few years scientists produced scores of cloned mice, frogs and cattle.

Part of the reason for this obscurity was that, while a few scientists were hoping to produce a new method of creating herds of identical animals, most clones were being created in experiments that sought to unravel the way animals work, many directed at unlocking the secrets of development. They wanted to understand more fully how an animal develops organs as varied as muscle, skin, bone, nerves and blood from a fertilised egg – an initial single cell. This sort of work has never attracted much public attention as it is too remote from everyday life.

In fact it wasn't even the birth of Dolly in the borders of Scotland that caught the media's attention. It was the publication of a paper describing her origins and birth in the respected science journal *Nature* seven months later on 27 February 1997 that triggered a media stampede. It let the world know that a new lamb had been created by uniting a cell taken from the udder of an adult sheep, with a specially doctored egg, before zapping with a small pulse of electricity. Even so the paper was written in typically complex and obscure language, and could easily have been overlooked by the world's media. Similarly it was the publication of Denis' letter, rather than the event itself, that sparked public reaction to, and gossip about, transfusion in seventeenth-century Paris, Oxford and London.

But why the fuss about Dolly? Well, although she was not the first clone, she was a new step in the journey of science because all previous experiments had used cells from embryos and foetuses, while this little lamb had started life as a cell donated from an adult. This could be seen as merely another technical development, but the fact that adult cells could be used as genetic donors for a clone had vast implications. Furthermore, Dolly was a sheep, and a sheep is a mammal. This meant that biologically speaking she was relatively closely related to *Homo sapiens* – to us. Together, this raised the spectre that adult human beings could generate clones of themselves. Again, it was Denis' move to apply transfusion to humans that had triggered debate. While transfusion was limited to animal experiments, few people had become excited.

Once the spotlight of media attention had fallen on the little Scottish ewe, the growing sense of unease meant that there was no end to the debate. Most of it was poorly informed and highly emotive. Newspapers ran articles discussing the threat of multiple copies of notorious dictators, and ethicists talked about the potential abuse of human dignity. Some scientists ran a defensive line saying that they thought Dolly was not really a clone in any case; others came out saying that, even if she was, they had no intention of using the technology. Politicians performed knee-jerk reactions that called for bans on the technology, without considering whether this was possible in practice, beneficial for science or necessary for the protection of humanity. Popular mood seemed to be against the technology, and it was easy to jump on the bandwagon and give the impression of leadership.

As the story of Denis and his attempts at transfusing blood unfolds, we discover a similar pattern of hysterical reaction, uninformed debate and hasty decision-making. It's possible to argue that the decisions taken were the correct ones, but the reasoning behind the decisions seems at best to be highly suspect.

The third transfusion

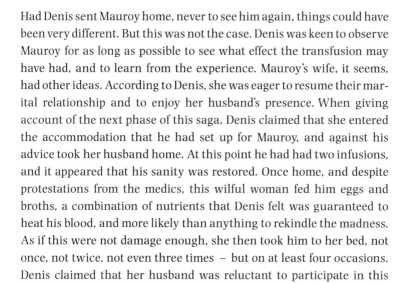

Had Denis sent Mauroy home, never to see him again, things could have been very different. But this was not the case. Denis was keen to observe Mauroy for as long as possible to see what effect the transfusion may have had, and to learn from the experience. Mauroy's wife, it seems, had other ideas. According to Denis, she was eager to resume their marital relationship and to enjoy her husband's presence. When giving account of the next phase of this saga, Denis claimed that she entered the accommodation that he had set up for Mauroy, and against his advice took her husband home. At this point he had had two infusions, and it appeared that his sanity was restored. Once home, and despite protestations from the medics, this wilful woman fed him eggs and broths, a combination of nutrients that Denis felt was guaranteed to heat his blood, and more likely than anything to rekindle the madness. As if this were not damage enough, she then took him to her bed, not once, not twice, not even three times – but on at least four occasions. Denis claimed that her husband was reluctant to participate in this exercise, but gave in to her enticement and persuasion. He was also sure that intimate sexual activity would heat a man's blood.

It came as no surprise to Denis, therefore, that within days the man was on fire inside and back to his old habits of visiting local cabarets and indulging in wine and women. This was a bad sign. Neighbours had also reported that the couple had started fighting. Despite his sick state, Madame Mauroy frequently hit him. Once, he struck back, boxing her on her ear. Her response was to scream that he should repent at once, or die if he didn't.

This blatant disregard for sensible instruction annoyed Denis intensely. Not only did he feel that it was it likely to injure the patient, but more critically it damaged his reputation. He was convinced that

Madame Mauroy's reckless action, and its all-too-obvious results, put into question the permanence of any cure. In addition he was anxious that such debauched behaviour could threaten the health of the new innocent blood Mauroy now had running in his veins. He had been at pains to transfuse blood from an animal that could never have been involved in licentiousness, and now all that care stood in ruin. Despite his misgivings, there was nothing he could do – the man had been taken from his care, and even though he was personally convinced of the wholesome benefits of transfusion, such was the temper of opposition to his work within the city, that this was no time to go chasing his patient.

Matters came to a head when Madame Mauroy accosted Denis in the street one day, asking him to perform a third infusion. Denis refused. She appeared again a few days later. Denis maintained that the only way he would be prepared to carry out the transfusion would be if she could gain permission for the operation from the Solicitor General. Given the strength of opinion running within the official circles of Paris, he felt it unlikely that the authorities would grant the permission.

Denis was in a quandary. Since starting work with transfusions he had become genuinely convinced of their power, and was eager to perform the operation as often as possible so that he could prove its use in medicine. After all, his profession called him to use his skills to save life and cure disease – surely it was his duty to give succour wherever possible?

On the other hand, Denis was anxious not to be accused of rushing with undue haste, and so had decided that the best thing to do was do nothing. He simply sat back, got on with life, and waited for events to unfold. And unfold they did. Madame Mauroy paid a third visit, this time calling on his home one morning. Denis was out at the time, but his servant, quite possibly Denis' first transfusion patient, took the message from the distraught woman: 'Please tell your master when he returns, that I have arranged a meeting at my house this evening to discuss the situation and it would be most helpful if he could be present, as I am sure he could make a valuable contribution. I beg you not to hold back now'.

Returning home, Denis received the message and, driven by curiosity alone, decided to attend. But when he arrived he was confronted by the sight of a calf tied up in the room, and his surgeon-colleague setting out his knives, ropes and tubes. On entering Denis stood still, struck by a state of considerable shock. Somehow Madame Mauroy had persuaded Monsieur Emmerey to perform the third infusion. He later claimed that he had been lured – straight into a trap.

His shock was compounded when he saw his patient. The last time he had set eyes on the man had been at Christmas, when he had sat up in bed and gently received communion from the local priest. He had looked pale and tired, but showed all the natural characteristics of a sane man. At that point he had spoken pleasantly and warmly embraced his wife. This had been in marked contrast to his unruly behaviour but a few days earlier. All in all, he had been the picture of a restored member of humanity – a man who had been wrested from the jaws of insanity by the wonder of new scientific medicine.

Mauroy was now barely recognisable. He was a torn and wild exhibit of humanity. The skin on his face was drawn tight, and small rivulets of dried blood streaked his arms and hands where he had struck them against objects – and people – during his bouts of fury. He was dirty and sat still only because, once again, he was bound to a chair with a stout rope, and the chair was strapped to a wooden beam of the house.

Denis' first inclination was to turn on his heels and run. This was no place to carry out the mighty art of advanced medicine, and the patient was clearly not fit to receive such a revolutionary therapy. The carriage he had hired for the journey was outside waiting for him – he could be gone with a simple word and a clatter of hooves. Indeed, for the rest of his life Denis wished he had followed that instinct. Instead, he hesitated. In a moment it was too late. Madame Mauroy fell at his feet and threw her hands around his legs. Kneeling on the stone floor she wept and pleaded, imploring the physician to have mercy. Instinctively, Denis tried to step back, and came close to tumbling to the ground. The woman was not about to let go, and was not about to let him walk out of the door.

He had been caught by surprise. An opportunity to meet the patient was one thing, but to walk into a room where the preparations for a transfusion were so clearly complete was far from his mind and against his better judgement. Quite clearly Emmerey had been persuaded of the need to perform a third transfusion and was keen to press ahead. He was testing the sharpness of his scalpel and honing it on a stone in preparation.

In the end, Denis felt he had no choice, but as he freed himself from the manacle grasp of the Madame Mauroy, he made his opinion clear:

this was not a good course of action. Having said that, he secretly hoped it would go well, that it would be very useful indeed.

Still, any enthusiasm Denis might have had was dashed just as quickly as it had been raised. The room was poorly lit. It was January and the sun had long since dived below the horizon – he saw the extent of Mauroy's degeneration only after he moved nearer. It was then that he realised that Mauroy was the origin of the putrid smell that filled the room, emphasising the extent to which the poor man had clearly degenerated over the last few weeks.

Denis and Emmerey proceeded to strap Mauroy's arm so that it was as near to being immobile as possible, and so that his veins were exposed. In preparation for the transfusion, Emmerey had forced a quill through the man's skin and into a vein. But before any blood could be donated, they would need to make room in his vessels. His leg was soon tied so that it couldn't move. Mauroy had been in no mood to co-operate, but was too weak to put up much resistance. An instant later Emmerey had plunged his lance into one prominently raised vessel on the upper surface of Mauroy's foot, and Denis had grabbed a porringer to catch the purple liquor.

'And that,' said Denis, 'was where the procedure ended. Within moments of the blood starting to pour from his foot, a violent fit seized Mauroy and his arms and legs began trembling violently.' Blood stopped flowing from the sliced vein in his foot, probably because the blood pressure inside the poor man was now so low, and Emmerey snatched the quill out of Mauroy's arm to prevent it getting broken, or the arm being injured.

Quite what happened next is cloaked in uncertainty, but one thing is clear. By the time the sun rose the following morning, Denis and Emmerey had gone home and Mauroy was dead.

CHAPTER TEN

The great debate

$\mathcal{A}$s word about Denis' human trials and Mauroy's death spread, Europe's ignorant masses as well as its key thinkers tried to make sense of what was occurring. For some this was an example of the way that new science was bound to reshape their view of the world and themselves, for others it was taken as an omen that this new way of looking at life was doomed to end in disaster. Prior to this, people had believed that reality had been revealed by the reasoned arguments of Aristotle and the like, and (literally) set in stone by the church. The great cathedrals were places to come and experience God's majestic splendour, not places in which to question understandings and make new discoveries. They were monuments that could not be moved, allowing people to experience something of a fixed understanding of an unchanging world. New science was breaking the mould. Reasoned arguments were important, but not on their own. Experience and experiment were becoming the new arbiters of truth.

The discussions that emerged on almost any subject were intriguing mixtures of ignorance and insight, permission and prejudice, and transfusion was no exception. As soon as word was out that Denis had cured a madman, he was held by some as a valiant warrior against illness, and by others as a hot-blooded youngster incapable of obeying orders from his superiors. Mauroy's death only fuelled the flames of gossip.

Throughout 1667 and 1668, many around Europe contributed to the debate in the form of letters and published pamphlets. Most fell neatly into pro-Denis or anti-Denis camps, although a few were prepared to express an open mind. Given the difficulties of travel, and the uncertain nature of European politics, many never met each other, but this restriction is one that this book is about to remove. In the decade after these events, Denis gained a reputation for organising conferences, and I have taken the liberty here of creating a conference that could never have occurred in reality at the time. However, while the meeting may be fiction, the arguments are those that each person contributed to the debate.

* * *

Denis' meetings were held in his apartments at Quai des Grands Augustins, and nearly 20 participants and observers sat on high-backed elegant chairs arranged in a rough oval around the room. On this occasion, the English contingent was on one side, consisting of Henry Oldenburg, Robert Boyle, Richard Lower, Thomas Willis, and a friend of Edmund King's by the name of Henry Sampson. Facing them were two groups of French participants. Louis de Basril, Claude Perrault, Claude Tardy and Louis Gadroy came with a cautiously curious mindset, while Pierre-Martin de la Martinière, George Lamy and a barber-dentist colleague had thrown transfusion to the devil and were decidedly antagonistic. At one end of the room nearest to Oldenburg and Perrault sat their host, Jean-Baptiste Denis, along with his colleague Paul Emmerey.

The first to speak was Oldenburg, who stood and smoothed down the white tabs that extended from his collar over his black tunic – his dress subtly reminded any who might not know that he had a training in divinity. 'Let us remember why we are here. Our meeting relates to a discovery made by none other than the most acute and curious geniuses of the age, namely the Virtuosi of the Royal Societies of London and Paris. The thing is this. A cherry or rose that does not ripen with the rest of the fruit on a tree is valuable, not because it has any worth in itself, but because it is rare. This novelty alone makes it an acceptable gift to princes. Likewise gentlemen, the experiments of healing by transfusion of blood, are both new and curious. I hope our reflections may cast some radiation of light upon the obscure and devious places of Nature, such as may perhaps discover some of her more hidden recesses, especially in her regiment of human bodies. But I would beg that wherever possible, we avoid using hard and obscure words. Yes there may be occasions when there is no alternative and you need to use a technical term to describe your ideas, but I do implore everyone to do all they can to explain any jargon. It should be possible, after all the technique is much simpler than some of those presented by touring physicians, who make a business out of selling new ideas.

'It is particularly exciting that we are gathered here to discuss the most worthy perhaps of all humane Sciences, namely the search for ways to provide comfort and health. All ancient cultures have sought after it, and many Kings have attributed greater value to medicine than to jewels. And although the ignorance and wild boasting of pseudo-chemists have almost brought the subject into contempt in this age, yet it is a most undoubted truth that recently a few medical pioneers like Jan Baptiste Van Helmont and Paracelsus have been able to conquer all diseases that Galenical physicians thought were incurable.'

As Oldenburg continued he was aware that this was going to be a fiery meeting. Mentioning Van Helmont and Paracelsus had already raised the temperature in the room, with many of the physicians gathered still being strongly opposed to anyone who challenged Galenic concepts. It was clearly time for Oldenburg to draw to a close: 'But Monsieur Denis' work, my learned friends, has given rise to this meeting and the opportunity for us to present our observations relating to health and the prolongation of life. I am glad to declare the meeting open.'

'Before we get too carried away with the fine details of this potential treatment, I too would like to make one plea.' The speaker was Perrault. Like Wren, Perrault had started out by concentrating on biological and medical pursuits, but in later life had exchanged this interest in living organisms for a career in architecture. This, however, did not stop him joining in the debate about blood transfusion. He was keen to make sense of the underlying science and determine the chain of events that led to Denis' appearance in court. 'Over the last few months I've made it my business to read and scrutinise all the relevant reports and pamphlets that many of the people gathered here today have been publishing, and I am currently collating the information into a report that the Académie Royale des Sciences will publish in 1688. I have an artist at this very moment working on two splendid watercolour illustrations that will bring the method to life. But my plea is this. Stick firmly to the truth with no exaggeration or deviation, it is the only way that we are going to make any progress.'

He paused, and surveyed the assembled group, sweeping his eyes across their faces and challenging any of them to contradict him. No one moved. No one, particularly in this age of new science, where carefully recorded observation was held as precious, wanted to argue against this point.

'We are,' Perrault continued, 'in grave danger of turning public opinion against us. Denis' trial will conclude shortly, and already the public is clamouring for gossip, thrilled once again to quench their thirst for scandal and conspiracy with the juicy chunks of slander and libel being thrown around. Meeting places abound with suggestions of bribery and corruption, and that Denis is about to file counter-claims against his accusers, all of whom are qualified doctors. It brings the medical profession into disrepute.'

'Quite so,' called out Oldenburg.

'It is not as if we can afford this assault. It's all too easy to get carried away by your enthusiastic work in laboratories and libraries, but to forget the need to bring public knowledge and opinion along with you at the same time. All your wonderful knowledge has clouded your vision so that you don't realise that people still prefer to go to amateur quacks rather than trained physicians. You may think it bizarre, but at first sight their reasoning seems sound – public opinion says that more people die at the hands of physicians than quacks. And it is probably true. But then think about it. Physicians only tend to get called to people who are severely ill. The situation would be rather like saying we should get rid of pilots because more ships get sunk if they have a pilot on board, without taking into consideration the fact that you only have a pilot on board when you are going through dangerous water. Yes, today's debate is about science. But the wider issue is our profession – let's keep the science pure so that medicine can win over public opinion,' said Perrault.[39]

'If I may reply?,' Denis had shot to his feet. 'Implicit in Monsieur Perrault's comments is the suggestion that I exaggerated, maybe even that I lied. I strongly reject this allegation. I didn't. My preliminary work was highly successful and I have done all in my power to report the patients in detail. Remember the adage; Nothing is as beautiful as the truth – the truth alone is good.'

From the seventeenth century to the twenty-first, nothing has angered scientists more than discovering that other workers have exaggerated or even falsified their reports. Whenever untruths are discovered, there is a scandal, which often shatters careers and leaves institutions fighting a public relations campaign. There is a more serious point. False reporting also damages science, because other researchers base their work on at best shaky foundations. In the area of health, the impact can be immediate as erroneous reports influence treatment decisions. It could be that one person's falsified research paper is another's death warrant.

Denis was also concerned that anyone should cast doubt on the validity of his word. He needed to have a purer than pure image if he was going to win the forthcoming court case.

Nevertheless, Perrault was clearly concerned about some of the reports of transfusions: 'There are so many reasons to believe that blood transfusions could never work', said Perrault, 'that you have to question the truth of some of the accounts, particularly those coming from England'.

It was Boyle's turn to respond: 'We have data to support all our statements', he shouted, instantly outraged.

'Ah ... Maybe, maybe,' said Perrault, appearing to consider this seriously. 'My problem, if you will forgive me, is that I have performed similar experiments and had very few successful outcomes. Even the animals that received blood and survived were weaker, more unhappy and depressed than those that had given blood. And this, I assure you, is not because the experiments were carried out badly.'

'But you didn't keep the transfusion pipes warm, did you?,' questioned Denis, stabbing his finger in Perrault's direction.

'I really don't believe that wrapping the transfusion tubes with warm cloths would have made any difference,' replied Perrault with a show of impatience.[40] 'Take, for instance, the report that Denis wrote to the Royal Society after his patient died. He says in the report that, and I quote, 'the transfusion succeeded so well that the patient was seen for two months after the transfusions in his good senses and in perfect health'. But how can this be? The poor man was dead just over a month after the second infusion was given. Clearly Denis exaggerates his claims of success, and does not hold to the rigorous demands of accurate reporting so essential to new science.'

A general hubbub broke out around the room as the delegates shouted their opinions on this.

Perrault stood, holding his hand in the air until calm was resumed. 'It may be that you were personally convinced of the power of this technique, but the problem is that you would not heed advice – advice that was calling for caution,' said Perrault, pressing his case.

'Caution? I had no need for excessive caution,' said Denis, his voice cracking slightly. 'Our results were so convincing that Emmerey and I would have been in error had we failed to give our assurances to the public that transfusion is safe and useful. To do otherwise would have been to lie. It would also have left others in foreign countries to gain the lead.'

'Quite so,' replied Perrault. 'It would, indeed, be wrong to blame Denis alone, because there were others, particularly foreigners,' his glance swung left from Denis towards Boyle and Lower who were sitting side-by-side on the opposite side of the room, 'who were pushing ahead with transfusion experiments. Nevertheless, it is a shame that the first experiments were not carried out with greater care and precision. For instance, it is impossible to tell how much blood really passed from one animal to another. As a result, when an animal dies we are left arguing whether it had received too little blood or too much. The haste is not solely confined to the pace, but to the lack of attention to detail that in retrospect would have been so useful. You might not be due in court had you sorted this out in animals before moving on to human trials.'[41]

'In no way did we think that we were rash to proceed and move on to a trial with a human. In fact we resisted pressure from some people to move with greater speed,' said Denis, speaking slowly and forcibly so as to keep control of his temper. 'Some even suggested using a condemned criminal as the first subject for a trial. It was an interesting idea, but not a good one. Think about it for a moment. A condemned person's condition will already have been disordered by the fear of death. He could then look at this trial as a new form of death and this far-fetched comparison could make him faint or even die. People would then accuse the technique of having injured him, something that would be unfortunate and untrue. Being seen to kill a person would put us at risk and would inevitably trouble his majesty Louis XIV, who has been watching our work with keen interest.'

There was a ripple of guarded laughter as people took on board the understatement – troubling the King would have meant signing your own death warrant.

'Having considered all opinions,' said Denis once people were listening again, 'we were more content to try it first in someone who had confidence in us and our theories. This might mean that we would need to wait for a bit, but the wait would be worthwhile. It was, therefore, in this frame of mind that we were introduced to the sick 15-year-old youth whom many of you know so well because he is now restored to health and serves in my household. You see, we were cautious. We didn't rush. We did wait for the right moment.'

'We too were cautious in moving to human experiments. In fact it was this very caution that gave time for Denis to steal the prize of performing the first transfusion on a human being,' said Oldenburg.

'Despite my anxieties, I look forward to today's proceedings in the hope that they will clarify the issues. For my part I think that the lack of success is likely to put an end to transfusions, rather than public opposition to the therapy,' concluded Perrault. 'To understand why this is the case, you will need to start by removing any sense of prejudice that may come from the excitement caused by the possibility of finding such a powerful medical treatment.'

Perrault's anxiety that hype should not rule over reality has continued to be problematic. In more recent times, scientists and politicians have debated whether to push forward with research into 'therapeutic cloning'. If the method works, it will mean taking a cell from a patient and fusing it to a specially prepared human egg. Under the right conditions, this could start to develop into an embryo – a clone of the patient. The idea would then be to divert this embryo's development so that scientists harvest individual cells, instead of allowing it to develop into a baby. If you believe the most enthusiastic of the pundits, these cells may cure almost all chronic diseases as well as repair the sort of nerve damage that can come from severe accidents, such as broken backs. Like the people gathered in Denis' room, present-day decision-makers need to distinguish over-inflated hype from genuine hope, a task made all the more difficult because so many of the people supplying the information have vested interests. Some, like Denis, hope to benefit professionally and financially from the work. Others, like the members of the Faculty of Medicine, are seeking to guard long-standing principles – in the case of therapeutic cloning, the principles being defended are the rights of a human being to be given protection from conception to death.

Sitting immediately to Denis' left, Louis de Basril, a physician from out of town, cleared his throat: 'Can I say how pleased I am to be invited to this gathering, and take the opportunity of thanking Monsieur Denis for hosting this conference in his wonderful apartment? The view over the Seine is striking. I do trust, however, that we will not spend too much time discussing the tedious arguments surrounding the case of poor Mauroy. I for one am irritated by those who through jealousy or ignorance spend their time trying to put down pioneers like Monsieur Denis. Let's take a look at the detractors for a moment. What picture do we make of their activity? They have attempted to use verbal smoke screens rather than solid argument to win their case. Their aim has been to defend the Faculty of Medicine rather than to work at finding or evaluating new discoveries. They seem to think they are better than, and can see further than, all the learned people gathered here today.'

All eyes flicked back and forth between de Basril and the three members of the faculty who had come along. Unsurprisingly, they sat at opposing ends of the room.

'I find it sad, therefore, that the Faculty did not see fit to send a senior member along,' continued de Basril. 'Instead it has chosen to hide behind a barber who yanks out teeth, as well as Dr George Lamy and Dr Pierre-Martin de la Martinière, names that you will be familiar with if you have kept up with the stream of abusive pamphlets being written recently. Let me remind you before you take them too seriously that Dr Lamy here is a 20-year-old medical student who has recently struggled to pass his exams, and de la Martinière might have the title of a physician to the King, but he is better known among the rabble on Pont Neuf than in any seat of learning. I am sorry gentlemen, but even mentioning their names leaves a bad taste in my mouth. All the same, we welcome you today – perhaps you will learn something.'

The accusations were distinctly harsh, but logic was giving way to rhetoric.

De Basril took a slow, mocking bow in their direction.

'Does the college really expect us to believe that young Lamy here is one of their best thinkers?,' said Parisian physician Gadroy, who had recently co-authored a paper with Denis. 'I think not.'

The three shot to their feet. 'For the moment we will ignore the outburst,' said de Basril, calmly waving his two friends down, and assuming an air of authority. 'You, Monsieur Perrault, mentioned truth earlier,' he continued, like a lawyer arguing a case. 'I believe these "philosophers" have abandoned themselves to their senses and are completely uninterested in truth for its own sake. They have declared themselves the sworn enemies of all those who discover, or more truthfully, these are people who have abandoned themselves to their senses, who are indifferent to the real truth.'

The nature of blood

'Before we forget our reason for meeting, let's remember that we came here today to talk about the science and the potential uses of transfusion. Yes, Denis' impetuous actions and subsequent personal problems were part of the stimulus, but let us try to leave them to one side if possible,' said Lower, breaking into the debate. 'Could I suggest that we start by reviewing what we know about blood. It is, I believe, central to this issue?'

A generalised nod of agreement signalled that the meeting could move on, but Denis sat and stared at Perrault. He had positioned himself close to Perrault, expecting to gain support from him, and was alarmed that someone whom he had seen as being impartial in the debate had been so quick to come out with criticism.

'I hope we can take it that everyone in this room is now convinced that there is only one type of blood in the body, by which I mean that arterial and venous blood are one and the same thing,' Lower was now onto his pet subject. He was in the process of writing *Tractatus de Corde*, his book on blood and the heart. 'This being so, the question we must ask is what gives arterial blood this deep red colour. My recent experiments show that this must be attributed entirely to the lungs. I have found that when blood enters the lungs it is completely venous and dark in colour – when it returns it is quite arterial and bright. I've also shown that it is the presence of air in the lungs that causes this change. I have evidence for this conclusion, not just argument. The evidence comes from two experiments. In one I prevented air entering the dog's lungs. Looking inside the chest I saw that the blood leaving the lungs remained a venous colour – it became bright red almost the instant I allowed air back into the lungs. In the second experiment I cut away the front of a dog's chest and pricked the lungs with a needle so that air could flow through. I then constantly pumped air into the lungs using a pair of bellows inserted into the windpipe. When I cut the pulmonary vein near to the point where it enters the heart, the blood that flowed out was completely bright red in colour. It was no longer venous, but was now arterial blood. Stop pumping air in and the blood remains dark and venous. We now have clear evidence that the dark blue and the red are clearly one and the same. Harvey showed us that it circulates, and now we know how it changes colour. At one point I believed the argument maintaining that the colour change occurred in the heart, but now I know that this occurs in the lungs – I know because I have seen.'[42]

'Yes, but we are still unclear what blood is,' said Boyle, rising to his feet and pleased that the debate had moved on to some serious science. 'I am one of the first to acknowledge that many physicians have, with great learning and skill, set forth the praises of the blood. They clearly show that it is a noble and excellent liquor, but I must beg their pardon, because I worry that their writings have simply sung blood's praises, without doing anything to reveal to us its nature. Sure enough, modern curiosity has acquainted us with several things that the ancients did not know. Yet, if I am not mistaken, what is generally known of human blood, is as yet imperfect enough, and consists much more of observations than experiments. We know only what Nature has been kind enough to reveal voluntarily, and have little information from experiments aimed at discovering the properties of this fluid that she has chosen to keep hidden.

'If I were being mean, I could say that, all too often, anatomists have concentrated on the solid parts of the body, and forgotten to enquire into the fluids, and especially the blood. This, my friends, would be akin to a vintner taking great care over the structure of his cask, but neglecting the wine it contains. Far be it from me to make this accusation, but all the same, just think about blood's importance in the human body. When it is healthy and moves in an orderly manner, blood conveys nourishment and vigour throughout the body. It sets the body in motion and in a word it delivers health to the rest of the living engine. Any corruption or disruption of this blood lies at the root of most diseases, and curing the patient depends mainly upon the rectifying of the blood. Consequently, looking at the importance of blood, made me realise that our lack of knowledge was a huge omission – an omission I have set out to rectify. To start with, did you realise that blood was heavier than water? You won't deduce that from philosophy, only careful measurement can reveal critical information like that.'

'So, then tell us …', encouraged Lower.

Boyle didn't wait to be asked: 'I was in the fortunate position to be able to collect the entire volume of blood from a single healthy man. It was a goodly quantity, but I managed to find a glass vessel large enough for it. Having shaken it down and let it settle so that all of the air bubbles had left, I used a diamond to make a mark on the glass, level with the top of the blood and weighed it carefully. This complete, I poured the blood out, washed the vessel and weighed it again. Subtracting the second weight from the first gave me the weight of the blood. I then refilled the vessel with water right to the very mark I had made previously and weighed it for a third time. Now I could calculate the weight of water. The blood turned out to be 1/25 heavier than the same volume of water, an important observation, but as always in good science, we need to repeat the observation.'

While many could not see the importance of knowing its weight relative to water, most nodded in order to look intelligent. Having got going, Boyle was not about to be deterred.

'But of more interest to many of you will be the experiments I did to test blood's heat.' Boyle paused. He was right, this did bring people to the front of their seats, as the nature of blood's heat had been debated since ancient Greek times. It was something they all knew about and could relate to. 'To study this I placed the ball of a weather gauge into the stream of blood coming both from a young woman and from an older man. In both cases the alcohol rose above the highest mark. Just think about it. This means that blood is substantially hotter than any recorded weather temperature. And these were in healthy people, not people with disease-induced fevers.'

'So where does this heat come from?' called the barber-dentist. 'Can your science shed light on that?'

'I believe it can,' Boyle replied, keen to expound some more of his work. 'The heart still seems to me the most probable source of blood's heat, but blood itself contains oil, and is thus packed with flammable energy.' Boyle had their attention, and was enjoying himself. 'I have dried it, powdered it and held it in a candle flame. It burnt with a yellow flame and "crackled" much like that of sea salt thrown into a fire. I also took a lump and placed it between hot coals. It caught fire, burnt with a yellow flame and was reduced to a black residue. Blowing powdered blood into a flame caused an explosion. The result was so extreme I tried it on a number of occasions and the same thing happened each time.

Blood might not need any external source of heat, it is very obviously packed with its own heat-generating material.'

Imprinting individuality

'Fascinating, fascinating,' said Perrault, 'but can I suggest we concentrate on transfusion. Like Mr Boyle, our friend from overseas, I too am keen to see what nature had taught us, and then ask additional questions.'

'Nature and experience has surely taught us that transfusion is an abomination. Monsieur Denis is keen to talk about the patients who got away, but remember the Swedish dignitary, he was dead within hours of receiving blood. And now Mauroy. What more proof do we need that this process is an abomination?' called out de la Martinière.

'Good science often starts in failure, young man,' continued Perrault. 'Let's look at a foetus, because there surely we have a situation of transfusion occurring. I want to ask, why, if transfusion is so simple, does a foetus in its mother's womb have a placenta? Surely the mother's blood could simply be passed to the growing baby without having to negotiate this enormous organ?'

Learned opinion had taught that the heart impressed its image on chyle and thus turned it into blood. This meant that maternal blood was marked by the mother's heart, but Perrault maintained that the foetus needed blood marked by its heart. While the blood of the mother and the foetus look similar, Perrault maintained that they must be crucially different. There must, therefore, be some mechanism for removing the maternal mark and replacing it with a stamp of the foetus. His suggestion was that the answer lay in the placenta. This organ existed only during pregnancy and was packed with blood vessels. It made sense, therefore, that its specialised vessels 'naturalised' the blood before it flowed to the foetus: 'So, the placenta's special vessels can make maternal blood safe for the foetus, but in transfusion there is no placenta and therefore no transformation can occur. This transfused blood cannot be safe for the recipient,' Perrault concluded. 'From this I also conclude that, if a mother's blood needs to be transformed before it is compatible with her own child, there is no way that transfusing blood between animals of different species could ever work.'[43]

'But this is a poor analogy,' said de la Martinière, 'because the mother and the foetus are in effect one and the same flesh.'

'Not so,' Denis replied. 'Quite often the father's seed predominates over the mother's contribution. Consequently the child's constitution is very different from the mother, even though the child was nourished by the mother's blood.'

It was an interesting argument and convinced many in the room. Intriguingly, it was right, but for the wrong reasons. The mother's blood is totally foreign to her developing baby. In fact the two should never mix. The placenta does not act to neutralise the maternal blood, but provides a barrier that keeps maternal and foetal blood strictly separate while allowing gases and nutrients to pass from mother to foetus. If they did mix, there would be a risk of a severe incompatibility reaction.

'Fascinating ideas, but this is conjecture, and experiments of thought. Where is the solid proof? Where are the data showing that blood from two different people will be incompatible?' asked Boyle.

'If you want proof, just look at all the experiments that report blood clotting in the veins of the receiving animal – is that not evidence that the two bloods were incompatible,' Perrault replied.[44]

Boyle pursed his lips, widened his eyes, and nodded slowly. 'Maybe,' he said. 'Maybe.'

'I have other evidence,' Gayant chipped into the discussion. He told the gathered dignitaries of science that on one occasion he had removed three dishes of blood from one dog, before transfusing blood from a second dog. Despite surviving the operation, the receiving dog died five days later. This, he maintained, was due to the large volume of blood that had been transfused in one go. The thrust of his argument was that blood contained the 'principle of life', and that this principle was given to the blood by the animal in which the blood flowed. Consequently, the blood and the animal were intrinsically linked. When blood was moved to another animal, this link was severed, and it would take time for a new link to be formed within the receiving beast. 'The blood was separated from the Principle of Life in the emittent, and yet destitute of the stamp necessary to live the life of the recipient. In this case, so much blood had been moved at once, that the dog did not have enough time to reform this life distributing link before the animal died.'

'Isn't a more straightforward suggestion that the dog died because it had been wounded in the neck,' said the barber-surgeon. 'For a dog this is distinctly problematic because it would not be able to lick its own neck and therefore the dog had no way of helping its wound heal.'

'I don't agree,' Gayant replied, 'I have performed much more severe operations on the necks of dogs without seeing them die over subsequent days.'[45]

Boyle thought for a few moments before leading the discussion on again. 'And there is of course another issue. All transfusions performed so far have taken animal blood and given it to humans. Does anyone have any evidence that this movement from one species to another causes additional problems?'

The first to respond to this question was Sampson, a good friend of the transfusionist Edmund King. Sampson was an English Nonconformist minister who had left England after the Restoration of the monarchy in 1660 and had studied medicine in Montpellier, Padua and Leiden, Holland. 'I fear that transfusion will have no practical use because it will always be difficult to obtain human arterial blood. No person will be so charitable to his sick decrepit neighbour, as to suffer a severed artery. They might give venous blood, but this will be no good because its strength is already spent in the nutrition of the parts of the body it has travelled through. Finally I don't believe that the blood of brutes will suit the body of man.'

'There are certainly many who hold these views,' said Denis. 'Some of the people who witnessed our transfusions on animals, as well as many who have only heard about them, were convinced that even if they worked on animals they would fail in humans, but …'

De la Martinière interrupted. For him it seemed obvious – the blood of a healthy person was very different from that in someone who was diseased. One was pure, the other impure. Mixing the two would never produce pure blood. The two were in effect opposites, and attempting to mix them would generate a feud. 'The result must be the destruction of the subject who received this unfortunate cocktail,' he said, convinced that he had delivered a *coup de grâce*.

'But surely sir, you display your ignorance in saying this,' retorted Denis. 'I can see no reason why the continual circulation that repeatedly passes the blood through the purifying heat of the heart's ventricles should not be capable of perfecting the mixture and removing any damaging properties from the blood.'

'Evidence, gentlemen, where is the evidence?' called out Boyle.

'I have the experiments to back my side of the argument. I have seen it work, I have seen mixing occur,' replied Denis. 'Only a few days ago I syringed a quarter of a pint of milk into the veins of an animal. When I drew blood from this beast a few hours later there was no sign of it. Quite obviously the milk had mixed with the blood and become refined and perfected by the heart. If anything the blood was better than usual because it was more liquid, and less prone to coagulate.'

De la Martinière was undeterred and launched another attack: 'If pure and impure blood mixed, the pure would lose its perfection. As soon as the newly transfused pure blood arrived at the liver it would be stripped of all of its goodness, and in an instant become like the whole corrupted mass of the sick person. The liver is, after all, the great organ of sanguification, the place where blood is made and receives all its qualities. This loss of quality would render the procedure useless.'

'An interesting idea, but again it is deeply flawed,' rebutted Denis. 'You claim that blood is made in the liver, but we know from recent experiments that blood forms in a developing embryo long before there is any sign of a liver, much less the appearance of chyle. Quite obviously blood is formed in many different places in the body. Consequently I don't think that this argument is worth pursuing any further.'

'Fascinating, I am sure,' said Perrault, 'but as I sit here I have begun to wonder whether we give too great a value to blood? If it is true that you can give up your blood and receive some from a donor, then you could argue that blood is not a very important fluid. It is in many ways just like a shirt that you can change whenever you like. In fact it is not even as important as a shirt, because there are occasions when you would die without a shirt, but you can live if you lose some of your blood!'[46]

No one answered.

'Wasn't it Hippocrates who said that blood will inevitably be corrupted if it leaves the veins?' asked Oldenburg, bringing the discussion back to the subject.

'The best way to defend this great person's honour is to understand the underlying meaning in his words, rather than to simplistically take them at face value,' replied Denis. 'Hippocrates was pointing out that blood is corrupted because whenever it leaves vessels it loses its heat and natural motion and blood requires this combination of heat and motion to continually keep itself pure. Yes, if you pour blood into a dish it stops moving and coagulates. Then after a few minutes its constitution changes. This is a process we have all witnessed many a time. But contrary to the saying that "whatever will be corrupted, will be corrupted when transferred to another place", blood can become corrupt even inside its vessels. Just block the flow inside a vein and watch what happens. Rapidly the blood clots.'

Denis was enjoying being the centre of attention and was not about to give up: 'In transfusion, a very natural process moves blood from one animal into another. I acknowledge that the conduits through which it passes are unnatural, but if we keep them warm and don't allow air bubbles to get inside they should cause no more alteration to the blood than occurs in arteries or veins. I have little time for people who say that the process will inevitably cause clots, and once these clots have passed to the heart they will trigger fatal palpitations, because I have never seen this happen. It might be an interesting idea in theory, but it has no grounding in practical reality. If you want, I can show you many animals, and people, who have had transfusions and are still very much alive.'

Perrault was up again: 'Even supposing blood isn't physically corrupted when it enters a foreign body, the violence and suddenness of the change and the accompanying movement of humours and spirits must be too much for the body to support. Nature just wouldn't allow it. She jealously guards her right to supervise any alteration of the humours, and will not endure anyone who tries to usurp her authority. If you doubt this, just consider the passions that can kill someone. The attack disrupts the heart's normal movement, messing up the humours and so death comes about because the underlying principles of life and health are disturbed.'[47]

Lamy jumped up to contribute: 'I wonder whether sickness or age might irrevocably damage a person's arteries, veins and heart. In this state these damaged vessels and organs would probably transmit evil properties to any blood that is placed inside them. It strikes me that the idea has support both from analogous examples and from experiments. The well-used analogy, of course, is a small barrel that has previously held vinegar. Any liquid you put into it, at any point in the future, will be infected with its sourness. The experimental evidence is more complex, but is probably best seen in the English experiment carried out by Thomas Coxe, in which he transfused blood of a mangy dog into a sound one. Bleeding cured the mangy dog, but the sound one did not pick up the infection.'

'Let's take them one at a time,' said Oldenburg, trying to get some order back into the meeting. 'I suggest you start with the vinegar barrel.'

'It is true,' said Perrault. 'And, indeed a number of philosophers have pointed out that containers not only preserve materials, but in some cases they can also perfect it. Blood is actively being changed as it passes through veins or arteries. In some cases the change can be beneficial, in others it can be detrimental. While Hippocrates was the first person to recognise that blood was always corrupted when it left the body, other philosophers say that blood can also become corrupted while it is still inside the body. Take varicose veins, as an example. Here we find corrupted and clotted blood inside a vessel.'[48]

'Well, first of all,' said Denis, 'I don't believe that blood could ever become so corrupted by illness that it was irredeemable. Or if this is the case it must be so rare that we don't have to worry about it. Something that infrequent would obviously require us to find some other forms of medical treatment to solve the situation, and I look forward to searching for them. The alternative argument would be that this total corruption is very common. The problem I have there is to see any purpose in this – it would, after all, undermine all of our understanding of how the body works.'

'I too doubt the analogy, but I wanted to know your views,' said Perrault. 'Any thought that blood changes its nature when it enters another animal must be incorrect. After all, we all know that water does not change into wine just by being poured into a full wine barrel. No concept is more distant to true philosophy than the idea that you can change things in ways that are novel to Nature. Blood changing itself after transfusion is just as fabulous as stories of wheat turning into crab grass, spinal cords becoming serpents, lead being transformed into gold, or a man mutating into a frog. Water can only become wine by being perfected in the vine. Similarly chyle needs to be perfected in its intended animal so that it can form the appropriate blood.'[49]

Having spent much of his time and money on alchemy, Boyle winced slightly at Perrault's decision to group all concepts of transformation together in such a disparaging way, but chose not to rise to the bait.

For a moment the participants sat in silence. Under question was the ability of blood to change its nature. For Denis there were opposing arguments. If blood could change its character, then new blood could be corrupted in the vessels and transfusion would then be rendered useless. If it couldn't change, then the infused blood would never be able to conform to the recipient's body. It would always be foreign, and unlikely to work well.

Having thought for a moment, Denis responded with an idea that attempted to solve both issues at once. By transfusing blood into the jugular vein he hoped to avoid the issue, because this blood would pass directly to the heart. It would therefore avoid all the tiny convoluted vessels where corruption could occur, and be immediately imprinted with the body's own 'principle'. Only having been naturalised would it pass into the rest of the body.

'As far as I can see, many physicians agree with me on this,' continued Denis. 'Even if they didn't, the "barrel of vinegar" argument would not change my mind. For sourness is the last quality that wine assumes, and because its original sweetness can never be recovered this transformation is the equivalent to its death. I can't see that there is any change that can occur to blood that can never be rectified. Blood can always be purified, except, I suppose, in a small number of remarkable and incurable diseases that we don't need to discuss at the moment.' He paused and thought for a moment. 'But wine can be used to make a good comparison. We all know that you can sweeten the roughest wines, clarify the foulest, strengthen the weakest, and remove fatness from any that are oily. Basically, if you know what you are doing you can add appropriate liquors to wine to remedy almost any problem. In the same way, it is reasonable to believe that mixing the right types of blood by using the technique of transfusion could refine and thin blood that is too thick, or heat blood that has become too cold,' said Denis.

Even so, Denis explained that he didn't expect transfusions to help patients whose blood had become 'exceedingly putrid and foul, or ... completely saturated with extraneous ferments and poisons'. He did not expect the treatment to cure anyone who had swallowed poisons, or whose body has become polluted and weakened by scurvy, syphilis, leprosy, or other long-standing illnesses as a result of which tissues waste away. For Denis, the problem was that, as impure blood circulated repeatedly around the body, it would poison the living reactions that occurred in the individual organs. Any new blood would be damaged by this poisoned environment before it had time to put things to rights.[50]

Denis' dismissal of the ability of transfusion to cure syphilis is amusing in the light of modern reflection on the Mauroy case. One of the symptoms of syphilis is violent insanity, and Mauroy's history, which included his frequent use of brothels, would fit the bill. We now know that syphilis is caused by a particular species of spiral-shaped bacterium – *Treponema pallidum* – and among its destructive effects this sexually acquired germ can cause brain damage. It is, however, highly sensitive to heat – so much so that a person can sometimes be cured by being placed in a steam room for a few hours at a time. There is therefore the possibility that the fevers that followed the two transfusions Mauroy received in Denis' house killed off the bacteria and did in effect cure him of his primary disease, relieving his insanity. In effect, transfusion could potentially cure syphilis, but this was a very dangerous way of going about it.

'The other problem, as I see it, is dilution,' offered Lamy, who was not about to sit quietly listening to his elders. 'Any transfused blood running down the jugular will meet the mass of blood in the *vena cava* and be overwhelmed before it enters the heart. It will surely lose its purity before it can perform any benefit. Consider the size of the jugular, in comparison with the other veins. It is just one of a number of veins that all discharge into a common canal before entering the heart. You will judge, without fear of contradiction, that the small quantity of foreign blood will be diluted by the great amount of blood from the patient.'

A question of mange

'And the mangy dog?' asked Oldenburg. 'Any thoughts on this experiment of my absent friend Thomas Coxe?'

'Yes,' volunteered Denis. 'I'm not convinced that the mangy dog's blood was necessarily corrupted in its veins? It may be that the blood was purified within the dog because it passed all of the impurities out through the pores in its skin. These impurities were seen as the mange on the dog's skin, but the blood was consequently kept clean. Surely it is always the case that producing many scabs in a disease is good, because this is a sign that all of the impurities are leaving the body and not remaining to circulate in the blood where they could damage some "noble" part of the body causing severe damage?'

Oldenburg was again back on his feet: 'I too have been wondering how is it that when Coxe infused blood from a mangy animal into a sound one, the mangy dog was cured without passing the disease to the sound one. But then the experiment is all the more confusing because the two dogs were not of the same type. It demands further enquiry, but I believe that Monsieur Denis has simply missed the point. He inquires whether the blood of the mangy dog was putrefied and corrupted in his veins, as if putrefaction of the blood were necessarily the root cause of the disease. This idea, however, runs against common experience of anatomy, in that blood does not putrefy within the vein many days after death. It is even less likely to putrefy in the veins of a living animal, because its constant circulation should prevent coagulation, which we all know is the beginning of putrefaction.'

Denis looked as if he was about to respond, but Oldenburg held up his hand, demanding silence. He continued. 'Now as to the disease itself. It looks to me as if mange is an excretion of an acid salt from the blood. This salt is driven out onto the skin, but is then not capable of being volatilised and so it sticks and turns into the mange. It seems to me that the sound dog was much more likely to catch the disease if he had been tied up to the mangy one for long enough for some of this salt to have rubbed off, than if he received a trifling transfusion of blood.'

'I don't agree,' said Denis butting in again and effectively ignoring anything that Oldenburg had just said. 'Even if the mangy dog's blood was corrupt, is it guaranteed that the receiving dog would catch the disease? No, again I think not. Why couldn't the damaged blood become purified when it mixes with the healthy blood in the recipient? It is easy to see how the gentle temperature in the second animal could cool the great heat that caused the scabs to appear in the ill dog. The disease would then not be spread.'

Now Oldenburg launched a gentle attack. 'But even by your own logic, cooling this disease-inducing blood is more likely to kill the dog. Your argument is that, in a process more powerful than fire, blood's heat is needed to make the damaging elements volatile and force them out through the pores in the skin. No heat – no purification. No purification – no cure. Your argument needs to take all the evidence into account.'

'If I am being accused of failing to account for all details,' Denis went on, stress once more making his voice sound very dry, 'I would like to point out the missing evidence in Coxe's reports of his experiment. What is the *evidence* that the disease was not passed to the healthy dog? There is nothing in the report to say that the experimenters opened this dog up to look at its organs a few days after the transfusion, so I can't see they can validate their claim that transfusion didn't transmit disease to the receiving dog.'

Grafting

'I would be interested to know what others think about another analogy,' said Lower, restarting the meeting after a five-minute refreshment break. 'Some observers have suggested that infusing blood is similar to grafting branches into citrus trees. An orange branch grafted into a stem produces oranges, while a lemon branch in the same stem produces lemons. In these trees, the stem strains the juice supplied from the roots and produces appropriate fruit.'

'What do you think?' asked Boyle, nudging his friend Lower.

'Me?' Lower was caught off-guard. 'I fail to see that there is any equivalent 'percolation' that will strain the blood and enable its nature to be changed. It seems reasonable to guess that infusing blood will not alter the nature of the receiving animal, though it would be well worth testing this with a few well performed experiments.'

'But can't we learn from Nature?' asked Perrault. 'After all, trees readily accept grafts, and some people have reported occasions when mutilated parts of bodies have been sewn on and survived. Nature always aspires to perfection and surely it is doubtful that she would turn down such a generous gift as a transfusion of blood.'[51]

'Are you talking about the wild Italian claims of transplanting noses, ears and teeth?' asked Oldenburg.

'No,' replied Perrault, 'but people who have difficulty believing those reports also will have difficulty believing that there is any truth in the reports that Nature will allow blood transfusion.'[52]

'Nature. Nature – what is this Nature?' asked Lower puffing out his cheeks in a display of mild exasperation.

'You see,' interjected Oldenburg, 'some people are worried about the great difference between generating blood by eating flesh, and simply receiving blood via transfusion. They say that Nature has arranged things so that as blood is produced from flesh it is altered to suit the individual animal, but if it is received via a transfusion the blood cannot experience this alteration.'

'This is the crux of the issue. Transfusion is abhorrent, it is equivalent to cannibalism,' called out de la Martinière. 'It comes directly from the courts of Satan.'

'As far as I can see, Monsieur Denis' recent pamphlet goes one step further. He makes the fanciful suggestion that there may be advantages to receiving foreign blood over building your own blood by digesting food,' added Lamy with a sneer. 'This artificial remedy, he would have us believe, is better than Nature itself.'

'Quite so,' replied Denis. 'The path from food to blood must be fraught with difficulty, and infusing blood will remove some of the ways that it could potentially become corrupted. Let's face it, transfusion moves nutrients directly from one body to another, and avoids the recipient's body having to expend work transforming food to blood. Meat, after all, contains bad as well as good juices and therefore requires the acidic juices in the stomach to purify the mixture so that only cleaned-up chyle gets forced into the veins. Surely, transfusing blood is just a simple way of giving a person more blood and bypassing all these energy- and time-consuming processes.'

'Some people say that manufacturing blood uses a lot of the body's heat and spirits,' said Perrault. 'It is a fair assumption that in a weak person these could be better used elsewhere in the body, so replacing blood that is in poor condition with healthy blood could make better uses of the body's resources.'[53]

At this point Denis started to relax a little. Perrault may have started by being aggressive, but it appeared he was at least prepared to think about the issues. It increased the chances of his giving a balanced report when he next went to the Académie Royale des Sciences.

'To realise where these arguments fall down, we need to begin by understanding that there are three principal digestions in the body.' Oldenburg's portly frame was once again on its feet. 'The first occurs in the stomach, and is the most minor. The other two turn this digested product into chyle and blood and occur predominantly in the liver and heart respectively. The grafting analogy is useful for clarifying this problem. Consider for a moment a tree. The juices in the tree are a concoction of juices in the earth and in the root and trunk. But the fruit that the tree produces will depend on the final branches that it passes through. If a bough of an apple tree is grafted in, then the juices will be filtered through small fibres in that branch and produce apples. If part of a pear tree is grafted in, the same juice will be filtered so that this time pears grow on the branch. Now in the case of blood transfusion of animal blood into a human, it is true that the blood will miss out the first digestion, but as it circulates around the body it will be refined and altered by the liver and heart so that it is changed into a human substance. It is the final stage, the equivalent of percolation in the grafted branches, that has the most important effect.'

'But the analogy with trees does not work,' interrupted Perrault. 'It may be that fluids in grafted plants mix well, but there is a great difference between plants and animals. There is no more reason to presume that plants and animals share this same ability, as there is to suggest that horses are as intelligent as human beings. There is a clear rule that nature devotes more care to animals than plants. For example, plant nutrition is less perfect. In plants the roots serve as the mouth and stomach, possibly even the heart. But these are easily replaced. Simply cut off a branch and stick it into the ground and it will grow new roots. The equivalent cannot be done with animals. For them the process is so perfect that if something goes wrong it is much harder to repair. By analogy, you might be able to build a hut using stones that you find lying around, or by taking stones from some other dilapidated building, but if you want to build a palace you need carefully cut stones, each of which has a specific role. Similarly, an animal can only be nourished by blood made to nourish that particular species, or more probably an animal can only be nourished by its own personally made blood. Transfusing blood would be equivalent to giving an architect stones cut to build a slanting wall when he had asked for stones that would produce a wall that stands straight up.'

'This is therefore the admirable way that animals work,' Perrault pressed on. 'In every way the different parts of the body work together within each individual for their common good, and combine to generate each person's individual character. It simply would not be possible for part of the body that has been made by one individual to fulfil the needs of another. Thus, the heart can impress its spirit onto the chyle and make this useful for its body, but I remain convinced. Blood prepared by one heart will be of little use for the body of another animal.'[54]

'I quite agree,' chipped in Denis, wanting to keep Perrault on his side as much as possible. 'Blood does need to be tailored for the individual, and transfusion will be dangerous if a person had strange blood placed in his veins that couldn't be transformed to suit his or her individual needs. This transformation is likely to take time, and I take it for granted that no one would be so bold as to replace the entire mass of person's blood in one go. Rather, we should always perform partial transfusions, and then only if the patient's body is strong enough. A partial transfusion would allow the recipient's spirits and blood to master the transfused blood and convert it into its own nature by a gentle ebullition.

'It goes without saying, that the more closely you match the donor to the recipient, the less work the blood will need to do to make it compatible,' continued Denis. 'Though I am convinced that at some point we will discover a substance that is so like blood that it could be transfused without the need for it to be transformed. This artificial blood will indeed be a miraculous substance.'

However, while a couple of centuries later people have worked out how to transfuse blood safely, and to give artificial fluids that could boost blood volume, the complexity of blood means that a total replacement has proved elusive to this day.

Different bloods

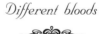

'With respect, Monsieur Perrault, I don't think your concerns add up to much, but let me give you one of the most powerful reasons that I have heard for doubting transfusion,' said Denis. 'Some say that the complexions of blood are so diverse in different animals that it would be poison and venom if transfused to another. I do acknowledge that there may well be different complexions and qualities of blood, but to go as far as saying that this means it would act as a poison must surely overstate the situation. If you take this view you would also condemn the meat. After all, blood is simply an elixir or quintessence of that meat and, as the meat comes from a different animal it would presumably produce blood that is unsuited to the person who eats it. On the contrary, we know that you can use cooling meats and certain medications to prevent blood boiling in the veins, or hot food and medical science to excite new vigour in old people or those with diseases. Meats are quite clearly not poisons, but are good for you. So if mixing meats is healthy it is quite reasonable to suppose that mixing bloods ought also to be good for your health. Why shouldn't an infusion of hot blood strengthen someone whose blood has run cold?

'I don't doubt that there are extreme differences in the blood coming from different animals, and that they will not easily mix – not unless they are subject to fermentation.'

'Fermentation?' called out Lower. 'Dr Willis, I believe this is your area – do you think fermentation could match different bloods?'

'I never considered the issue of transfusion in my book *De Fermentatione*,' said Lower's friend, colleague and former teacher Dr Willis, rising to his feet and brushing off some dust from his blue cloak. He was of average height with grey streaks running through his dark-red hair, and he stammered as he spoke. 'But let's consider the process and see whether it might. Ferm … Ferm … Fermentation is at the heart of existence. Understanding it is essential if you are going to understand any physiological process, including the life of blood and the effect of trans … transfusing it from one animal to the other.

'Going back to basics for a moment, everything is made of minuscule particles, and these particles can be divided into one of five classes. They may be spirit, sulphur, salt, water or earth. Now for today's discussion we need to concentrate on the fiery nature of sulphurous p … p … p …'. He paused, took a breath and forced out the next word: '… particles, because it is these that determine what we casually call heat. If sulphur particles in a substance are moving fast then the substance will appear to be hot. Faster still and the body will burst into flames. When they move slowly the m … material will mature and may simply become "sweet".'

Willis went on to explain his theory that materials changed their nature when particles belonging to different classes joined together. A salt may become volatile when combined with a sulphur or a spirit, or the same salt could become fixed if it linked to an earthy particle. This basic understanding then showed how blood changed colour from dark blue in the veins to bright red in the arteries. The cause was a 'fermentation' in which sulphurous particles in the blood joined with those of salt and spirit to produce a more volatilised salt. This was the process that imprinted life, vigour and individuality to blood.

'And where does this fermentation occur?' asked Willis, looking around to check he had everyone's attention. 'In the heart, of course, that n ... noble organ, which imprints life and heat into blood. It is in the heart that blood is made in that great ferment of sanguification. I am all too aware that the English physiologist and anatomist George Ent believes that the heart becomes warm because nitre particles from the air fuel a flame within the very fabric of the heart, and that Descartes, before his untimely death, concluded that this heat was simply passed to the blood. But I believe the heart to be the vessel that contains the process, not the supplier of heat itself. It is in the ventricles of that mighty organ that the spirituous and sulphurous particles break forth in motion, filling the blood with heat – heat that is then carried throughout the body.'

'And what are the practical applications of this theory?' asked Denis.

This, concluded Willis, led to an understanding of disease – in that diseases that created fever were ones where the ferment was excessive and the sulphurous or spirituous particles set in too great a motion. In the same way that an expert wine-maker could regulate the ferment within a wine cask, a physician must be able to influence the ferment within his patients' blood. 'What is needed is a more thorough understanding of the chemical nature of b ... blood so that we can be in a better position to influence its behaviour,' said Willis, relieved to have got to the end of his speech.

The scraping of a chair leg on the floor caught his attention and he paused. 'I remember well your book, good friend, and I admit that until recently I too shared similar thoughts,' said Lower, who was now standing. 'But as I said earlier, my recent experiments have taught me to think again. For it is now clear to me that the nature of blood changes not in the heart, but in the lungs. If fermentation is the process, it must occur in the lungs.' Sitting to his left, Boyle nodded sagely: 'It is in the lungs, not the heart, that blood encounters air and it is this encounter that enables its nature to change from dark venous to bright arterial. If fermentation is the process, then the lung is where it occurs.'

'I am well aware of your experiments, my good man, and I watch them with interest. You may yet be right,' replied Willis, both nodding and smiling at the same time.

Uses of transfusion

'Can we move from theory to practice?' asked Oldenburg, moving on the proceedings.

'I will briefly list a few types of patient who I think could be helped by blood transfusions,' said Lower. 'If a healthy person loses a lot of blood, then replenishing it from elsewhere could bring distinct benefits. Furthermore, I believe that transfusion could help arthritic patients and those with lunacy so long as their bodies are basically healthy, their brains are not damaged and their blood hasn't become putrid. In any case, transfusion should have as good a chance of healing as does blood letting.'[55]

'As far as I can see, physicians seem to fall into one of three general groupings,' said Denis. 'There are those who approve the invention and maintain that it could be prescribed for a wide variety of diseases. Others look on it as a useless novelty, while those in the last group haven't made up their minds, and claim to be waiting for more evidence one way or another. For myself, I have no problems identifying myself with the first group. I am convinced of its benefits and usefulness. Everyone knows that blood loss and haemorrhages kill a good many people, and sentence others to a premature old age. Transfusing mild and laudable blood could prolong the life of many of these patients. It is possible to foresee that this wonderful technique could relieve suffering in people with pleurisy, smallpox, leprosy, cancer, with ulcers, St Anthony's fire, madness, dotage, or many, many other diseases where malevolence runs in the blood. I fully expect to produce proof of this in the very near future.'

'Transfusion may have some role to play in supporting a very sick person to give them time to recover,' added Lower. 'In some of my transfusion experiments I have shown that if you infuse bright crimson arterial blood into an animal that is gasping for air, then this suffocating animal relaxes and ceases to fight for breath. Clearly the new blood has refreshed the animal as it has been supplied with blood that is already imbued with the spirit of the air.'

In saying this, Lower foresaw the idea of what is now referred to as an ECMO (extra-corporeal membrane oxygenator), a piece of medical equipment used in bypass surgery that can add oxygen to blood while at the same time stripping out carbon dioxide.

'And infusing such vitalised blood stands a good chance of being even better than bleeding,' said Denis. 'There can't be a physician here who is going to deny that blood lies at the centre of most diseases. After all, we all know that many, if not most, are cured by bleeding. But, you must admit that while this may draw out corruption, it also weakens the patient. You may cure the fever, but the process can leave the patient prone to faintness.'

'But you can't tackle fevers by transfusion; certainly not if you take the blood from an artery,' shouted Lamy. 'Arterial blood is packed with heat and rather than refreshing the patient's blood, I believe it will increase the heating even more. This surely is the reason why the men who have received blood felt an extreme heat in their arms.'

Denis continued, ignoring the young man's intervention. 'Too much bleeding can even kill a person. Consequently many physicians are extremely cautious about using the technique. But those who use bleeding should find transfusion useful because they can immediately replace the lost damaged blood with a healthy alternative, while those who are anxious about bleeding should find transfusion a valuable way of strengthening the person with new blood.'

'I would agree,' said Lower, who explained that he had always felt that transfusion would most probably be used so that animals that are in need of blood or have blood that is damaged by disease could be supplied by others. He thought that the process may be less effective than it could be because the old diseased blood mixed with the new healthy blood, but even here there was a potential solution. How about letting the blood of two or three animals into the recipient, while at the same time drawing blood out. This should flush out the old, and leave only new blood present.

'The question then is, what is the best source of blood?' asked de Basril, warming to the possibilities that transfusion offered.

'It makes basic sense to use animal's blood,' replied Denis. 'This will contain fewer impurities than a man's because animals do not get involved in debauchery or irregular eating and drinking. In addition, emotions and passions such as sadness, envy, anger, melancholy and disquiet corrupt the whole substance of a man's blood, whereas the life of beasts is so much more regular and subject to fewer miseries that result from Adam's disobedience in Eden. Indeed, experience shows that just as it is very rare to find bad blood in animals, it is equally rare to find untainted blood in a human being. Even a suckling child is not without fault in some ways, because having been fed with his mother's milk he will have sucked corruption together with nourishment.'

'We can also be a little bolder in using an animal,' interjected Emmerey, who had remained silent thus far. 'There is good evidence that arterial blood is less easily corrupted and passes more freely through tubes from one animal to another. Opening an artery on a human, however, is risky as we all know that you might end up accidentally bleeding the donor to death. This obviously would not be a problem if the donor was an animal.'

'Beasts have one final advantage,' said Denis. 'Because you are in control of them you can be careful what they eat for the few days before a transfusion occurs. We know that the meat of calves tastes different if you grow them carefully, and that you can affect the taste of milk and the yolks of eggs by giving the animals appropriate feed. Its reasonable to assume that feeding the animals well will produce a richer blood that is better suited to the purpose of transfusion.'

'I wonder,' thought Perrault out loud, now actively seeking solutions to some of the problems, 'could the deaths and ill effects in some of the operations have been caused by too little blood being bled from the animal before the transfusion began?'

'This is always a concern,' replied Emmerey.

'Would using two sets of tubes solve the problem?' continued Perrault. 'In that case each animal could bleed into the other allowing the two bloods to mix and unite in a more natural way.'

Emmerey agreed. 'Quite possibly, but it would only be possible in larger animals because of the technical difficulties of getting enough pipes into a small space.'

Fear

'One objection relates directly to the transfusion given to the young Parisian man,' said Oldenburg, flicking through a wad of letters he had received. 'Some people suggest that it was the fear of the procedure rather than the transfusion itself, that jolted him out of his lethargy.' The claim was that the anxiety roused his spirits, and sent them racing so fast that they knocked away whatever had been blocking their passage around the body. It was this clearing of the spiritual passages rather than the transfusion that had healed him.

Denis left no time for anyone else to answer before giving his response, stating that the idea did not stand up to investigation. If anxiety and fright were the key features that cured the youth, then he should have been set free from the lethargy some 24 hours earlier. The reason being that the day before Denis met him, he had fallen down a flight of stairs; that should have frightened him. 'Besides this,' said Denis, 'the boy was so far from being anxious that he seemed to be totally unaware that we were even transfusing blood into him. In fact he seemed to think that the lamb had been attached to his arm to act like an enormous leech and suck the blood from him.'

Philosophy or experiment

'Thinking the whole thing through, I do wonder whether any of these transfusions ever took place,' said Perrault, leaning back and massaging his temples. 'Take for example the dog that lay on its back for half an hour while its blood was drained and replaced by blood from another dog. We are supposed to believe that after a considerable transfusion of blood the dog merely shook its ear and suffered no more. It strikes me that a more likely explanation is that as soon as the transfusion started, blood coagulated in the vein blocking any further entry of blood. The animal probably benefited from having some of its own blood let out because it had too much in the first place. Sadly there was little or no attempt to measure exactly how much blood had passed from one to the other, so there is no way of verifying either the official account or my alternative proposal.'

'I am sad, although not surprised, at the extent to which our discussion today has returned to philosophy, rather than resting on the foundation of experimental evidence,' said Oldenburg. 'Too often the objectors to transfusion have refuted the experiments by using logic and a system of carefully constructed arguments taught in academic schools, clearly believing that this process is all that you need to build a debate for and against any ideas. Experiments, however, are better than any argument and data should be left to give the verdict and last decision, especially in matters of natural philosophy and medicine.'[56]

'Quite so,' said de Basril. 'And our learned colleague needs to remember a bit of history. For example, one hundred years ago the Faculté de Médecine discovered that certain chemicals made you sick and listed them as poisons.'

'You are referring to antimony?' asked Oldenburg.

'Yes, and mercury and rhubarb,' replied de Basril. 'But then the King was cured with antimony and consequently issued a Royal Decree against the Faculté saying that it was a good cure and that they had been too quick to reject it.'

'Now it is seen as a very valuable purgative and an important weapon in a physician's armoury,' Oldenburg took over. 'And that same Faculty of Physicians not only permits, but even ordains, its use. Why the change in view? Data. When it was seen to cure many people including the Most Christian King, then everyone was convinced, and all the clever arguments in the world to the contrary were thrown out. It's the same for all remedies that doctors use. At some point other members of the profession have forbidden each one of them. Indeed, the most rational person is the one who is guided by experience.

'Blood transfusion is a new thing, and as far as we know was not performed in former ages. In this case ingenious men, as well as those who wish to see humanity prosper, can do no more than to present the little that is known so that other generous and unprejudiced physicians can try it. In this way we will build up our body of experience and will be in a better position to judge whether it is agreeable to the human body. But it is not straightforward. On the one hand people argue that because it concerns the health and life of human beings no amount of investigation could be considered excessive. On the other hand, these conceited people ...', Oldenburg gestured in the direction of the three representatives of the college, '... dismiss any fact or argument that they have not thought of themselves. The best people are those who come with no preconceived verdict, perform many carefully conducted experiments and then form an opinion. It is for this reason that I ask those in power to order that a number of trustworthy and open-minded physicians and surgeons perform many experiments aimed at finding out the true potential of this technique.'[57]

'But don't neglect either,' said Perrault. 'Reasoning and experiments combine as two excellent instruments and neither are exempt from error. You need to correct experiments by reason and reason by experiments. This demands an exactitude and an application greater, to my mind, than that which has been employed by those who have no doubt at all of the advantages which the transfusion of blood from one animal to another can bring. From the experiments so far, you can't conclude that transfusions work, but at the same time it would probably be incorrect to call them objectionable and pernicious. All the same, it seems most likely that animals survive the assault of a transfusion, rather than that they are helped or even cured by the procedure. It might be that they would have done just as well if they had been infused with muddy water or some other foreign fluid.'

'Gentlemen, blood transfusion is a highly original invention,' said Lamy, wishing to sum up his views before the meeting closed. 'If it works, our century will be pleased to have found a means so simple and so quick to get rid of cruel illnesses that trouble our peace and prevent us from enjoying the gentleness of life. Sadly I remain convinced that once we look at it carefully we will find it has few benefits to offer. You may end up "putting people out of their misery" rather than healing them.'

'I am afraid that I can't agree,' said Denis, his eyes searching the floor for inspiration and trying to work out whether the day would help or hinder his forthcoming appearance before the magistrate. On the whole, he was relatively pleased. This roomful of thinkers had not destroyed his concept, so the court shouldn't be able to present any crippling blows. 'Nothing that I have heard or seen diverts me from my opinion that transfusion is a useful technique, possibly even the ultimate cure for all disease.'

'But surely, good friend, you must admit there is room for doubt?' pressed Perrault. 'Some of the claims are so difficult to believe. Take curing insanity, for example. If good or bad blood confers or takes away wits and good sense, giving someone calf blood must surely leave him with the stupidity of this animal!' Denis didn't join in the laughter that followed.[58]

'But equally you can't dismiss it entirely,' contributed de Basril. 'There are now many dogs that have survived for a year or more with transfused blood. There is the old dog that received blood from a deer and regained its appetite and became more energetic after eight days. As well as the men who have received blood, Denis has recently informed me of a woman who has been healed of paralysis down half of her body, an outcome that is quite amazing. What we need is to follow the example of our English colleagues and recommend a series of trials that are performed carefully and recorded well – then we might get a clearer picture of the truth. Notwithstanding this, I beg M. Denis not to give up because he has enemies. I have always heard say that it is better to envy than to pity. I exalt him in the name of all those who are curious to continue his conferences and to share with the public the new data he discovers every day on other matters, and I will continue on my side to be one of the listeners who defend the justice of his interest in all types of situations.'

It seemed a good place to draw the meeting to a close.

CHAPTER ELEVEN

Mistake, malice or murder?

Once more the stave struck the floor, and this time the conversations died down. In walked the presiding magistrate, the Lieutenant in Criminal Causes, Monsieur D'Ormesson. 'The court of Le Grand Chastelet, Paris, will come to order on this day, Saturday, April the 17th in the year of our beloved Lord, sixteen hundred and sixty-eight,' called the official, pleased that people were at last taking some notice of him. D'Ormesson took his time making himself comfortable and the assembled people waited – there was no point in having authority and power if it did not impinge on others' time and freedoms. When finally ready, he gave an expansive gesture and bow in the direction of Denis' assembled dignitaries in the gallery, before turning to the distinguished lawyer, and gently nodding his head. He finally signalled to an official who read out the charge.

'The case against Monsieur Denis, is that in the last days of January this year, he and his accomplice did unlawfully kill a patient, one Monsieur Antoine Mauroy. The accusation is that, despite protestations from learned gentlemen within the Faculté de Médecine, he performed a series of unnatural operations, transfusing blood from calves into the victim's veins. He did this not once, but three times. The day after the third transfusion being the day the patient died. The inference is clear. Denis killed Mauroy.'

'My learned and distinguished Lord, I wish to present the case for the defence,' announced Monsieur Lamoignon, Denis' lawyer, rising to his feet and bowing first to the judge and then to the gallery. There might have been no jury, but getting the right reaction from the crowd was always useful in winning a case, and a little courtesy went a long way.

'You are, I am sure, well acquainted with the opening chapters of this episode, with the remarkable cure that was given to a man whose destructive insanity had brought him to the attention of the entire population of this mighty city of Paris. Removing some of the depraved man's contaminated blood, and replenishing his system with cool, innocent blood from a docile calf transformed him, so much so that within days the church authorities declared him sane and allowed Mauroy to partake of holy ritual. Should you be interested, I am more than willing to call the two priests who attended him the days before Christmas just passed, who can witness to his sanity.'

The magistrate did not appear to be interested.

'It is my contention,' continued the lawyer, 'that in this action for murder, the wrong person is accused. I wish to present the case, and indicate the evidence against another member of the public who by rights should be at present within these walls, but curiously seems to be absent.' Lamoignon shaded his eyes and made a play of scanning the galleries, as if searching for a spy. 'It is my belief that Madame Mauroy should be present to answer for her actions, as it would appear she has much to answer for. At the very least she should answer for her inability to follow sound advice.'

'That may be the case, but the accusation currently rests against Monsieur Denis, and there are questions that he needs to answer,' replied the magistrate. 'You complain at the woman's blatant disregard of advice, but isn't it the case that Denis too paid little or no heed to the calls for caution from the medical profession?'

'If you are inclined to doubt his caution and reluctance, note this. It was not Denis who sought Mauroy, but his wife who pestered and pleaded with him. If you are suggesting that he ignored his superiors, then again that is not true. The calls for a cessation of this technique came from the Parisian medical school, but Denis was trained in Montpellier. Why should he listen to the inflexible minds of Paris?'

'But, Monsieur Denis, would it be fair to say that you would have eagerly sought to perform the operation given the opportunity?' pressed the magistrate.

'I believe in its power, so I of course look for all prudent times to employ the technique – this, however, was not one of those opportunities.'

'But you went ahead and infused blood.'

'No, my Lord,' replied Denis. 'The night was full of confusion, but at no point during this operation did we get around to opening the artery on the calf and connecting it to the quill in Mauroy's arm. The man went into such violent fits as soon as we tried to start the procedure that we had to desist. There is no way that we could have performed an infusion on this occasion. It might have saved his life if we had, but given his terrible state of health we were not in a position to continue. His times were in God's hands and he was clearly beyond any restorative art that medicine could offer.'

'And you are sure of this?' pressed the magistrate.

'Quite so.'

'You have witnesses?'

'Not of this event. The only people present at the time were myself, Emmerey and the two Mauroys.'

'How convenient,' said the magistrate, scribbling down a note. 'And there was no examination of the body either?'

'This was not my client's doing, my Lord,' stepped in the defence lawyer. 'For Monsieur Denis the next move was obvious. He needed to perform a post-mortem, and do it rapidly. He was keen to do this for two reasons. First of all this was a matter of science. Mauroy had received two transfusions, and my client was keen to see if there was any internal evidence of what the calves' blood had done. Secondly, he wanted to look for any signs of poisoning, yes poisoning. There were, you see, rumours that in desperation at receiving so much violence, Mauroy's wife had on a number of occasions threatened to dispatch him given the chance. At the time, the comments were taken as black humour, but a good physician looks at every possibility before forming a diagnosis.'

Denis butted in. 'So, in order that our word would be trusted, we gathered together seven or eight eminent physicians who could act as witnesses, and headed for Mauroy's home. In marked contrast to the previous visit, I got no welcome. Instead this widow was adamant that we shouldn't come into her home. She was determined that we would not examine her husband's corpse. Don't you think this strange? Only a day before, I had been dragged to his side – now I was banished. According to neighbours, as soon as we left she had spent the rest of the day frantically trying to make arrangements for his burial, but was unable to complete the task that day. You will be aware how quickly news of the incident hit the cafés and meeting places of Paris, so it is with no surprise that one of the most eminent members of the Paris medical faculty heard about Mauroy's death that evening. He was no supporter of my work and saw this as an opportunity to gain evidence against me. He sent surgeons to examine the corpse, but once again, Madame Mauroy refused access to the body. This time she even lied, saying that the burial had already occurred.

'Then in a rare meeting of minds, I and the physician agreed that the only thing to do was for both of us to go to her house and take the body by force. We agreed to the adventure in the morning, but by the time we got there we discovered that she had indeed had the body buried a matter of hours earlier, under the cover of darkness and just before the dawn.'

And this, he continued to relate, could so easily have been the end of the experiment, and the last anyone heard of this unfortunate couple. Indeed, claimed Denis, he decided to leave it alone and say nothing more. Soon, however, this was no longer an option, because those 'enemies of the experiment' had been thrilled at the tragic chain of events, and had sought to make use of it. Their first move had been to publish a pamphlet decrying the whole concept of the therapy. 'When I remained silent, they set the rumour running that this was because I agreed with them and wanted no more to do with the art,' said Denis.

'You are, I presume, referring to these?' queried D'Ormesson, lifting a sheaf of letters and magazines into the air. 'Let's take a look at them for a moment, if we may. To start with there is this letter from the eminent philosopher Justel to his English colleague Mr Oldenburg, dated February the third. He clearly believes your actions were rash and unsupported by philosophical debate or the evidence of new science. Let's pick a quote from his letter shall we – "This will decry Transfusion, and now no one will dare to perform it on man". It would be fair to say he was sceptical, I think. Then there are these two letters written by George Lamy. He displays his scorn for your work and seems to envisage tragedy for any recipient of the treatment. We could add to this the numerous articles coming from Martin de la Martinière, who is convinced that your work is an immoral scandal.'

'We are very happy to explain that,' said the lawyer, trying to take control of his presentation again. 'There is clearly a difference of opinion. The official line is sceptical about transfusion and sees these pioneers as meddling nuisances or on occasions as immoral villains. But they raise bluster and argument without engaging in experiments and observation. Listen to them and we will never move from the state of understanding established in ancient Greece. But moreover, I wish to present evidence that among these learned gentlemen are those who are prepared to subvert the course of justice in order to achieve their goals. Please listen to Monsieur Denis' account of the next episode in this drama.'

Denis took the floor again. 'Imagine my surprise when I discovered that two months after this untimely death, Madame Mauroy was being pestered by three of these physicians. Were they trying to help her in her grief? I think not. It turns out that they were offering her money, in return for her word in court that by performing transfusions, I had murdered her husband.

'This event not only casts doubt on the integrity of my attackers, it also reveals a little more of Madame Mauroy's character. Any law-abiding person would see the injustice and evil intent behind the bribery and instantly turn from the offer. Not she. She didn't even take the pieces of silver and go Judas-like to the courts to turn over an innocent man; rather she came to me in secret. At first it appeared that she came out of a generous spirit with the sole intention of protecting my good name and reputation. She went on at length about the good service and kindness I had showed her late husband, acknowledging that I had given him the most technical therapy that new science could offer a man and consequently offering to stand witness in my defence should that ever be needed. At this point, however, her tone changed as it became obvious that this offer was not free of cost. Unlike my generous actions performed at no cost to her or her family, Madame Mauroy's services in court would require a fee. And the price she asked? All I had to do was offer a higher sum than had my opponents. Her sole desire, she claimed, was to have enough money to return to the country of her birth and hence start a new life.

'I didn't know whether indignity or rage got the upper hand. Quite simply, I sent her away saying that those physicians and herself stood more in need of the transfusion than ever her husband had done, and that for my part I cared not for their threats. It is my belief that all the evidence against me is based on false information, inflated by jealousy and the desire to subvert justice with scandal.'

Three witnesses

'And my Lord, we have witnesses,' said Lamoignon, beckoning Denis to sit down.

At this point two witnesses came forward, one corroborating Denis' story and saying that Madame Mauroy had indeed attempted to blackmail the honourable doctor. The other claimed that a physician had offered him 12 Gold Louis if he would come to court and say that Mauroy had died in the very act of the third transfusion – an accusation that could turn Denis into a murderer and leave him fighting for his own life.

'There is one other witness I would like to call, if your lordship would grant it?' asked Lamoignon, bowing slightly. D'Ormesson nodded. 'I would like to call Madame Mauroy's neighbour.'

The witness was sitting waiting and shot to her feet as if suddenly energised by a bolt of electricity. She played incessantly with a ring on one of her fingers and looked distinctly ill-at-ease in the formal surroundings of the law court. A rumble of conversation spread throughout the room as people swapped ideas and gossip, trying to predict the information she was about to present.

'You saw some worrying episodes I believe?' prompted the lawyer, when the court was calm once more. 'It started when you heard something? Do tell us.'

'It would have been a week, maybe two, before Mauroy died,' she paused and looked around nervously.

'Yes?' enquired D'Ormesson.

'Well, sir, I overheard an argument.' She faltered again and Denis stared at the floor. There was every indication that his key witness was about to fail.

'An argument?' prodded Lamoignon. 'Between whom?'

'Mauroy and his wife, of course.' She looked surprised at the question, and then suddenly gained inspiration and spouted the rest of her story. 'I mean, there was nothing unusual about this. You see our houses join and the walls, well they are mighty thin – we hear everything. You even see through in a couple of places because there are cracks in the wall. One of the cracks is getting quite large at the moment after they hit it during one of their disputes. I keep asking them to sort it out. If things get rough, you see, you know all about it. And then, like I said, two weeks ago the argument was louder than usual; arguments and fights were a regular part of their lives, you see. Always had been. Still on this occasion Monsieur Mauroy was complaining about the food. He was arguing that the physician had commanded that he ate nothing that would heat his blood, but that all she would serve were strong drinks and strong broth. "Anyone would think you are trying to poison me", he called out one evening. "You could hide arsenic in that broth and I would never know." You might think this was a strange thing for him to say, but then his wife had been mixing curious pouches of powders with his broth. She said they were potions from the apothecary, and to prove her case she made a great show of drinking a spoonful of the broth.'

'How did you know? Could you hear the slurp or were you standing with an eye to that crack in the wall you so wonderfully described?' asked D'Ormesson, sending a ripple of laughter around the court.

'No, my Lord,' she replied, warming to the occasion, 'by this point I had stepped outside and was watching through the window.'

'So she drank a spoonful of broth – what of it?'

'No, my Lord, she didn't. This is just it. She just pretended to drink it, and then a moment later I saw her flick it from the spoon so that it fell to the floor.'

'It was never eaten, then?' he enquired.

'Not by man. No. But it did not lie there for long, because the last I saw was it being licked up by a cat.'

'How fascinating,' yawned D'Ormesson, stretching out his arms and leaning back in his chair to make his lack of interest in this low-class witness all the more apparent. The movement drew a murmur from the crowd, and one or two responded in sympathy with involuntary yawns. A few started talking and Denis panicked that the critical punchline was about to be lost.

'But the cat died.'

'All cats die – it is in the nature of cats to die.'

'Not after eating spilt broth. They don't die in my house after eating my broth, I can assure you.' For once the court was quiet. 'This cat was young and healthy at mid-day and dead before midnight, found curled in contortions in a mass of its own blood-stained vomit and diarrhoea. This was no natural death.'

A pin dropped, and everyone heard it.

SENTENCE RENDUE AU CHASTELET
par Monsieur le Lieutenant Criminel le 17. Auril 1668.

A TOUS Ceux qui ces presentes Lettres verront, Pierre Seguier Cheualier Marquis de Saint Brisson, Seigneur des Ruaux & de Saint Firmin, Gentilhomme ordinaire de sa Chambre, & Garde de la Preuosté & Vicomté de Paris; Salut. Sçauoir faisons, Que sur la Requeste faite en Iugement deuant Nous en la Chambre criminelle du Chastelet de Paris par Maistre François Mulot Procureur de M. Iean Denis Docteur en Medecine demandeur & complaignant; le Procureur du Roy joint, & aux fins de sa Requeste, & exploit du 9. de ce mois, tendant afin qu'en prononçant sur sa plainte & informations, deffenses soient faites à l'acousée cy-apres nomée de rescidiuer ses discours, & inuectiues, & de reparation, amande, & despens. Contre Maistre Gilles de Trappu Procureur de Perine Pesson vefue d'Anthoine Mauroy presente en personne, deffenderesse & accusée, & demanderesse & complaignante; Parties ouyes on leurs playdoyers & remonstrances, & ouy Noble homme Maistre André le Febure sieur Dormesson Aduocat du Roy en son plaidoyer, qui a dit que par les informations dont il a eu communication, il y a preuues de sept faits considerables.

1. Qu'on a fait deux fois l'operation de la transfusion sur le nommé Mauroy, & qu'on l'a tentée vne troisiéme. Qu'elle a si bien reussy ces deux fois, qu'on l'a veu depuis pendant deux mois dans son bon sens, & en parfaite fanté

Plate 17   Reproduction of the front page of a French pamphlet giving court sentencing at Chastelet.

'Thank you,' said Lamoignon after a suitably long pause, dismissing the witness with such a deep and solemn bow that the humble woman blushed. 'You see, my Lord,' he continued with a studied calm and turning slowly to D'Ormesson, 'we have one other suspect for this murder. One who knew the victim well and had cause and occasion to carry out the deed. One who had suffered violence at his hands in the past, and had threatened retaliation recently. One who had the outward appearance of a caring wife in search of a cure, but the hidden motive of an adulterer seeking to free herself of the marriage she had willingly entered but a few years earlier. I refer of course to Madame Mauroy. Indeed her behaviour since her husband's death serves only to increase the level of suspicion.'

After withdrawing to consider the evidence and the implications of any verdict he might give, D'Ormesson returned and drew the case to a close, issuing a written judgment. It had catches – but at least it meant Denis could walk free.

Won the battle, lost the war

Leaving the court, Denis and his entourage crossed the Seine over Pont Neuf heading for his house on Quai des Grands Augustins to digest the verdict. They could have been forgiven for walking fast, putting distance between themselves and the court. But for the moment the sun was out and the weather was fine – it was a great day to be alive, and their passage was slow. The gloom of a long winter had given way to a perfect spring day and the streets were a seething mass of humanity.

On a normal day, Pont Neuf was always crowded, some people pushing as they went about their business, others just standing and staring at the magnificent Louvre, the impressive terraced apartments and the hundreds of boats that navigated cautiously around each other on the busy river. This was the only bridge across the river not to be lined with houses, and as such gave a unique and magnificent view of the flowing torrent that gave Paris its life. Today the bridge was unusually full.

It was one of the last days of the Saint-Germain fair, a month-long celebration that had been initiated by monks a century before to mark the Lenten period that precedes Easter, but had in recent years become a celebration of the obscure. The bridge and the roads immediately ahead of the group were packed with soldiers and beggars, guardsmen and prostitutes. The fair was a melting pot of Parisian life, a long-drawn-out event that allowed the most refined courtesans, the prettiest girls and the subtlest pickpockets to become entwined. Masters wandered with their valets, and thieves sat and drank with honest men. Clerks, shopkeepers, lackeys, students and porters all jostled for space. For noble aristocrats the fair was an opportunity to step out of the strict monotony of their formal life, and a chance to scoff at the vulgar inferiority of the peasants. Similarly, the lowly were suddenly brought to an equal level with their superiors, as together they strained their necks to view the entertainment. And there was plenty on offer.

With a deliberate show of annoyance, Denis and his crowd passed one tent where a man was professing to demonstrate the wonders of science, but was in fact an illusionist, who with sleight of hand, smoke and mirrors duped a gullible audience into thinking he had carried out remarkable feats. The result may have lined his pocket, but in Denis' mind it also devalued true science, and would make more difficult his task of convincing a sceptical public and legislature of the value of his work. The show confirmed in popular debate the idea that science and magic were one and the same. With more than eight percent of Paris illiterate, Denis was painfully aware that it was not going to be easy to drag the nation into an enlightened age.

The tightrope walkers, acrobats, tumblers and fire-eaters were more enjoyable, as each vied with the other to perform ever more incredible acts. The more impossible the feat, the larger the crowd. One performer crouched low, buckled into a contorted position on the floor, and then leapt in one explosive movement to sit on a chair balanced on top of an eight-foot pole. A tightrope-walker defied gravity as he played his violin in truly suspended animation. A supposedly two-year-old child spun herself around while sharpened swords pointed at her eyes, throat and stomach – one slip would be messy indeed.

But it was not this display of perfect and well-honed humanity that drew most of Denis' attention. Each time he walked through the fair he was drawn to the spectacles of deformity – those with additional fingers on their hands raised a little interest, but those with grossly deformed heads or wildly contorted bodies had a fascination of their own. There were two-foot dwarfs on display alongside eight-foot giants, and a boy who had no arms or legs but could hold a stick in his mouth and play a drum. Many simply sat looking dejected. Others were prone to strike out, forcing their keepers to restrain them with chains or keep them in elaborate cages that reinforced the sense of fear and asked questions about the cut-off between humanity and the rest of the beasts that roamed the face of the earth.

Looking at one badly misshapen individual who was displayed wearing the minimum of clothing to emphasise his covering mass of hair, a question played back in Denis' mind. How much blood would you have to transfuse from a sheep to a man, before the man became part sheep? And then another surfaced alongside it: how much would you need to transfuse from a man to a sheep, before the sheep achieved a status at least as high as did this poor fellow?

The question seemed to become more complex as he looked at the adjacent cage holding a large ape that sat appearing to question him with great intensity and at least an appearance of intellect. In the open sunlit square behind him, another chimpanzee danced a minuet and exercised military drills, though the shaved bear dressed in the clothes of a Parisian trader was a more pitiful attempt to smudge any distinction between Adam's descendants and the rest of God's magnificent creation.

Paris in charge — time to change

The 10-minute walk had taken an hour, and in the process many of the entourage had become so 'involved' with the entertainment that they failed to reach Denis' apartment. Those that did were soon embroiled in a debate about the consequences of the morning's decision.

They sat and read the judgment, which stated:

That there was cause enough to cross-examine this woman and answer a series of questions: Where had she obtained those powders? Why she had given them to her husband? And by whose order? Why had she lied in order to hinder the opening of the body? To enable this, [D'Ormesson] ordered that in the meantime she should be taken into custody.

That as to the three physicians who had solicited her with money to prosecute those that had made the operation, and who had been seen with her, he demanded that a day might be set for them to appear in person.

Lastly, that since the transfusion had succeeded well the two first times, and had only been undertaken the third at the earnest request of the woman (who otherwise had so ill observed the orders of those that had made the operation, and who was suspected to have caused the death of her husband) he demanded that the execution of the decree of ordering Denis to appear in court should be cancelled – he was innocent of the charges and free to leave.

Whereupon it was decreed that the widow of Mauroy should on a set day appear personally, and undergo the examination upon the alleged information; and that more ample information should be made of the contents in the complaint of M. Denis; and, that for the future no transfusion should be made upon any human body without the approval of the physicians of the Parisian Faculty.

There was general relief and hearty back-slapping that the case against Denis had been dropped; any ruling against him could have led to the raising of a catalogue of other complaints. In reality, transfusing blood was unusual, but in many ways it was less extreme than drilling holes in people's heads, or other forms of treatment currently being investigated. A few people asked guarded questions about the origins of the witnesses they had so conveniently found, but no one was in a mood to press this detail too far – all that would be looked over in the future court hearing.

Despite the camaraderie, Denis was subdued – he had won the battle, but most probably lost the war. The major problem was the magistrate's closing remark: 'that for the future no transfusion should be made upon any human body without the approval of the physicians of the Parisian Faculty'. Awarding a power of veto to the Parisian Faculty of Medicine was the same as banning transfusion. They had made their opposition plain and they would be thrilled to gain this boost to their status and ability to control medical activity.

Although Denis was a physician, he was not a member of the Parisian Faculty. His medical origin and ongoing affiliation was with the

Montpellier faculty of medicine, and many of the people gathered in the room were from either that group or the rival college in Rheims. Together they were furious. The verdict as it stood applied to all of France. If no one challenged it, this would mean that the Parisian physicians had suddenly assumed the role of judge and jury over all of their work. 'Why,' they asked, 'should we have to bow and scrape to some Parisian doctor?'

His colleagues drifted away into the night, and Denis sat hunched at his desk recording the day's events in a letter penned to his colleague in England, Mr Oldenburg:

> ... Mean time, if ever the Faculty of the Parisian physicians meets to discuss this, I'd not believe that they will act rashly. In reality we will have to wait for Parliament to rule, and I can't see them wanting to strike this treatment down unless new evidence from future experiments suddenly shows that the procedure is dangerous.
>
> As far as the Parisian college is concerned, we need to remember the case of Antimony. They listed it as a poison, while other colleges recommended its use as a therapy. After it had successfully treated the King, the Parisians had to change their minds and they even started to demand that it was used more frequently.
>
> This example alone will make them act with more caution. Besides, the time we are living in is much more favourable to new discoveries. Despite having a kingdom to run, the King himself is keen to encourage learned and inquisitive men. At the time when the King sends money and favours around the world to cultivate science, I can't see a magistrate who is going to condemn a man for no other crime than concentrating all their interest and labour to the progress and advancement of knowledge.
>
> I will certainly let you know of any developments in this affair.
>
> In the meantime believe me
>
> Yours etc.
>
> Denis J-B

Prudence or prejudice?

Events did not unfold as Denis had hoped. He saw his fame and future prosperity being linked to blood transfusion, but this didn't happen. In reality there was no mass rush to test the technique, and rumours that the few attempts made over the following few months ended with the patient in a box and six feet below ground. With the French authorities becoming ever more sceptical, the Pope signed an order in 1675 outlawing the procedure, and in 1678 the English parliament stepped in and banned the technique from being used in England. It took another 150 years before transfusion moved on again and eventually developed into the multimillion-pound multinational industry it is today.

These prohibitions are intriguing as they form one of the earliest examples of a moratorium placed on an aspect of scientific endeavour. In this case the legislators felt themselves unprepared to adjudicate, and passed the issue back to the medical community for them to sort out. The result was an effective ban. The scientists, however, didn't pack up bags and abandon science. Rather, they directed their attentions elsewhere, with a niggling feeling that once other basic research was complete, they or their successors might be able to revisit this territory.

The echoes with the call for moratoria relating to current cloning-based research are also intriguing. Looking back at transfusion, it is easy now to see how so many of the decisions were based on poor information. Neither Lower, Denis, Boyle nor Perrault had a clue what real issues would need addressing before transfusion became a reality. They were far from developing a language of blood groups and agglutination, and they were unaware that blood is a streaming mass of living cells suspended in fluid. The precaution was forced on them from political masters who were ignorant of the state of science then, and from medical practitioners who were afraid that they might lose their livelihoods if transfusion was successful.

This episode serves to remind scientists that, as they work to push the boundaries of knowledge, they necessarily step forward into the unknown. Their ignorance of the true mechanisms underlying their results is, and will always be, vast.

Denis' dream of instant fame and fortune was over, but his life hadn't come to an end. He seems to have lost enthusiasm for pursuing medical research and turned his attention back to the safer grounds of mathematics, philosophy and astronomy, and added to this portfolio by running general scientific conferences. Medicine, however, remained part of his life, as in 1673 we find him walking the streets of London, having been invited by Charles II to explain his experience with transfusion and give his opinion on other remedies. He appears now as a man living well by making the most of his memoirs, rather than an investigator who is forging ahead with new discoveries. Denis showed no signs of challenging the generalisation that most scientists only have one big idea in their life. It is interesting to see how many people have an innovative phase of life, while working for their PhDs and in the first years of post-doctoral research, but their ongoing success depends on drawing a team of young minds around them. If all goes well, they assume the role of mentor and manager and have an enjoyable time roving around the international conference circuit presenting their team-members' work. Denis' failure was therefore less that he never came up with another earth-shattering idea, but that he didn't create a team.

And what of Madame Mauroy? In reality the court case had come down to a battle of witnesses and a comparison of supporters. The whole episode has the air of injustice hanging about the outcome of this particular fight. In one corner was a poor, recently widowed peasant trying to scrape together enough cash to make a new start in life. She wasn't in court that day, but it is a fair bet that when her case was heard a few weeks later the gallery would be empty – she had few friends and no financial support. In the other corner was a man with powerful friends and a convenient collection of witnesses. In fact, the collection looked so convenient that it raises the question as to whether Denis had performed the same manoeuvre that had offended him most in the physicians of the Faculty of Medicine. Could he have offered his witnesses a little incentive?

There is no evidence that bribery occurred, but what really were the chances of someone seeing the spoonful of soup hit the floor and later being eaten by a cat that subsequently died? How fortunate that Denis had witnesses who had been offered bribes and could testify that Madame Mauroy had also been offered money. More curious, though, are the various accounts Denis gave of the final evening with Mauroy. The court record says they never got around to opening the calf's artery before Mauroy went into a fit. In his letter to Oldenburg, however, Denis says that a pipe was inserted, but that no blood was transfused. But with a pipe inserted, it is very likely that some blood would have passed into the patient. As we have seen before, Denis was also prone to exaggerate the length of time between the first two transfusions and this later event, an exaggeration that meant the process looked better than it really was.

On top of this, Denis showed a general disregard for detail. The letter he wrote to Montmor that so enraged the English workers was dated 25 June. But this must have been an error. Oldenburg had received it and translated it by the time he was arrested on 20 June. And Denis' claim for precedence in his work on transfusion rests on his statement that he heard Benedictine friar Dom Robert de Gabets talk about it at one of the Montmor Academy meetings 10 years earlier. While 1657 was the most active time for the Montmor group, Denis would have been only 17 at the time, and it is most unlikely he would have attended the meeting. Also, remember that the rules specified that only members could be present – observers were not allowed. And there are other inconsistencies.

Whatever did occur on that evening, Denis' description of the events was not totally consistent, and has the appearance of being adjusted to meet the needs of clearing his name. It seems highly reasonable, though, that Denis did attempt the third transfusion, and that the small amount of blood that entered Mauroy's body was enough to tip the balance between life and death. Mauroy was a sick man, and yet another adverse reaction was more than he could take. There seems to have been little time for his wife to administer the alleged fatal broth, even if she had wanted to. The patient died immediately after Denis' third attempt. Sadly, a fire that destroyed the court and all court records means that there is no way of seeing what Mauroy's wife had to say of the matter.

Nor do we know her fate. While the accounts of Denis' trial were of interest in England and were therefore recorded by Oldenburg, he had no concern for any of the following action. Madame Mauroy's decision to bury the corpse at the earliest possible moment was not desperately unusual, although it may well have been encouraged by offers of money from meddling members of the medical profession. All the same, there seems little in her story, other than the 'convenient' witnesses, to brand her as a murderer. But given the harsh treatment of prisoners who had no high-profile support or personal wealth, and the harshness of punishment handed out in seventeenth-century Paris, it is doubtful that her history went on for much longer.

So, was Denis a murderer? Almost certainly not. It seems more than likely that his therapy weakened Mauroy. The murder requires proof of an intent to kill, and this was the last thing Denis wanted. Did he commit manslaughter? Well, that is a charge that quite possibly could have stuck if the crime had existed at the time.

Around the world, blood transfusion now saves millions of lives each year, and it would be fair to say that Denis played a small part in setting the wheels in motion. The technique had to pause while science moved on to the point that his dream could become reality. In his lifetime, Denis achieved a small measure of the fame he had hoped for, but it is certain that he would be thrilled with the long-term results of his work. Open almost any text book on blood transfusion and there will undoubtedly be mention of his adventurous work somewhere in the introductory paragraphs. As is so often the case, history has given him bigger recognition than he achieved from his peers.

The whole episode outlined here, certainly involved a little science and a lot of blood, but did anyone really get justice?

Notes

1. Harvey, W., *De Motu Cordis* (1624).

2. Aubrey, J., *Brief Lives* (1681).

3. Ibid.

4. Harvey, W, op. cit.

5. Quoted from Gibson, W. C., 'The biomedical pursuits of Christopher Wren', *Medical History* (1970) 14: 334.

6. Ibid.

7. Boyle, R., *Some Considerations Touching the Usefulness of Experimental Naturall Philosophy* (Oxford) 1663, Part II, p. 64.

8. Hoff, E. C. and Hoff, P. M., 'The life and times of Richard Lower, physiologist and physician', *Bulletin of the Institute of the History of Medicine* (1936) 7: 517–35.

9. Translated from Lower, R., *Tractatus de Corde* (1671).

10. (With modifications) from Brown, Harcourt, *Scientific Organisations in Seventeenth Century France* (Baltimore: The Williams and Wilkins Company), 1934, ch IV, pp. 64–65.

11. Ibid., p. 66.

12. Ibid., p. 67.

13. Ibid., p. 125.

14. Weld, Charles Richard, *History of the Royal Society* (London: John W. Parker), 1848, p. 37.

15. Ibid., p. 42.

16. Fellows signature book of the Royal Society.

17. Birch, *History of the Royal Society*, 1: 107.

18. Intriguingly, Pepys says that the meeting was at Gresham College, though all other historians record that meetings of the Royal Society over this period occurred at Arundel House. Most probably

the meeting was at Arundel House, but Pepys was using 'Gresham College' as his shorthand for the Royal Society.

19. Shadwell, Thomas, *The Virtuoso*, ed Marjorie Hope Nicholson and David Stuart Rodes (Lincoln and London: University of Nebraska Press), 1966, II.ii 108–33.

20. *Philosophical Transactions* (1667) 27: 489–504.

21. Ibid.

22. *Philosophical Transactions* (1667) 28: 517–24.

23. State papers (Domestic), Entry Book 23, 485.

24. Ibid.

25. Correspondence of Oldenburg, 3 October 1666.

26. Correspondence of Oldenburg, 29 January 1667.

27. State Papers (Domestic), Charles II, 1667, 208/46.

28. Ibid.

29. State Papers (Domestic), Charles II, 1667, 209/123.

30. State Papers (Domestic), Charles II, 1667, 210/59.

31. State Papers (Domestic), Charles II, 1667, 210/59.

32. *Boyle's Works*, ed. T. Birch (London), 1772, 6: 237–38

33. Quoted in Riesman, D., 'Bourdelot, a physician of Queen Christina of Sweden', *Annals of Medical History* (1937) 9: 191.

34. Ray, J., Correspondence, 1848, p. 23.

35. Gunther, R. T., *Early Science in Oxford* (1932), Vol. 9.

36. Libavius, A., *Appendix Necessaria Syntagmatis Arcanorum Chymicorum Contra Heningum Sheunemanum*, (Frankfurt), 1615, IV, 8.

37. Translated by Mrs A. H. Lloyd and quoted in Keynes, G., *Blood Transfusion* (Bristol: John Wright & Sons), 1949.

38. A copy of the book exists in the Bibliothek der Leopoldina, Halle, Germany.

39. Adapted from quotes in Hoff, H. and Guillemin, R., The first experiments on transfusion in France, *Journal of the History of Medicine* (1963) 18: 103–24.

40. Ibid.

41. Adapted from Hoff and Guillemin, op cit.

42. Adapted from Lower, R., op cit.

43. Adapted from the Hoff and Guillemin, op. cit.

44. Ibid.

45. Ibid.

46. Ibid.

47. Ibid.

48. Ibid.

49. Ibid.

50. Ibid.

51. Adapted from Hoff and Guillemin, op. cit.

52. Ibid.

53. Ibid.

54. Ibid.

55. Adapted from Lower, R., op. cit.

56. Adapted from *Philosophical Transactions* (1667), pp. 559 – 60.

57. Ibid.

58. Adapted from Hoff and Guillemin, op. cit.

Timeline

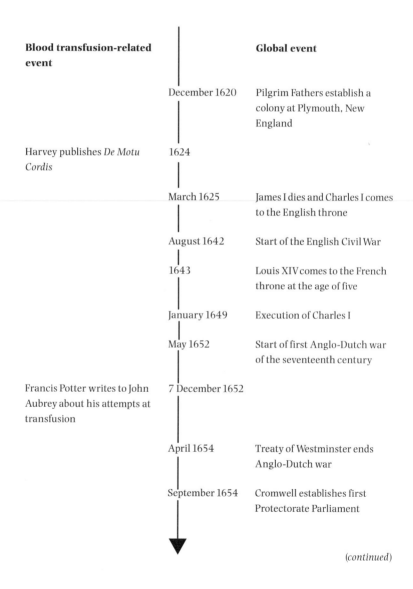

Blood transfusion-related event		Global event
	December 1620	Pilgrim Fathers establish a colony at Plymouth, New England
Harvey publishes *De Motu Cordis*	1624	
	March 1625	James I dies and Charles I comes to the English throne
	August 1642	Start of the English Civil War
	1643	Louis XIV comes to the French throne at the age of five
	January 1649	Execution of Charles I
	May 1652	Start of first Anglo-Dutch war of the seventeenth century
Francis Potter writes to John Aubrey about his attempts at transfusion	7 December 1652	
	April 1654	Treaty of Westminster ends Anglo-Dutch war
	September 1654	Cromwell establishes first Protectorate Parliament

(*continued*)

Blood transfusion-related event		Global event
Wren, Wilkins and Boyle inject opium and other chemicals into dogs	1656	
Wren and Clarke inject an extract of *crocus metallorum* into a man-servant	Autumn 1657	
	September 1658	Cromwell dies
	1659	Peace of the Pyrenees means that France replaces Spain as Western Europe's greatest power
	May 1660	The monarchy is restored in England and Charles II is crowned King
	1660	Louis XIV marries Maria Theresa, Infanta of Spain
The forerunner of the Royal Society is formally established	28 November 1660	
	10 March 1661	Louis XIV claims supreme authority in France
	1661	England acquires Bombay and increases trade with India
	September 1661	Nicholas Foquet arrested in France, effectively removing any potential challenge to Louis XIV's authority

(continued)

TIMELINE

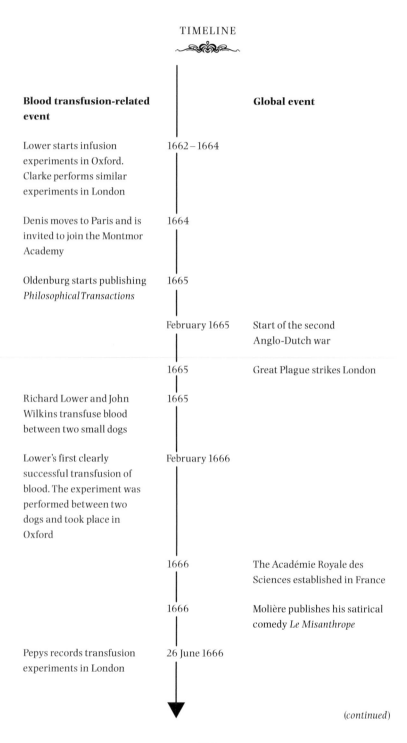

Blood transfusion-related event

Global event

Lower starts infusion experiments in Oxford. Clarke performs similar experiments in London	1662 – 1664	
Denis moves to Paris and is invited to join the Montmor Academy	1664	
Oldenburg starts publishing *Philosophical Transactions*	1665	
	February 1665	Start of the second Anglo-Dutch war
	1665	Great Plague strikes London
Richard Lower and John Wilkins transfuse blood between two small dogs	1665	
Lower's first clearly successful transfusion of blood. The experiment was performed between two dogs and took place in Oxford	February 1666	
	1666	The Académie Royale des Sciences established in France
	1666	Molière publishes his satirical comedy *Le Misanthrope*
Pepys records transfusion experiments in London	26 June 1666	

(*continued*)

TIMELINE

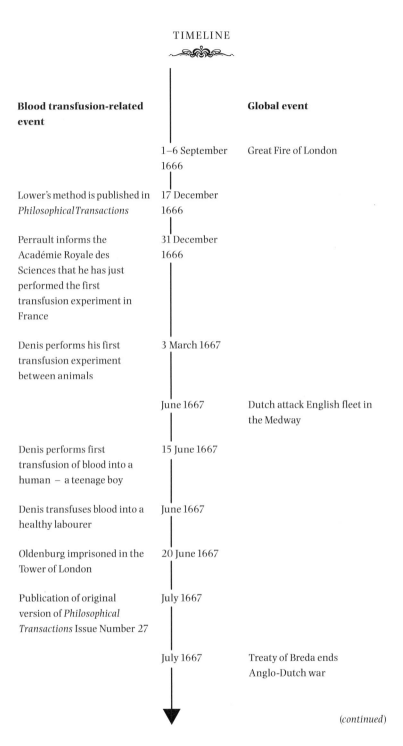

Blood transfusion-related event		Global event
	1–6 September 1666	Great Fire of London
Lower's method is published in *Philosophical Transactions*	17 December 1666	
Perrault informs the Académie Royale des Sciences that he has just performed the first transfusion experiment in France	31 December 1666	
Denis performs his first transfusion experiment between animals	3 March 1667	
	June 1667	Dutch attack English fleet in the Medway
Denis performs first transfusion of blood into a human – a teenage boy	15 June 1667	
Denis transfuses blood into a healthy labourer	June 1667	
Oldenburg imprisoned in the Tower of London	20 June 1667	
Publication of original version of *Philosophical Transactions* Issue Number 27	July 1667	
	July 1667	Treaty of Breda ends Anglo-Dutch war

(continued)

TIMELINE

Blood transfusion-related event		Global event
Oldenburg released from the Tower of London	26 August 1667	
Publication of second version of *Philosophical Transactions* Issue No. 27	September 1667	
First transfusion of lamb's blood into Arthur Coga in London	23 November 1667	
Second transfusion of lamb's blood into Arthur Coga	14 December 1667	
Denis' first transfusion of calf's blood into Antoine Mauroy	19 December 1667	
Denis' second transfusion of calf's blood into Antoine Mauroy	21 December 1667	
Denis' third encounter with the Mauroys	January 1668	
Denis' trial in Chastelet, Paris	16 April 1668	
	March 1672	Start of third Anglo-Dutch war
Charles II invites Denis to England	1673	
Pope bans blood transfusions	1675	

Bibliography

Papers in the Philosophical Transactions

'An Account of the rife and attempts, of a way to conveigh Liquors immediately into the mass of blood', *Philosophical Transactions* (1665) 1: 128–30.

Lower, R., 'The method observed in transfusing the bloud out of one animal into another', *Philosophical Transactions* (1666) 1: 353–58.

Boyle, R., 'Trials proposed by Mr Boyle to Dr Lower to be made by him, for the improvement of transfusing blood out of one live animal into another; promised Numb 20 p 357', *Philosophical Transactions* (1666) 1: 385–88.

'An account of an easier and safer way of transfusing blood: An experiment of bleeding a mangy into a sound dog; an extract of a letter written by a French philosopher concerning the same subject of transfusion', *Philosophical Transactions* (1667) 2: 449–53.

Denis, J.-B., 'A letter concerning a new way of curing sundry diseases by transfusion of blood, written to Monsieur de Montmor, Counsellor to the French King, and master of requests. By J: Denis Professor of philosophy and mathematicks', *Philosophical Transactions* (1667) 2: 489–504. [Retracted version].

'An advertisement concerning the invention of the transfusion of blood – and – an account of some experiments of injecting liquors into the veins of animals, lately made in Italy by Signor Fracassati, Professor of Anatomy at Pisa', *Philosophical Transactions* (1667) 2: 489–91.

'Of more trials of transfusion accompanied with some considerations thereon, chiefly in reference to its circumspect practice on man; together with a farther vindication of this invention from usurpers', *Philosophical Transactions* (1667) 2: 517–25.

'An account of the experiment of transfusion, practised on a man in London', *Philosophical Transactions* (1667) 2: 557–59.

'A relation of some trials of the same operation lately made in France', *Philosophical Transactions* (1667) 2: 559–64.

'Of injecting medicated liquors into veins, together with the considerable cures perform'd thereby', *Philosophical Transactions* (1667) 2: 564–65.

'Of a letter written by J. Denis, Doctor of Physic, and Professor of philosophy and the mathematicks at Paris, touching a late cure of an inveterate phrensy by the transfusion of blood', *Philosophical Transactions* (1667) 2: 617–24.

'Of a printed letter, addressed to the publisher, by Jean Denis D. of physick and prof of the mathematics at Paris, touching the differences risen about the transfusion of bloud. Including an extract of the sentence, given at Chastelet, by the Lieutenant in Criminal causes, April 17, 1668, in Paris', *Philosophical Transactions* (1668) 3: 710–15.

'Out of the Italian Giornale de letterati, about two considerable experiments of the transfusion of the blood', *Philosophical Transactions* (1667) 3: 840–41.

Register Book of the Royal Society

Lower, R., Boyle, R., King, E. and Cox, T., 'Blood transfusion', *Register Book of the Royal Society* 1666, copy II.

Pamphlets in the British Library (Shelf mark 783.g.23)

'Lettre ecrite a Monsieur * * * * par J. Denis docteur en medecine, & professeur de philosophie & de mathematique. Touchant une folie inveterée, qui a esté guérie depuis peu par la transfusion du sang', 12 January 1667.

'Lettre ecrite a monsieur sorbiere docteur en medecine, par Jean Denis aussi docteur en medecine; Touchant l'origine de la transfusion du sang, & la maniere de la pratiquer sur les hommes. Avec le recit d;une cure faire depuis peu sur une personne paralitique', 2 March 1667.

'Sentence rendue au chastelet par Monsieur le Lieutenant Criminel le 17. Avril 1668', 15 May 1667.

'Copie d'une lettre escrite a Monsieur de Montmor, conseiller du Roy en ses conseils, & premier maistre des requestes. Par I. Denis professeur de philosophie & de mathematique. Touchant une nouvelle maniere de guarir plusieurs maladies par la transfusion du sang, confirmée par deux experiences faites sur des hommes', 25 June 1667.

'Lettre escrite a monsieur Moreau, docteur en medecine de la Faculté, conseiller, medecin, lecteur & professeur ordinaire du Roy, par G. Lamy, maistre aux arts en l'Université de Paris; Contre les pretenduës utilitiés de la transfusion du sang pour la guerison des maladies, avec la réponse aux raisons & experiences de Monsieur Denis', 8 July 1667.

'L'ombre d'apollon, decouvrant les abus de cette pretenduë maniere de guerir les maladies par la transfusion du sang. Ensemble. Une lettre servant de response à la premiere & seconde lettre de Monsieur Denis & Gadroys. Par le Sieur de la Martiniere, medecin chymique & operateur ordinaire du Roy', 15 September 1667.

'Lettre ecrite a monsieur l'abbe Bourdelot, docteur en medecine de la Faculté de Paris, premier medecin de la Reine Christine de Suede, á present auprés de Monsegneur le Prince à Chantilly, Par Gaspard de Gurye Ecuier Sieur de Mont-polly, Lieutenant au Regiment de Bourgongne; sur la transfusion du sang, contenant des raisons & des experiences pour & contre', 16 September 1667.

'Lettre escrite a monsieur l'Abbe Bourdelot Docteur en medecine de la facultè de Paris, & premier medecin de la Reine de Suede, Par C. G. pour servir de rèponse au Sr Lamy, & confirmer en meme temps la transfusion du sang par de nouvelles experiences', 8 August 1667.

'Lettre escrite a Mr Moreau docteur en medecine de la Faculté de Paris, conseiller, medecin, lecteur & professeur ordinaire du Roy; Par G. Lamy: Dan laquelle il confirme les raisons qu'il avoit apportées dans sa premiere lettre, contre la trans-fusion du sang, en répondant aux objections qu'on luy a faites', 26 August 1667.

'Reflexions de Louis de Basril – advocat en parlement, sur les disputes qui se sont à l'occasion de la transfusion', 1667.

'Euthyphronis philosophi et medici, de nova curandorum morborum ratione per transfusionem sangvinis, dissertatio ad amicum', 1667.

'Lettre ecrite a monsieur Oldenburg gentilhomme anglois, & secretaire de l'aca-demie Royalle d'Angleterre. Par Jean Denis docteur en medecine, & profes-seur éz mathematiques. Touchant les differents qui sont arrivez à l'occasion de la transfusion du sang', 1667.

'Physical reflections upon a letter written by J Denis Professor of Philosophy and the mathematicks, to Monsieur de Montmor Counsellor to the French King and Master of Requests. Concerning a new way of curing sundry diseases by transfusion of blood', 1668.

'Relatione dell'esperienze fatte en Inghilterra, Francia, ed Italia. Intorno alla celebre,e famosa transfusione del sangue', 1668.

'Discours de Monsieur de Sorbiere, touchant diverses experiences de la transfu-sion du sang', 1 December 1668.

'De nova et inavdita medico-chyrvrgica operatione sangvinem transfundente de individvo ad individuum; Prius in Brutis, & deinde in homine Roma experta. Opusclum singulare avctore avlo Manfredo Lucense ex camaiore philosopho & medici Romano, & in vrbis archilyceo medicine practica pro-fessore extraordinario', 1668.

Pamphlets in the Bibliothèque Nationale de France

'Discours de Monsieur de Sorbiere, touchant diverses experiences de la transfu-sion du sang à Monsiegneur le Duc de Chaulnes, pair de France, cheualier des ordres du Roy, & son ambassadeur extraordinaire auprés de sa sainteté', 1 December 1668.

'Lettre escrite a monsieur le Breton docteur Regent en la faculté de medecine de Paris & medecin ordinaire de monsigneur le prince, par M. Claude Tardy aussi docteur Regent en la mesme Faculté. Pour confirmer les utilitez de la transfusion du sang, & responder à ceux qui les estendent trop', 30 October 1667.

'Lettre ecrite a monsieur l'abbe Bourdelot, Docteur en Medecine de la Faculté de ˙ Paris, Premier Medecin de la Reine Christine de Suede, á present auprés de Monsegneur le Prince à Chantilly, Par Gaspard de Gurye Ecuier Sieur de Montpolly, Lieutenant au Regiment de Bourgongne; Sur la Transfusion du sang, Contenant des Raisons & des Experiences pour & contre', 16 September 1667

'Traité de l'ecoulement du sang d'un homme dans les veines d'un autre et de ses utilitez, par M. C. Tardy', 12 June 1667.

Journal des Sçavans (Bibliothèque Nationale de France)

'Extrait du journal d'angleterre. Contenant la maniere de faire passer le sang d'un animal dans un autre', *Journal des Sçavans*, Monday 31 January 1667; 1: 31–36.

Translation into French of Lower's method of transfusing blood from the carotid artery of one dog into the vein of another.

'Extract d'une letter de M. Denis Professor de philosophie et de mathematique à M. *** touchant la transfusion du Sang. Du 9 Mars 1667', *Journal des Sçavans*, Monday, 14 March 1667; 4: 69–72.

'Extrait d'une letter de M. Denis professeur de philosophie & mathematique, à M. *** touchant la transfusion du sang. Du 2. Avril 1667', *Journal des Sçavans*, Monday 25 April 1667; 8: 96.

'Lettre de M. Denis Professeur de Philosophie et de mathematique, à M. de Montmor premier Maitre des Requestes; touchant deux experiences de la transfusion faites sur des hommes. Jn 4', *Journal des Sçavans*, Monday 28 June 1667; 11: 134–36.

'Extrait du journal d'angleterre, contenant quelques nouvelles experiences de L'infusion des medicamens dans les veines', *Journal des Sçavans*, Monday 23 January 1668; 1: 10–12.

'Diverses pieces touchant la Transfusion du sang

- Lettre de G Lamy a M. Moreau, Docteur en Medecine de la Faculté de Paris, contre les pretenduës utilitez de la transfusion.
- Lettre de C. Gadroy a M. L'abbe Bourdelot Docteur en Medec. De la Faculté de

Paris, pour servir de Response à la lettre écrite par M. Lamy contre la Transfusion.

● Seconde lettre ecrite a M. Moreau Docteur en medecin de la faculté de Paris par G. Lamy, pour confirmer les raisons qu'il a apportées dans sa premiere Lettre contre la Transfusion.

● Lettre de G. de Gurye Sr De Montpolly à M. l'Abbé Bourdelot Docteur en Medecin de la Faculté de Paris, touchant la transfusion.

● Eutyphronis Philosophi et medici de nova curandorumm ratione per transfusionem sanguinis dissertatio.

● Lettre de M. Tardy Docteur en la Faculté de Medecin de Paris, à M. le Breton Docteur en la mesme Faculté, touchant l'usage de la transfusion.

● Extrait du journal d'angleterre, contenant quelques experiences de la Transfusion.

● Lettre de J Denis Docteur en medecin & Professeur de Philosophie & de mathematique, touchant une folie inveterée qui a été guerie par la transfusion du sang'

Journal des Sçavans, Monday 6 February 1668; 2 : 13 – 24.

'Relatione dell'esperienze fatte in Inghilterra, Francia, ed Italia intorno la transfusione del sangue in Roma', *Journal des Sçavans*, Monday 2 July 1668, pp. 50 – 52.

'Extrait du Journal d'Angleterre contenant le succez des experiences faites à Dantzic, de l'infusion des medicamens dans les veins de quelques personnes maladies', *Journal des Sçavans*, Monday 12 November 1668, p. 108.

'Extrait du journal d'Italie contenant deux experiences de la transfusion du sang', *Journal des Sçavans*, Monday 19 November 1668, p. 117.

Books

Harvey, W., *On the motion of the heart and blood in animals*, 1628 (English translation of *De Motu Cordis*).

Boyle, R., *Usefulness of experimental philosophy*, 1663.

Lower, R., *Tractatus de Corde*, 1670.

Boyle, R., *Memoirs for the Natural History or Humane Blood, esp. the spirit of that liquor* (London: Samuel Smith), 1684.

Pepys, S. *The diary of Samuel Pepys, 1660 – 1699*.

Hall, A. and Hall, M., *The correspondence of Henry Oldenburg, volumes 1 – 13*, (London: Taylor and Francis), 1986.

Hall, M., *Henry Oldenburg: shaping up the Royal Society*, (Oxford: Oxford University Press), 2002.

Further reading

Shadwell, Thomas, *The Virtuoso*, ed. Marjorie Hope Nicholson and David Stuart Rodes (Lincoln and London: University of Nebraska Press), 1966.
A seventeenth-century play that discusses the Royal Society and blood transfusion.

Pears, Iain, *An Instance of the Fingerpost* (1997), (London: Vintage), 1998.
A novel involving blood transfusion and many of the characters in this book.

Coward, Barry, *The Stuart Age – England 1603–1714* (London: Longman Group UK Limited), 2nd edn, 1994.
An accessible introduction to this period of English history, with comments on the rise of science and medicine within English society.

Loux, François, *Pierre-Martin de la Martinière, un médecin au XVIIe siècle* (Paris: Imago) 1988.
A biography of one of Denis' most vocal detractors – chapter 5 looks specifically at his stance against transfusion.

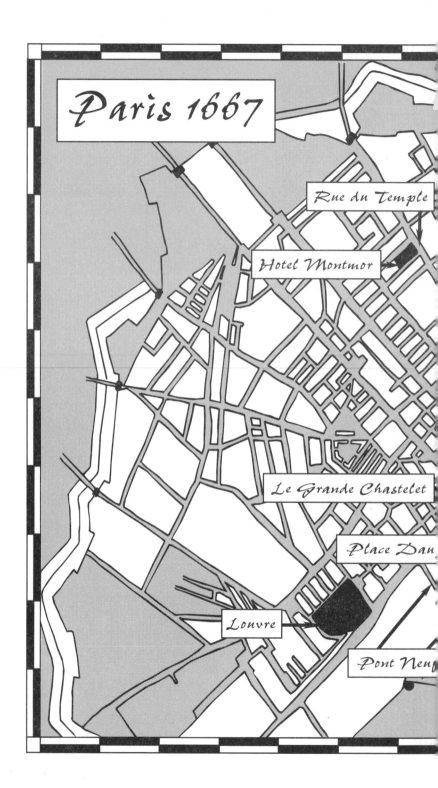

Paris 1667

Rue du Temple

Hotel Montmor

Le Grande Chastelet

Place Dau

Louvre

Pont Neu